Folklore Research around the World:

A North American Point of View

edited, with an introduction,

BY RICHARD M. DORSON

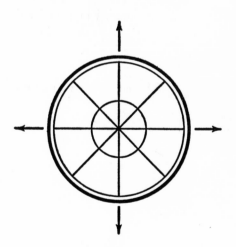

Indiana University Folklore Series Number 16
Indiana University, Bloomington, Indiana

PUBLICATION COMMITTEE
Editor: Richard M. Dorson
Consulting Editor: John W. Ashton

Assistant editors: W. Edson Richmond, Warren E. Roberts, Thomas A. Sebeok, Erminie Wheeler-Voegelin

Editorial assistants: Pamela Casagrande, Maurice D. Schmaier

The Indiana University Folklore Series was founded in 1939 for the publication of occasional papers and monographs by members of the faculty.

CONTENTS

RICHARD M. DORSON

INTRODUCTION BY THE EDITOR

BY ITS very nature the study of folklore requires an international breadth of vision. The materials of folklore transcend all barriers of language and culture, traversing continents and spanning oceans in vast leaps and drifting across borders in easy stages. "Cinderella" has circled the globe. The "Shanghai gesture," popular among American schoolboys as a thumb and finger wiggle of derision, roamed all over Europe in the past four centuries. One extended family of water goblins unites the Japanese *kappa* with the Scottish kelpie.[1] In ballad and legend, romance and epos, the same protean hero performs the same sequence of marvelous exploits. Proverbs and riddles glide from one tongue to another to settle comfortably in a new idiom.

Yet in seeming paradox folklore studies have developed most energetically along national lines. Individual scholars of eminence, such as Archer Taylor and Stith Thompson in the present volume, have pursued their researches in a truly international spirit, following their materials wherever they wander. But the galvanic force behind concerted, subsidized, and firmly organized folklore studies is the force of nationalism. Folklore has served national interests of various sorts: the anxious pride of the small country seeking its cultural identity; the *hubris* of the racist state, glorying in the solidarity of the *Herrenvolk;* the aspirations of an emergent nation, hoping to crystallize its myths; the ideology of the socialist state, extolling the creative powers of the anonymous masses. The same impulses that have led to the self-study of national history and national literature have urged the pursuit of national folklore. Today the well-equipped political state possesses its accredited historical records, its approved literary masterpieces, and its classified folklore archives.

The present collection of essays builds a picture of the international folklore scene through successive comments on the status of folklore research in various parts of the world. At the summer 1958 Folklore Institute of America held at Indiana University, the writer arranged a seminar on "International Relations in Folklore," in which visiting and resident faculty members spoke on folklore scholarship in countries and continents of their special interest. This volume is an outgrowth, with additions, of those lectures.[2] The seminar was designed to pool information gathered by American folklorists abroad, and to examine the character of folklore studies as they have developed on the five continents. Thanks to the John Simon Guggenheim Memorial Foundation, Senator Fulbright, and the State Department, American professors, including folklore scholars, have enjoyed unprecedented opportunity for foreign residence, study, and travel, in a dispersion recalling the Victorian age of the British Empire. England's colonial administrators, missionaries, and travelers are now matched by America's cultural attachés, visiting professors, and specialist lecturers. While the Victorians produced many volumes of collected texts, made possible by their long tenures overseas, Americans stay usually one or two years abroad, and cannot undertake comparable fieldwork. Furthermore the situation has radically altered in countries where Englishmen were once pioneer collectors, and the American visitor today is confronted by an impressive pile of publications and a mass of archival manuscripts. The problem now is to locate the folklorists, not the folklore.

International communications among folklorists have improved over the past forty years, from the nadir when scholars in the United States knew virtually nothing of European developments. Stith Thompson tells of the unawareness among his Harvard mentors in 1914 of the Type-Index by Antti Aarne published four years earlier in Finland. Consequently Thompson had to execute his doctoral dissertation and subsequent research on the intrusion of European tales among the North American Indians without benefit of a major tool. When he did establish contact with the Finnish folklorists in 1926, Kaarle Krohn suggested he revise the Aarne index, and the edition of the Aarne-Thompson *Types of the Folk-Tale* published two years later—currently in press for its second expansion—attests the fruitfulness of transoceanic cooperation in folklore scholarship. But the problem of maintaining exchange of monographs, field collections, and journals becomes evermore insistent, particularly with the extension of folklore investigations to other continents besides Europe. The *Internationale Volkskundliche Bibliographie,* valiantly prosecuted by Robert Wildhaber in Basel, lags half a dozen years behind the current year. Exchange of books may well be less rewarding than exchange of persons, for if one knows the dedicated folklorists in a given country, he can become oriented far more readily, and safely, than if he forages for himself in the library. The Irish Folklore Commission is the creation of James H. Delargy, the Japanese Folklore Institute of Kunio Yanagita, the Swedish Folklife Research Institute in Stockholm of Sigurd Erixon.

The plan for the lectures, and the essays into which they grew, called for an account by the American observers of the resources—bibliographical, physical, and human— open to the student of folklore in a given country. References to and comments upon representative works would serve to lead the interested student further into the scholarly literature. Physical resources could include folklore archives, museums, institutes, and libraries. Identification of leading folklorists and their research interests should also assist the outsider. The picture that emerged would reveal something of the character of folklore studies in the national state or culture area.

This character can be viewed from a double perspective: the point reached by folklorists in their progression from field collecting to systematic study of folk materials, and the direction taken by the mature study. On the first score, we may divide the world along the lines roughed out by anthropological and humanistic folklorists. The anthropologists investigate cultures predominantly oral and traditional, cultures in which the concept and self-conscious examination of indigenous folklore (or oral literature) are not yet understood, although the raw materials are present in flourishing abundance. In the following pages, Luomala for Polynesia and Herskovits and Crowley for subSaharan Africa report on such culture areas. Australia presents a special case, neatly divided between aboriginal and colonial folk literatures, unlike Latin America where the Indian and the European—with an admixture of the African—have effected a partial blend. Quite appropriately, the commentator for Australia, Greenway, himself is trained both as anthropologist and as humanist. In the countries of Europe, where long established distinctions of social classes have produced a peasant "folk" readily identifiable by scholars, literati, and intellectuals generally, the folklorists delve into the customs and beliefs of their submerged countrymen. Nineteenth century collectors frankly referred to the folk at home as "the lower orders," and the folk of uncivilized (i.e. non-European) societies as "savages." Theoretical schools have waged their controversies to explain the ancestry of folk ideas, but all, whatever their positions—celestial mythologists, Indianists, survivalists, ritualists, Freudians—shared a common premise, that the culture of the folk differed from and trailed behind the culture of civilization, to which it adhered like a picturesque fungus. Even in the United States, with its more mobile population and its democratic doctrine, the same notion of a backward, backcountry folk, dwelling chiefly in the southern mountains, has governed much of the fieldwork. Childlike savages are available both in aboriginal and imported African stocks. French Canada, whose folklore work is described herein by Lacourcière, is a European folk culture transplanted wholesale into the wilderness.

Folklore as studied in Europe and North America embodies a quite different conceptual approach from that employed by American ethnologists in Asia and Africa. The anthropologists deal with the total culture, and their approach is holistic; the traditions of the unlettered belong to the entire society, for there are no lower illiterate orders. Hence the controversy between anthropological and humanistic folklorists over the content and usefulness of the term "folklore," and its restriction by the ethnologists to the verbal arts. In the nonliterate society the entire institutional structure and cosmogonical system involve traditional "custom" and "belief." Even the intellectual classes of Asia and the Middle East stay close to their folk inheritance; the gulf between industrialized and traditional cultures has not yet riven their societies; the aspiring folklorists from Thailand, Pakistan, India, Indonesia, Egypt are usually informants as well as collectors.

The romantic haze that surrounded the folk in the nineteenth century has given way to pragmatic and political attitudes in the twentieth. The folk serve as repositories of the ancient language and popular traditions of the nation, and this legacy must be firmly recorded and made known to the citizens of the modern state. What kind of Finn is ignorant of the *Kalevala?* What good Norwegian who does not treasure the tales of Asbjørnsen and Moe? Publishing the national folklore in the school primers acquaints each youthful citizen with selected hero-tales and hero-songs that glorify the national genius. Recognizing the propaganda potentialities in folklore, the totalitarian states have decreed the erasure of the nineteenth century theory of *gesunkenes Kulturgut* and compelled their scholars to advance the party line through folklore. In Nazi Germany, the folklorists of the Third Reich abandoned the concept of peasant folklore for a racial theory of Germanic *Volksüberlieferung* uniting Teutonic peoples everywhere in a mystic kinship of blood and lore. Instead of dividing Germans into classes, folklore would weld them into a whole. In Soviet Russia, and her satellites, the folk—i.e., the people—have replaced the decadent aristocracy and bourgeoisie as originators of folkstuff, by party decree of 1933. Folklore is the vigorous creative expression of a revolutionary people against the landlords, the tsars, and the factory bosses, and it is the spontaneous hymn of praise—stimulated by prize competitions—to the Red Army generals and Kremlin leaders.

Folklorists from the United States visiting Europe accordingly are faced with a far different situation from anthropologists prospecting in Africa. The reporter in the European country meets an established and honored field of inquiry. Because ties between folklorists in Scandinavia and the United States have been close in recent years, our information about the active scholarship in those four countries is reasonably full and up-to-date. But of developments in, say, Turkey or Spain, neither well represented at the Stockholm and Kiel international congresses of 1951 and 1959, we have received little word, and the papers by Jansen and Gillmor now reveal considerable interest and activity there in folklore research. Contrary to the general impression, Spain is indeed folklore-minded, so much so that Gillmor found the man and woman in-the-street thoroughly conversant with the word "folklore."

Even allowing for the difference in treatment required for countries in different stages of research, the editor has not sought a rigid uniformity in the essays that follow. Some, like those of Simeone for Italy, Richmond for Finland, and Luomala for Polynesia, survey the growth of the field in historical perspective. Others have given impressionistic accounts of their visits. The history of humanistic learning can profit greatly from the autobiographical asides which scholars tend to suppress as unscholarly. Yet the chance encounter, the casual suggestion, the gift of serendipity, may very well determine the destiny of the creative scholar, and particularly of the folklorist who depends so heavily on his associates in his undermanned field. Cecil Sharp learned of the ballad riches in the southern mountains from a bundle of manuscripts brought him on his sickbed in Lincoln, Massachusetts. Thompson began his life's work when Kittredge in a Harvard seminar suggested he examine northeast Indian tales for instances of European intrusions.[3] Rarely indeed does a chatty volume such as the *Memories* of Edward Clodd sketch in the network of personal relationships that give vitality and spark to a field of learning. Any student of the English folklore movement soon appreciates the interdependence of the active London group, but only Clodd actually set down vignettes of his discourse with Lang and Gomme and Hartland. The late R. M. Dawkins of Oxford and André Varagnac of the Sorbonne told me a revelatory anecdote about Frazer. The serious-minded young scholar was accustomed to dine at the same Parisian restaurant with friends; to pull his leg, they informed him that Frazer's gallantries had smitten the waitress, who now believed herself compromised. The courteous Frazer wedded the waitress, but his companions suffered the consequence, for she barred the door to all his soulmates and made him sit at his desk writing his books. Accordingly he never received any new ideas, and while he wrote many books, they were all identical.[4] Like the visible crack in the tale of the tame trout, who fell through a crack in the bridge and was drowned, Sir James's volumes uphold the story.

The present symposium records some personal associations and impressions gained by American folklorists abroad during the past decade, along with more formal facts, and so offers a new chapter to the history of international folklore studies.

NOTES

1. See Marian R. Cox, *Cinderella* (London, 1897), and Anna Birgitta Rooth, *The Cinderella Cycle* (Lund, 1951); Archer Taylor, *The Shanghai Gesture*, FF Communications, Vol. LXVI, No. 166 (1956); Eiichiro Ishida, "The *Kappa* Legend," *Folklore Studies,* IX (Peking, 1950), 1-152.

2. The only seminar lecturer not represented in the present volume is the late R. D. Jameson, who spoke on "Folklore in China."
After the International Congress of Western and European Ethnology held at Stockholm in 1951, I talked with W. Edson Richmond, editor of *Midwest Folklore,* about a series of short surveys on folklore research abroad, to be written by folklore scholars of their respective countries. The following articles have since appeared in that journal: Demetrios Petropoulos, "The Study of Ethnography in Greece," II (1952), 15-20; Eeva Makela-Henriksson, "Recent Folklore Research in Finland," II (1952), 151-158; Brita Gjerdalen Skre, "Folk Life Research in Norway," II (1952), 221-228; Naoe Hiroji, "Post-War Folklore Research Work in Japan," III (1953), 213-222; K. D. Upadhyaya, "A General Survey of Folklore Activities in India," IV (1954), 201-212; Salvatore Nania, "A Glimpse at the History of Folklore in Italy," V (1955), 153-158; J. Podolak, "The Development of Ethnography in Slovakia," VIII (1958), 69-84.

3. A. H. Fox Strangways and Maud Karpeles, *Cecil Sharp* (2nd ed., London, New York, Toronto, 1955), pp. 129-130; Stith Thompson, "Folklorist's Progress" (1956, typescript, 320 pp., Folklore Library, Indiana University), pp. 59-60.

4. This pleasantry is supported by the ringing critique of Frazer in Edmund R. Leach, "Golden Bough or Gilded Twig?," *Daedalus* (Spring, 1961), 371-387.

EUROPE

ARCHER TAYLOR

CHARACTERISTICS OF GERMAN
FOLKLORE STUDIES

COMPARED with more stable disciplines such as history or the natural sciences, the study of folklore has a special character differing from country to country. The reasons for its variability are that folklore deals with local or national materials of varying kinds, and that its late origin, development, and achievement of academic recognition differed in various nations. Let us consider Finland first, because we look upon it in some ways as the motherland, where folklore scholarship has enjoyed the most generous recognition as a subject of study. Its special importance there is explained readily by the fact that the center of Finnish literary studies and the beginning of Finnish literature is the *Kalevala,* an epic which Elias Lönnrot based on folksongs. Since the time of Lönnrot, folklore always has been regarded as the core of Finland's national literature and culture; hence the history of folklore studies in Finland is more a history of methods than one of changing emphases.

The history of folklore in England has been clarified by Richard M. Dorson, but his studies begin somewhere near the middle rather than at the beginning.[1] English folklore scholarship had an antiquarian stage without international context or contacts, prior to the stages discussed by Dorson. I am thinking of a period of non-comparative study covering almost the entire seventeenth century, from William Camden's *Remaines Concerning Britaine* (London, 1605), to John Aubrey's writings in the century's last decades. These men, and others who collected traditions in the same spirit, might have made folklore into a recognized discipline. Why they did not arrive at a purpose and method is not altogether apparent, but we should remember that science was in much the same stage as folklore in that century. Scientists of the time were collecting, classifying, and organizing the curiosities of plant or animal life, wherever these might be found. In the seventeenth century folklorists were collecting their materials in much the same spirit, and in a comparable antiquarian fashion.

From the middle of the eighteenth century until the rise of Romanticism, English folklore study was in a second stage of development. The predominantly literary approach of the time is conspicuous in Bishop Percy's *Reliques,* and having been altered and enlarged by influences from Germany, is characteristic of the works of Sir Walter Scott. Following Scott is the third period, and the first in which Dorson has been interested.

With marked historical, local-historical, and antiquarian characteristics, the third stage in the history of English folklore scholarship was inspired to a certain extent from Germany and, interestingly enough, also from Denmark and the Scandinavian north. The materials collected extended beyond folksongs to include customs, superstitions, and other survivals of the past.[2] In the latter part of the nineteenth century, with recognition of England's status as an international or colonial power, the subject was enlarged even further to include primitive cultures. This fourth stage in English folklore also was characterized by considerable growth of interest in local history, by the publication of collectors' handbooks, and by the establishment of journals called *Notes and Queries* in almost every county. The founding of such journals is worth stressing, for the original *Notes and Queries* was started by W. J. Thoms, who coined the word "folk-lore." Thoms's journal maintained a pronounced interest in the subject until about 1900, and the smaller local journals modeled after it followed its lead. Over the last generation, though, the study of folklore in England has become fragmented. Lacking any coherent body of collectors and students, the English, as evidenced by the contents of *Folklore,* seem to have returned to a markedly antiquarian approach to the subject.

In other parts of Europe, the history of folklore studies presents an entirely different picture from either of the two preceding ones. With the exception of Italy, relatively little folklore activity has occurred in the south. Spanish folklore journals of the past, like *El Folklore andaluz,* were all short-lived, and the leading contemporary review, *Revista de Dialectología y Tradiciones Populares,* emphasizes dialect studies. Folklore in Portugal characteristically remains associated with *Revista Lusitana,* a journal devoted to what can be described as literary history. In the Scandinavian north, though, folklore scholarship has developed into a study of the entire folk-culture. Surprisingly different from the Finnish approach to the subject, folklore research in the nearby Scandinavian countries, though not anthropological or sociological in character, has taken form in the very remarkable folk museums like the Nordiska Museet (Northern Museum) in Stockholm and its open-air counterpart at Skansen. In such museums the realia of folk-art and folk-culture are brought together.

When we turn to Germany, the picture is different once more, mainly because in a very real sense the study of German folklore began about A.D. 100 and not in Germany. I am referring to Tacitus' *Germania,* a description of Germany written by a Roman for his countrymen at a time when rampant luxury promised to destroy the Roman city and state. In this essay, which is ethnographic as well as sociopolitical, Tacitus tried to describe primitive life and its virtues as a desirable alternative to the conditions prevailing in Rome, in order to correct conditions and to set up new and better ideals.[3] Since the book lay hidden for centuries and was not rediscovered until the late fifteenth century just before the Reformation, it came on the scene at a critical time when German humanists were ready to receive it with enthusiasm. Widely read and frequently edited, its influence was enormous, and was responsible, I believe, for steering German folklore studies into descriptive, historical, and markedly ethnographical directions. Two early examples of these trends are Joannes Boemus, *Omnium Gentium Mores, Leges, et Ritus* (1520), which is an ethnography international in scope, and the contemporary (ca. 1530) writings of Sebastian Franck, such as the *Weltbuch* of 1534, which deal chiefly with Germany. But descriptions of particular German provinces and cities had preceded these works and continued to be written. Like their more national or international counterparts, these more limited descriptions contain a considerable amount of material which we would consider today as folklore. For instance, a characteristic and flourishing literary genre of the time—the city poem which celebrated the site, history, and population of a city—often utilized folkloristic materials.[4]

During the sixteenth and seventeenth centuries, there was also a German tradition of antiquarianism that expressed itself when scores of authors published collections of miscellaneous information. Comparable to the antiquarian tradition in England,

German antiquarianism became especially popular in the seventeenth century, and miscellanies of that time include particularly large quantities of folklore. These compilations first consisted only of miscellaneous notes that were not very often classified. Later books of this kind, though, were provided with good indexes and hence can be utilized today by scholars.[5] By the end of the seventeenth century, the historico-ethnographical and antiquarian traditions had developed sufficiently enough for Germans to set folklore materials apart as something peculiar, outside of themselves, and worthy of study. Though random folklore collections had been made outside of Germany as early as the Middle Ages, I think we can regard this period in German history as the time when folklore became something to be seriously collected and studied.

During this pioneer period, German students at the universities already were writing dissertations on such strictly folkloristic subjects as superstitions and ghosts. There were large books of this sort, such as Erasmus Francisci's *Der höllische Proteus* (1695). But there were also late seventeenth-century works typical of the rising tide of European rationalism, which, in the eighteenth century, would cause many of such folklore materials to be looked upon no longer as objects of particular interest in themselves but as curious phenomena to be condemned or explained away. An early study of this kind is a German theologian's treatise on the Ten Commandments, which contains a list of superstitions that he condemns.[6] Though their presence makes the treatise a folklore document, it is clear that the author never regarded these superstitions as objects worthy of academic examination.

We owe the foundation of modern folklore scholarship, in the sense in which we know it, to Jacob Grimm in the early years of the nineteenth century. The emphasis that he gave to the discipline still remains characteristic of folklore activities in Germany. Grimm derived some of his materials from earlier collections; he made vast collections of several kinds himself; and he inspired others to record and study national traditions. Owing a great deal to the Romantic spirit of the age, Grimm was moved by a feeling that everything characteristically German ought to be preserved, especially because it was threatened by the imperialism and internationalism of Napoleon. His interest in things German fell in line, of course, with the earlier ethnographical tradition; it extended to the rejection of Christianity as a foreign religion that had been imposed upon his countrymen; and it stimulated the study of pre-Christian heathendom as something typically native and German. These developments contrast sharply with the course of events in nearby France.

Though there is a Celtic background to French traditions, at least in certain parts of France, and it has been an object of active study,[7] this background never became something to be investigated because it was uniquely and characteristically French. That is, Frenchmen regard their pre-Christian traditions merely as objects of historical interest, and not as a heritage they almost had lost because of the unfortunate migration of alien cultures. In contrast, the Germans have placed much greater value upon their pre-Christian past, and thereby have considerably enlarged the field of folklore. Grimm created a strong emphasis on heathen mythology, customs, superstitions, and legal practices; and since much could be learned by studying the etymologies of words associated with these traditions, he also made free use of linguistic evidence. He can be said to have established the general pattern for modern German folklore studies, a pattern which other German folklorists have actively developed and constantly maintained.

In Germany there is now, and always has been, a strong local tradition. We have already noted its existence during the age of humanism. Flourishing in the nineteenth century, this tradition gave rise to the establishment of many local historical journals. Literally hundreds of these journals still are published today, for they serve local pride, which has survived the abolition of the many small states that once constituted Germany. These publications give more attention and space to folklore and local literature, which contains a great deal of traditional material, than do our American local historical journals. I can scarcely imagine a local historical journal in Missouri finding room for an article on Mark Twain, even though he lived in Hannibal in that state. Its editor almost certainly would not be interested in a study of Twain's writings in relation to the local folklore, and would be even less likely to print a more specialized article on, for example, local proverbs in Twain's works. Yet in Germany local historical journals will enthusiastically publish articles on local authors, especially if their use of folklore materials reveals an historico-ethnographical, pre-Christian mythological, or antiquarian point of view.

All of these remarks on the major pattern of modern German folklore studies, and upon the local folklore tradition as well, suggest that there is a certain degree of splintering in the collection and study of German folklore. This is true, and is revealed even further by Germany's long history of publishing folklore materials in journals of literary history as well as local history. As early as 1855, moreover, a German folklore journal was established, but it survived only for four years.[8] Influenced by various schools of thought and their respective interpretations of folklore materials, the editor of this journal, after its first two years, caused a sharp change in the magazine's underlying theories, thereby changing the character of articles accepted and alienating many former contributors. Finally, in the twentieth century the lack of sympathetic association between German anthropological and folkloristic studies has accentuated the splintering tendencies even further. No longer following the same path as anthropology, as it did in the latter half of the nineteenth century,[9] folklore scholarship in Germany has borrowed additional characteristics from the students of literary history, the local historians, and the curators of local museums. These people are the ones who attend folklore meetings in Germany today.

Because there are local folklore societies, historical societies, and museums to an even greater extent than there are in the United States, the consequence has been the establishment of a central organization. This organization, the League of German Folklore Societies (Verband deutscher Vereine für Volkskunde), exerts no pressure on the activities of the local organizations and does not direct them in any way. It merely holds an annual meeting which representatives of the local societies attend. Like meetings of German learned societies in general, this meeting differs somewhat from annual American gatherings of a comparable nature because those who attend are invited guests whose names are printed on the program in advance. The number of people present therefore is relatively small, about fifty or sixty, and their interests definitely are concentrated on folklore on this particular occasion. Those who attend have backgrounds in historical or literary studies, or they may be directors of folk-museums, or professors of law, medicine, or music who have shown an interest in the traditional aspects of their subject. Such a meeting as this serves to counteract the splintering tendency that might develop in the local organizations.[10]

Another way in which the splintering of folklore is counteracted is seen in the growth of general treatises that the Germans call *Handbücher*. Having written such general histories and introductions to folklore for several generations, the Germans have produced more of them than scholars of any other nation.[11] An early one is Elard Hugo Meyer's *Deutsche Volkskunde* (Strasbourg, 1898). It contains much information about the traditional shapes of villages and houses; discusses peasant costumes briefly; but devotes less space than English and American folklorists might expect to tales, songs, proverbs, riddles, and the like. Among the many later handbooks of this sort are Erich Schmidt's *Deutsche Volkskunde im Zeitalter des Humanismus und der Reformation* (1904); John Meier's *Deutsche Volkskunde* (Berlin, 1926); Wilhelm Pessler's *Handbuch der deutschen Volkskunde* (3 vols., Berlin, n. d.); and Adolph Spamer's *Die deutsche Volkskunde* (2 vols., Leipzig, 1934). Of these works, Meier's handbook is the best. It was written as a teachers' handbook during the early days of Nazism, but it contains none of Hitler's ideas. The works by Pessler and Spamer are encyclopedic, historical, critical, and interpretative. They provide a history of folklore studies, a description of the various branches of the subject, and an extensive bibliography. One of the large quarto volumes edited by Spamer is devoted entirely to illustrations! The pictorial side of German folklore has always been fully cared for.[12]

If we turn to the different fields of study that we regard as folklore, we note that, in Germany as elsewhere, the existence of a single great collection written at an early time in the development of folklore exerts a continuing influence. Thus, the collection called *Des Knaben Wunderhorn* that Achim von Arnim and Clemens Brentano published in 1808 continues to arouse general interest in folksongs in much the same manner that the *Kinder- und Hausmärchen* (Berlin, 1812) of the Brothers Grimm still evokes interest in tales. Such books have stimulated and directed study, and in areas of folklore where they are lacking, study has languished. For example, there has been no such important book in Germany for the proverb or the riddle. Or, if we turn to England, we see that folklore study has been hindered there by the lack of an easily available and generally accepted collection of children's rhymes.[13] It is instructive, then, to see how as standard a work as Jacob Grimm's *Deutsche Rechtsaltertümer* (2 vols., 1828) had led German folklorists into a subject that their English and American colleagues have never dealt with at all. Grimm's collection, classification, and study of German legal antiquities contains historical references to such matters as the kinds of punishments inflicted for various crimes and the time limits of contracts, such as "seven years" or "a year and a day." Because it was Jacob Grimm who wrote the book, German folklorists have maintained an interest in legal antiquities ever since. Despite its failure to attain the standards of critical editing of the time, much less those of today, Grimm's book has had a positive effect in stimulating the publication of similar volumes for each of the small German states,[14] and in establishing a solid scholarly tradition which contrasts sharply with the somewhat scattered antiquarian tradition, let us say, in England. In England and America, moreover, interest in legal antiquities remains almost exclusively limited to legal historians.

A characteristic of German folklore studies has been the collecting of parallels and the writing of annotations. These tasks have assumed an importance in Germany comparable to the production of monographs on individual tales or songs in Finland and in America.[15] Collecting analogues and annotating folklore, of course, are activities which others than German scholars have performed, but more of this kind of work has been done in Germany than elsewhere. The most convenient notes to Boccaccio's *Decameron,* for example, were written by a German and not by an Italian.

The Germans have naturally been most enthusiastic about annotating their own books. Because these books, especially the older collections of tales or songs and the older jestbooks,[16] naturally include items of international currency, their abundant and elaborate notes are important guides to the folklore of all nations.[17]

Although the Germans have collected and annotated parallels to all kinds of texts, they have not, as indicated already, shown a great deal of interest in writing monographs on individual tales or songs. Collecting and indexing remain their major tasks, especially with regard to folksong, which is the outstanding branch of folklore studies in Germany. The center of such study is the Deutsches Volksliedarchiv at Freiburg im Breisgau in southwestern Germany. The world's largest institute devoted to folksong, the Freiburg archive contains hundreds of thousands of texts, all of them admirably indexed. Started fifty years ago, the great collection entitled *Deutsche Volkslieder* (Berlin, 1935-), edited by John Meier and Erich Seemann, is still being expanded, and the fourth volume has just been completed for publication. This series is a work of international importance, since the volumes already in print contain ballads known throughout Europe. Much local publication of folksongs has likewise taken place, however. The Germans have a great many excellent collections from various provinces comparable to the various state collections in the United States.[18] And the first attempt at popularizing folksong was made not, as we might guess, in England or the United States, but by an Austrian who began publishing a folksong journal for the encouragement of German groups of folksingers over sixty years ago.[19]

Like the *Deutsche Volkslieder*, Kurt Ranke's folktale collection *Schleswig-Holsteinische Volksmärchen* (Kiel, 1955-58) is a work of international significance. To date two volumes have appeared, but more is yet to come. Although the title of this work suggests a regional collection and the tales were recorded in the two northernmost provinces of Germany, the notes are so extensive that the book is an essential guide to the study of international folktales. And here we might return to our previous remarks about the importance of a standard collection of materials. The *Household Tales* of the Brothers Grimm comprised such a standard collection and, like Ranke's collection, owed their importance in large part to the comparative notes. As early as 1822 these notes were printed in a separate volume, and the greatly expanded notes published in 1856 as the third volume in the set were a guide to tales for two generations. In 1912 Johannes Bolte began publication of a new, five-volume edition of these notes, a task which he and Georg Polívka completed in 1932. This book, the *Anmerkungen zu den Kinder- und Hausmärchen der Brüder Grimm* (5 vols., Leipzig, 1913-32), is the encyclopedia of the folktale. I have used the word "encyclopedia" somewhat colloquially, however, for Kurt Ranke at present is organizing what he calls the *Encyclopädie des Märchens,* which will be a truly encyclopedic work of eight to ten volumes.

For some reason the Grimm tales have proved a discouragement to further German collecting of *Märchen*.[20] Therefore, another kind of tale, the *Sage,* has attracted a great deal of attention in Germany. *Sagen* collections have been made in great numbers for almost a century and a half,[21] but German folklorists have never studied these narratives in an adequate, systematic way. Though they continue to collect such stories about the Devil, ghosts, water spirits, dwarfs, and the like, in order to gain information about their nation's pre-Christian background, these scholars have not yet found their efforts in this direction too successful. We may expect increased interest in such tales, though, because Will-Erich Peuckert is preparing a *Hand-wörterbuch der Sage* that will be as large as Ranke's encyclopedia of the *Märchen*. At present, the only encyclopedic work dealing with the *Sage* is Waldemar Liungman's *Sveriges Sägner i Ord och Bild* (3 vols., Stockholm, 1957-59), written in Swedish.

The collection of German proverbs began auspiciously in the sixteenth century, and during the following hundred years some very large collections appeared.[22] But since then proverbs have been somewhat neglected in Germany. To be sure, a large five-volume collection was published by K. F. W. Wander, but he had succumbed to the disease that so often infects students of proverbs: he believed that he could invent them. Consequently, his *Deutsches Spirchwörterlexikon* (1863-80) is regarded today with considerable suspicion. That is, his data are accepted only when he gives specific sources for a given proverb. Wander's book has been a handicap to the making of more solid, subsequent collections. Nevertheless, the German contribution to proverb studies in more recent times is noteworthy for the best general book on the subject, Friedrich Seiler's *Deutsche Sprichwörterkunde,* and for a book of a very special kind. This book is Georg Büchmann's *Geflügelte Worte,* which since its first appearance in 1864 has had an amazingly successful career. A twenty-seventh edition was published in 1925, and various new editions, which no longer take account of numbers, have appeared since 1945. All of these, at least down to the edition of 1925, show constant enlargement and improvement, but such recent editions as I have seen are condensations and popularizations of less value. Büchmann's annotated collection contains a special kind of popular saying that lies on the boundary between the familiar quotation and the proverb. It is concerned with those sayings, such as "Let them eat cake," that can be ascribed more or less correctly to particular persons like Marie Antoinette. Making every effort to trace such sayings to their sources, Büchmann has given folklorists a work of international reference value. By comparison, our books of familiar quotations in English are very often mere compilations of praiseworthy sentiments.[23]

There remain two more general reference works in other fields of German folklore. The first of these is the *Handwörterbuch des deutschen Aberglaubens* (10 vols., Berlin, 1927-42), which began as an enlarged revision of a mid-nineteenth-century book of German superstitions[24] but almost immediately outgrew the limits of this work. Originally an alphabetical, annotated list of the materials that the nineteenth-century volume contains, the *Handwörterbuch* became a vast dictionary that not only includes superstitions, but also many references to tales of all kinds. Despite the title, the sources quoted go far beyond those in German. International in scope, these ten volumes include numerous references to classical materials, Orientalia, and to sources in English as well.[25]

The last of these general reference works is Paul Sartori's *Sitte und Brauch* (3 vols., Leipzig, 1910-14). This encyclopedia of manners and customs contains very rich references, but these almost exclusively pertain to German sources. The first volume contains descriptions of manners and customs related to the human life cycle; the second, descriptions of comparable traditions connected with seasons of the year; and the third focuses upon German calendar customs.

This survey will have given some general notions of the ways in which the German approach to folklore differs from approaches to the subject in other nations. It should also have indicated that folklore scholarship even within one country is not held together by a unified and generally accepted concept as rigidly as, for instance, is the study of history. And, finally, it will have suggested the wealth of excellent reference books available to the student who wishes to probe more deeply into German folklore.[26]

NOTES

1. "The Great Team of English Folklorists," *Journal of American Folklore,* LXIV (1951), 1-10; "The First Group of British Folklorists," *Journal of American Folklore,* LXVIII (1955), 1-8, 333-340; "The Eclipse of Solar Mythology," *Journal of American Folklore,* LXVIII (1955), 393-416.

2. See, for example, Benjamin Thorpe, *Northern Mythology, comprising the principal Popular Traditions and Superstitions of Scandinavia, North Germany, and the Netherlands* (3 vols., London, 1851-52).

3. This may, or may not, be a correct interpretation of the *Germania,* for students of the classics dispute over the matter. At any rate, all students would agree that even though it is primarily socio-political, it also has a conspicuous ethnographical and descriptive nature.

4. Conrad Celtis, *Situs et Mores Germaniae* (n. d.).

5. Unfortunately, copies of most of them are difficult to locate.

6. Nikolaus von Dinkelsbühl, *De Preceptis Decalogi* (Strassburg, 1516).

7. The French have journals devoted to their early Celtic background and to Celtic studies in general. Three of these are *Annales de Bretagne; Études celtiques;* and *Memoires de la Société d'Histoire et d'Archéologie de Bretagne.*

8. *Zeitschrift für deutsche Mythologie und Sittenkunde* (4 vols., 1853-59), edited by J. W. Wolf and, after his death, by Wilhelm Mannhardt.

9. Of course, folklore and anthropology have drawn further apart in other countries, too, as in France and the United States.

10. Little of this interest in local tradition exists in France. Though there are many learned societies in the French provinces, by and large they do not collect and publish items of folklore peculiar to their locality. For example, the local historical and antiquarian society of Amiens published an excellent article on the rebus, partly because it had a strange and unexplained tradition in that area, and partly because they regarded it, so to speak, as a monument of culture "par tout." (Oct. Thorel, "Les Rebus de Picardie," *Mémoires de la Société des Antiquaires de Picardie,* 4th series, IV [1903], 499-700.) The same society undoubtedly would not print a collection of local proverbs or folksongs, however. And neither would a comparable society in the United States.

11. Yet the best general history of folklore, and one of the few international in scope, curiously enough, was written by an Italian. Guiseppe Cocchiara's recently published *Storia del Folklore in Europa* (Turin, 1952) has been reviewed very favorably by this writer in the *Journal of American Folklore,* LXVII (1954), 407, and deserves the attention of folklorists everywhere.

12. There is even a history of Austrian folklore studies by Leopold Schmidt, *Geschichte der österreichischen Volkskunde* (Wien, 1951). For a history of folklore studies in all of northern Europe, consult Inger M. Boberg, *Folkemindeforskningens Historie i Mellem og Nordeuropa* (Copenhagen, 1953), an excellent work on the subject in Danish. Boberg presents more of a summary of completed scholarship than an interpretative or critical history.

13. *Mother Goose* was neither a scholarly collection with popular appeal nor a definite limited body of materials.

14. See Johannes Bolte and Georg Polívka, *Anmerkungen zu den Kinder- und Hausmärchen der Brüder Grimm* (Leipzig, 1932), V, 1-24, for older publications; see Kurt Ranke, *Schleswig-Holsteinische Volksmärchen* (Kiel, 1955-58), I, 11-14; II, 7, for newer publications.

15. Of course, such monographs are acceptable as doctoral dissertations in Germany. But after a German student receives his degree, he is not likely to make any further investigations of this kind.

16. See, for example, Johannes Pauli, *Schimpf und Ernst* (2 vols., Berlin, 1924), and Bolte and Polívka.

17. Aside from American collections of ballads, collections outside of Germany are not so likely to be as well annotated.

18. Whereas German and American regional folksong collections are comparable, the same cannot be said in regard to regional collections in France, Italy, and Spain. Collections in these Romance nations contain little in the way of theoretical framework, and lack such scholarly apparatus as cross-references to each other, data on informants, and the like.

19. *Das deutsche Volkslied,* edited by Josef Pommer. Volume I was issued in 1899 in Leipzig.

20. The publication of these tales was also supposed to have had a similar effect outside Germany, but we realize today that even though they were translated into other languages, they

did not have the destructive effect on, let us say, Flemish or Swedish traditions that was postulated some years ago. A few of the Grimm tales did return to European oral traditions, but in general even these did not contaminate other stories with which they came in contact.

21. See, for example, Will-Erich Peuckert, *Deutsche Sagen* (Berlin, 1961); Richard Beitl, *Wörterbuch der deutschen Volkskunde* (Stuttgart, 1955); and *Handwörterbuch des deutschen Aberglaubens* (10 vols., Berlin, 1927-42).

22. See the references in Friedrich Seiler, *Deutsche Sprichwörterkunde* (Munich, 1922); and Archer Taylor, "An Introductory Bibliography for the Study of the Proverb," *Modern Philology*, XXX (1932), 195-210.

23. Aside from Seiler's work already mentioned, no twentieth-century proverb collections in Germany can compare with either the superb German collections published in the seventeenth century, or with those that are available today in English. Yet there are some good regional collections in Germany today, and some scholars are beginning the promising task of extracting proverbs from the works of individual German authors. Those of the sixteenth and seventeenth centuries are especially likely to yield good materials. No work is being done in Germany on the riddle, however. Ever since Richard Wossidlo made an excellent collection of riddles in northern Germany ("Rätsel," *Mecklenburgische Volksuberlieferungen*, I [Wismar, 1897]), everyone else has been content to let it go at that.

24. A. Wuttke, *Der deutsche Volksaberglauben der Gegenwart* (1860), 4th edition by E. H. Meyer (1925).

25. Bachtold-Stäubli, an intermediary between textile unions and employers by trade, nevertheless spent half his life compiling this reference work and literally killed himself over it, just twenty years ago. But this monumental work was published and is again characteristic of the encyclopedic nature of German folklore studies.

26. While the subjects discussed in this paper usually have not been treated monographically, an abundant number of individual monographs has been published in Germany on aspects of archaeological and physical folklore. These include comprehensive treatises on folk-costume, folk-architecture, and the traditional layout of German villages. See, for example, Adolph Bach, *Deutsche Volkskunde* (Heidelberg, 1960), and Richard Beitl, *Wörterbuch der deutschen Volkskunde* (Stuttgart, 1955).

Further general references can be found in Adolph Hauffen, "Geschichte der deutschen Volkskunde," *Zeitschrift der Vereins für Volkskunde*, XX (Berlin, 1910), 1-17, 129-141, 290-306.

University of California
Berkeley, California

RICHARD M. DORSON

FOLKLORE STUDIES IN ENGLAND

IN THE halcyon years of English folklore studies falling toward the close of Queen Victoria's reign, American and English folklorists enjoyed much closer communion than in this present day of jet air travel. At the international folklore congress in London sponsored by the English Folk-Lore Society in 1891, the peripatetic Yankee Charles Godfrey Leland personally presented a paper, as did his disciple Mary Alicia Owen, and the editor of the American Folklore Society, William Wells Newell, sent one in on "Lady Featherflight" which evoked a sharp disagreement from Andrew Lang, smarting at the thesis that folktales originated with civilized peoples.[1] Two years later at a similar congress held in Chicago by the old Chicago Folk-Lore Society, several well-known English and Scottish folklorists, including Lucy M. J. Garnett, David MacRitchie, and the Hon. John Abercromby, reciprocated by offering papers of their own.[2] But in the twentieth century the links between English and American folklorists (exclusive of folksong devotees) have snapped, while ties between the United States and the continent have steadily grown stronger.

The reasons for this estrangement can be found on both sides of the water. In England the cause of folklore has languished since the generation of Lang; British social anthropology has severed its once intimate relations with ethnologically minded folklorists, and the famous universities ignore the science of folklore initiated by Englishmen. In the United States, three main lines of influence have all bypassed the Victorian folklorists: the anthropology of Franz Boas, with its emphasis on tribal narratives of North American Indians; the historical-geographical methodology of the Finns, conveyed to America by Stith Thompson and Archer Taylor; and the collation of Anglo-American balladry, begun in the library by Child and continued in the field by Sharp. Since in England the gulf between "folklore" and "folksong" was so wide that a separate society represented each field, the American cultists of the Child ballad traced their ancestry to Percy and Ritson, in utter oblivion of Thoms and Gomme.

An aspiring American folklorist in the 1940's learned that he must master the foreign tongues before he could enter the holy chambers of folklore scholarship. He heard much about the magisterial monographs from Germany, Finland, and all three Scandinavian countries. The Irish were praised for exhaustive collecting labors among their Gaelic-speaking countrymen, and the Russians for attention to the cultural biography of Siberian folk-bards. Frenchmen had once speculated boldly about the Indian origins of European tales, and Italians had been the first to recognize the literary possibilities of traditional story. But of a folklore movement in England not a whisper was uttered.[3]

Yet the last of the dedicated group who organized and founded the English Folk-Lore Society, Edward Clodd and Sidney Hartland, lived on until 1924 and 1928. In one generation their names had passed into limbo. None of their numerous books remained in print, save only the multi-colored fairy tale series of Andrew Lang, which alone of his extensive folklore writings made no pretense at scholarship.

From July 1948 to December 1951, much of my time was spent in London on three different trips, reading the works of the nineteenth-century English folklorists in the Folk-Lore Society library and the British Museum. A purely personal circumstance led me to the Victorian folklorists; my sister had married an Englishman and resided in London, and I paid them a visit in the summer of 1948. One day I dropped in at the office of the Folk-Lore Society, at 21 Bedford Square—actually the quarters of the Royal Anthropological Institute, whose secretary also handled the business of the smaller society. The office secretary, Miss Felicia Stallman, informed me that a library belonging to the Folk-Lore Society was housed within the Medical Library of the University of London on Gower Street. There I went, and in that unlikely spot I found a treasure, several dusty and dilapidated rows of bookcases at the furthest end of a library devoted to medical literature. Here by arrangement with University College, London, since 1911, the Folk-Lore Society obtained space for the accumulation of books, periodicals, reprints, and clippings donated by its members, and by the reviewers in its journal *Folk-Lore,* since the founding of the society in 1878. In the whole summer—and I spent every day that summer in the Gower Street hideaway— perhaps three persons made their way briefly to the folklore library. I had the collection all to myself.

In 1948 the devastation of war still scarred London, and the direct bomb hit on University College gaped in the courtyard. The librarian of the university, F. M. C. Johnson, who was also the Hon. Librarian of the Folk-Lore Society, was salvaging his stocks and searching for new quarters, hence the makeshift arrangements for the folklore collection. Books were heaped on the floor and piled on window ledges, and when I blew the dust off them, great vaporous clouds arose to the grimy ceiling. Three years later the library was housed in its own alcove on open shelves in a readily accessible general reading room, well lighted and handsomely furnished. But my first impression was the true one, for the Victorian folklorists had been forgotten as completely as if the bomb had blown their books sky high.

In the fall of 1949 I returned to England for a year's stay on a Guggenheim fellowship, and again in June 1951 I came back to my old digs near Hyde Park for six months on sabbatical leave. My Guggenheim project called for a history of the English folklore movement, concentrating on the "great team" of Lang, Hartland, Gomme, Clodd, Nutt, and Clouston. But in fact I spent the whole year attempting to reach their period, from 1870 to 1912, and sailed home without having crossed the mid-century. In endeavoring to uncover the intellectual tradition from which Lang and his fellows had sprung, I came to realize that the story began early rather than late in the nineteenth century, and that another voluminous literature lay behind the productions of the great team, buried even deeper in the shadows. Eventually I fastened on 1813 as the foundation year for the continuous history of the folklore movement, for in 1813 the Ellis edition of Brand's *Popular Antiquities* gathered up the scattered chronicles and antiquarian treatises of past centuries into a vade mecum for Victorian gentlemen. From that point on one could trace a consecutive chain of influences and an increasing momentum that came to eruption in 1878 with the formation of the Folk-Lore Society. A brilliant period followed, in which George Laurence Gomme and his colleagues labored prodigiously to establish a science of folklore.[4]

And what was their heritage? The Folk-Lore Society lived on, and I regularly attended its meetings in the winter of 1949-50. Now the reason became increasingly clear for the eclipse of the Victorian folklorists; they had left no successors. Two world wars had taken their toll of Britain's manpower, and the elderly membership of the Society belonged indeed to the nineteenth rather than the twentieth century. The suppers and lectures at University College on one Wednesday each winter month were conducted in the wholesome spirit of archaeological, topographical, and antiquarian societies which flourished during the Pax Britannica. Lectures were given on methods of lighting, furniture styles, the folklore of the potato, and the Sutton Hoo burial mound.

A visitor from the States was immediately struck by the absence of academic people in the society. The president, W. L. Hildburgh, turned out to be an American, although years of bachelor residence in London had turned him into the veriest English antiquary, and in fact he belonged to the Royal Society of Antiquaries, as well as to the boards of several museums. Dr. Hildburgh had taken an engineering degree at Columbia University, subsequently traveled to the Far East for his father's export firm, and there had begun to write papers on Japanese household magic and talismans. His chief research interests lay in amulets and alabasters, and he was active in the Victoria and Albert Museum. Since my digs were close to his, we frequently lunched together, and I heard from him a good deal about the problems, chiefly financial, of the Folk-Lore Society. The chief factotum of the Society was Mrs. H. A. Lake Barnett, the Hon. Secretary and Hon. Treasurer, who tended its affairs with a strong maternal care. Equally energetic was Mrs. Mary Danielli, review editor of *Folk-Lore,* a young woman who had done fieldwork in Madagascar, but pressures of a home and young children shortly caused her to resign her duties. Margaret Murray, venerable and sturdy, attended the meetings frequently, while continuing her speculations about the undercover witch cult of western Europe. With some excitement I called on Allan Gomme, son of the vigorous and dedicated Sir George Laurence and Lady Alice Bertha Gomme. Gentle and kindly Allan Gomme succeeded Dr. Hildburgh to the presidency of the Society, but his interests in folklore were nominal. Another future president, Sona R. Burstein, had developed a concern with witchcraft through her work in gerontology, and presented a paper on the correlation between old crones and witches. From Germany had come Ellen Ettlinger to reside in Oxford, where she organized an Oxford folklore group, and often managed to attend the London meetings. Viola Alford occasionally came to the suppers, providing a link with the English Folk Dance and Song Society of Cecil Sharp House; she would publish a slight *Introduction to English Folklore* (1952), strewn with references to her research in folk dances and festivals of Spain and the Pyrenees, and heavily emphasizing the Mummers' Play. Thomas W. Bagshawe, whom I visited in Cambridge, upheld the folk museum movement, and contributed frequent notices to *Folk-Lore* on museum exhibits and acquisitions. By all odds the youngest person in evidence was Peter Opie, noted collector of children's rhymes, who was elected to the Council in 1952, but he and his attractive wife Iona lived in the south of England and rarely came to meetings. The one university don actively involved in the Society was the Hon. Editor, the Rev. Prof. E. O. James, Professor of the History of Religion at the University of London, who also lived outside London, and never attended a Society lecture all the time I was in England.[5]

One evening I arrived early at the monthly supper, and found myself alone with the ancient Mrs. M. MacLeod Banks, past president and compiler of three volumes of Scottish calendar customs, who never missed a meeting. This seemed a splendid opportunity to query her about the founding fathers of the Society, whom she had known personally, and I broached my inquiry into her ear trumpet. Several repetitions of increasing volume brought no response, and we sat it out in stony silence until the others arrived.

The contrast between the old and the new look in folklore activities would have forcefully struck any observer present the night James H. Delargy lectured to the Society. Founder and director of the flourishing Irish Folklore Commission, Professor Delargy spoke of the treasures of lore collected and archived in Dublin in the short period since the founding of the Commission in 1935, and exhorted his English listeners to initiate a comparable collecting program. The lack of any collecting enterprises, whether cooperative or individual, is indeed the great handicap of the current English folklore scene. Save for the work of the Opies with the traditions of school children, and excepting folksong publications which take their stimulus from Cecil Sharp House, no collections of any consequence have been added to the series of county volumes that appeared in the half century after 1860. Meanwhile the great European archives continue to swell with a regular and systematized inflow. In the decade since Professor Delargy's particular lecture, and with his encouragement, the School for Scottish Studies at Edinburgh has developed a substantial folklore archives and collecting program. But the English have at the present writing not solved their problems.

A major problem lies in the failure of folklore studies to attain academic recognition at Oxford, Cambridge, the red brick universities, or even the University of London, where the Society's library is housed. Hence the dearth of academic scholars, old or young, of funds for archives and field trips, of concerted intellectual effort. In the generation of Lang the private scholar possessed vigor enough, but it is a fact of contemporary life that any solid field of learning needs university sponsorship. Anthropology, once so closely linked with folklore that Gomme called the two subjects indistinguishable, did win its way into the great universities, but English social anthropology today has discarded folklore even more ruthlessly than has cultural anthropology in the United States.

American folklorists can sympathize with their English colleagues all the more since they are to some extent in the same boat, and at the First International Folktale Congress held in Kiel, Germany, in August 1959, participants from Great Britain and the States met together one evening to compare notes. Both sides commented on the difficulties of their national societies in maintaining a firm and growing membership, in competition with the professional organizations of the humanities and the social sciences anchored in the universities. The problem of popularization so prominent in America had not become acute in England, although the new editor of *Folk-Lore*, Christina Hole (who succeeded Professor James in 1956), is not a research scholar but a re-writer of older English works on witches, ghosts, heroes, and customs. New leadership has come to the Society with the appointment as Secretary of Professor C. S. Mundy of the Institute of Oriental Studies of the University of London. A standing committee was appointed on British-American folklore relations, with Mundy as chairman, Hamish Henderson representing Scotland, and R. M. Dorson the United States.

What had happened since the days when G. L. Gomme strove so energetically to establish a "science of folklore"? The moral for Americans, now in a stage of ferment and intensity comparable to that of the late Victorians, is clearly pertinent.

We cannot know the reasons for the decline of the folklore movement in England until the full history of that complex movement has been written, but I suggest as a general explanation the character that English folklore studies assumed from their very beginnings.

That character was antiquarian and amateur, in the best sense of those words. *Popular Antiquities,* the title of John Brand's celebrated compendium, perfectly describes the kind of interest that attracted Victorian gentlemen to this quaint subject. Brand himself had assembled the gleanings of earlier antiquaries.[6] Antiquarian zeal came to fruition in the nineteenth century, when England possessed the wealth, the leisure, the interest, and the educated upper middle class to unearth descriptions of old "customs and usages" in the British Museum, and to observe them in the countryside on walking tours. For the Victorians the fondling of antiquities provided moderate intellectual stimulus, innocent nationalistic satisfaction, and the serene joy of the hobbyist. Proliferating local societies, presided over by an earl, duke, or lord, delved into heraldry, genealogy, archaeology, topography, lexicography—and folklore. One of the first books to include "folklore" in its title was the second edition in 1852 of a work by Jabez Allies *On the Ancient British, Roman, and Saxon Antiquities and Folk-Lore of Worcestershire,* whose first edition in 1840 of course did not carry the uncoined word "folk-lore."[7]

The heart of antiquarian folklore lay in custom, and particularly in calendar custom. Brand constructed the *Popular Antiquities* around the calendrical festivals and local observances on special days of the year, and English folklore studies have followed this rubric right up to the present; scarcely a year passes but the same volume in slightly new design issues from the press, relating once again with the usual musty flavor the call of the Padstow Hobby Horse on May Day, the Pancake Scramble on Shrove Tuesday, the Dunmow Flitch trial on Whit-Monday.[8] Currently the Folk-Lore Society for its long range enterprise continues a comprehensive series on British Calendar Customs. When the spirited team of Gomme and his fellows sought to vitalize folklore science by applying the concepts of evolutionary anthropology to their field, their doctrine of survivals still retained the emphasis on archaic and ancient practice and belief, whose preservation among the "lower orders" of society furnished clues to the early history of mankind. Consequently, in spite of occasional pleas to consider "living" folklore, the anthropological school turned away from questions of function and process (save for the process of degeneration) in folk traditions, and sought instead to reconstruct their prehistoric forms. When anthropology rejected the theory of unilinear cultural evolution in favor of cultural pluralism, the scaffolding of English folklore research collapsed.

The debris could have been cleared were it not for the amateur status of folklore. Had a group of professional scholars emerged, they would necessarily have kept abreast of current developments on the continent, and have turned their attention to the tasks of collecting and archiving, as a necessary preliminary to new speculative theory. The survey of folklore scholarship by Ethel J. Lindgren included in a handbook of the social sciences, published in London in 1939, could admirably have served as a point of departure for a new generation of professional folklorists.[9] Such a new generation might never have equalled the prodigious labors of the gifted Victorian amateurs, who wrote their books in the evening after their day's work at the law office, the bank, the publishing house, the newspaper desk. But by their commitments as teachers and researchers, university professors of folklore can keep their subjects from falling exclusively into the hands of dilettantes. They did this in Europe, and are attempting to do so in America, but such professorships never emerged in England.[10]

The England of the nineteenth century—or more precisely, of the years from 1813 to 1912, from the Brand-Ellis edition of *Popular Antiquities* to the death of Lang—still needs to be visited by all students of folklore. Its vast and diversified output of folkloristic writings may be suggested under the following heads.

(1) *The older antiquaries.* Here is the amorphous literature upon which Brand levied: the older compendiums of marvels and oddities, like Wanley's Wonders and Turner's Providences; the ethnographic walking trips, such as Pennant's Tour; the polemics over witchcraft, notably Scot's *Discoverie of Witchcraft;* and other household tomes, Stow's *Survey of London,* or Strutt's *Sports and Pastimes,* each with its share of custom, belief, and usage to be extracted.[11]

(2) *The early 19th century antiquary-folklorists.* The transition from the antiquary to the folklorist is achieved by 1846, when William John Thoms replaces "popular antiquities" with "folk-lore." Fellow-enthusiasts of Thoms giving order and shape to the assembled antiquities were his friend the bibliophile Francis Douce; Thomas Keightley, author of *The Fairy Mythology;* James Orchard Halliwell-Phillips, compiler of nursery rhymes and children's games; the prolific medievalist Thomas Wright.[12]

(3) *The early literary folklorists.* The study of living folklore germinated when English observers began deliberately to describe the still surviving customs and usages ferreted from old tomes by the antiquaries. A leading spirit in stimulating country squires and vicars to report on archaic village ceremonies and superstitions was William Hone, who began in 1826 his *Every-Day Book and Table Book; or Everlasting Calendar of Popular Amusements, Sports, Pastimes, Ceremonies, Manners, Customs, and Events* (3 vols., 1838). The impulse to collect and record developed slowly and fitfully, and was diverted during the 1820's and '30's into the literature of topography and rural scenes and characters. Nevertheless these heavily landscaped musings and jottings displayed a keen sense for oral tradition in their prefaces and in their titles: Allan Cunningham's *Traditional Tales of the English and Scottish Peasantry* (2 vols., 1822), John Roby's *The Traditions of Lancashire* (2 vols., 1829), Andrew Picken's *Traditionary Stories of Old Families, and Legendary Illustrations of Family History* (2 vols., 1833), Samuel Lover's *Legends and Stories of Ireland* (1831). One preface announces its tales as "essentially *oral* in their character"; another declares the "old narrative fire-side mode of story-telling . . . has not been departed from," and thanks the "humble and wandering novelists" who supplied the author with his themes. The perspective of these writers is revealed in a third prefatory note, on Roby, who spent the leisure of six years "in collecting materials for the *Traditions of Lancashire,* and in weaving these into tales of romantic interest."[13]

(4) *The Scottish collectors.* The appreciation and respect for oral tradition emerges in Scotland sooner than in England, due in part to the transcendent influence of Sir Walter Scott in matters of demonology, witchcraft, and border legend. In 1835 the geologist Hugh Miller published his *Scenes and Legends of the North of Scotland, or the Traditional History of Cromarty,* in the mold of the romantic topographies, but with a firm grasp of the local traditions abounding in a hardy port town. Another disciple of Scott, the publisher Robert Chambers, brought out in 1825 an unusual assembling of city legends in *The Traditions of Edinburgh,* and the next year

issued his equally original *The Popular Rhymes of Scotland, with illustrations, chiefly collected from Oral Sources.* Over forty years later in the spirit of Brand and Hone he edited his well known *The Book of Days, A Miscellany of Popular Antiquities in connection with the Calendar* (2 vols., 1869), reserving one section for "Folk-Lore of the United Kingdom—namely, Popular Notions and Observances connected with Times and Seasons." In the latter decades of the century the supernatural lore of the Highlands attracted a number of collectors,[14] and the technique of recording oral narratives reached a high water mark in Campbell of Islay's *Popular Tales of the West Highlands* (4 vols., 1860-62).

(5) *The "savage" folklorists.* After mid-century the self-centered British interests of the antiquaries flowed into another current of inquiry, the behavior and beliefs of primitive peoples, or "savages" in the language of the day. The publication of Tylor's *Primitive Mankind* in 1871 crystallized the concept of cultural ascent for folklorists as well as for anthropologists. Key works in this transitional period, constantly cited by the later professional folklorists, are Kelly's *Curiosities of Indo-European Tradition and Folk-Lore*, Lubbock's *Pre-Historic Times*, Farrar's *Ancient Ways and Customs*, and Keary's *Outlines of Primitive Belief.*[15] Such syntheses of savage ideas gave a seemingly scientific basis to the doctrine of survivals cherished by the school of anthropological folklorists.

(6) *The scientific folklorists.* Building on the groundwork of these various groups, a nucleus of dedicated private scholars in 1878 founded the Folk-Lore Society, and devoted their considerable energies and talents to placing the study of folklore on a serious, scholarly basis. George Laurence Gomme was the chief spokesman for a "science of folklore," based on the doctrine of survivals. His notable colleagues included, in the inner circle, Edwin Sidney Hartland, Andrew Lang, Edward Clodd, and Alfred Nutt, all prolific scholars, who together combated and vanquished the solar mythologists led by Max Müller and George Cox. Other active folklorists of the anthropological school were Marian Roalfe Cox, who assembled the variants of Cinderella; Canon J. A. MacCulloch, author of *The Childhood of Fiction;* William Alexander Clouston, a self-taught Arabist especially interested in the tales of the Middle East; Moses Gaster, the erudite Rumanian rabbi who came to live in London, and published his *Rumanian Bird and Beast Stories* as a memoir of the Folk-Lore Society.[16]

(7) *The county collectors.* If the theoretical and speculative founders of the Folk-Lore Society never themselves engaged in collecting, they encouraged residents of the countryside to labor in the field, and trap survivals of once meaningful customs and beliefs. The typical English collection runs heavily to the items of local tradition, beginning usually with a chapter on the local geology and topography, and the traditions connected with the landscape. Then follow accounts of the demons, giants and ogres belonging to an older stratum of story; more modern specters, like witches and goblins; charms, beliefs, sayings, and rhymes of the peasantry; celebrations peculiar to particular villages or generally observed in the county; games and pastimes. Notably missing were international tales and large sheaves of balladry. Rarely did the collector venture into the field for any extended time, although Robert Hunt in his early (1865) volumes on *Popular Romances of the West of England; or the Drolls, Traditions, and Superstitions of Old Cornwall* tells of walking trips on which he made contact with the wandering storytellers who recited "drolls" or long, rambling narratives of magic and adventure. But typically the collector accumulated

notes on superstitions and customs in the county over a long period of residence, jotting down observations of the charwoman, the greengrocer, and the street vendor. Frequently he supplied comparative and discursive notes on points of origin and affinity. The same structure is visible in the cache of Burne from Shropshire, Leather from Herefordshire, Harland and Wilkinson, Hardwick and Henderson from Lancashire and the northern counties, MacCulloch from the Isle of Guernsey, and others. These sometimes massive county volumes were usually printed in tiny editions, often on a subscription basis.[17]

(8) *The popular folklorists.* While such facile writers as Andrew Lang and Edward Clodd reached wide audiences with their theoretical folklore books, a still larger circle, then as now, craved popular treatments of folklore. Often enough the village parson displayed talents as a folklore popularizer. Two clergymen in particular, Sabine Baring-Gould and Thomas F. Thiselton-Dyer, catered to the public with prodigious numbers of books. Baring-Gould published one hundred and twenty titles, running heavily to "Oddities" and "Strange Events." These Victorian bestsellers would probably be considered works of scholarship today, for they contain footnotes, extensive bibliographies, and summaries of considerable bodies of legends and customs. In fact they do sometimes make a contribution, for in works like *The Folk-Lore of Women* and *The Folk-Lore of Plants,* Thiselton-Dyer brought together scattered collectanea in compact form, while in his appendix to Henderson's *Folk Lore of the Northern Counties,* Baring-Gould analyzed "The Radicals of Folktales" in a manner suggestive of the type-indexes of the future.[18]

Another cleric, Rev. J. C. Atkinson, wrote in *Forty Years in a Moorland Parish* (1891) one of the most revealing field accounts of the whole period. From his secluded parishioners on the bleak Danby moors, he recorded beliefs in witchcraft and deviltry, in their complete ethnographical setting, and with human portraits vividly sketched. More gossipy is the reprinted series of newspaper jottings by Fletcher Moss, *Folk-Lore: Old Customs and Tales of my Neighbours* (Published by the Author from his home The Old Parsonage, Didsbury; and from his room in *The Spread Eagle Hotel,* Hanging Ditch, Manchester, March 1898).

(9) *The overseas folklorists.* In the glorious century of the Pax Britannica, Englishmen traveled, taught, preached, and administered all over the globe. From some of these missionaries, travelers, and colonial officers resident in Asia and Africa and browsing in Europe came important collections and translations of folk traditions, directly stimulated by the interest and theories in the subject at home. One thinks of the reports from Greece by Rodd; from Italy and Mongolia of Busk; from Scandinavia of Dasent, Craigie, and Thorpe; from Russia of Ralston; from India of Crooke and Knowles; from Africa of Callaway; from Polynesia of Grey and Gill; from Australia of Parker. Government officials and missionaries believed that a familiarity with native folklore would immeasurably aid their work.[19] The collective achievement of these skilled vocational collectors in many parts of the world awaits its due.

The characteristics of English folklore research may be summarized as follows. Folklore activities reached their height in the half century preceding the outbreak of the First World War. Gifted amateurs, i.e., nonacademic scholars, built upon the earlier work of antiquaries extending back for three centuries. The doctrine of survivals, adapted from the theory of biological evolution, unified the work of the late Victorian scholars. English folklore study from the beginning has been marked by a strong interest in custom and usage, and by a sharp distinction between folklore in this sense, and folksong. The full sweep of the English achievement includes the work of Englishmen abroad as well as at home. For the most part English folklore investigations have proceeded independently of European influence, save for the theories of Jacob Grimm. In the British Isles the center of activity has shifted in the period since World War II from London to Dublin and, more recently, Edinburgh. Folklife research is developing in Wales, where a new journal devoted to that subject, *Gwerin,* is now issued. The chapter of English folklore leadership is closed, but it makes magnificent reading.

NOTES

1. Published in *The International Folk-Lore Congress 1891. Papers and Transactions,* ed. Joseph Jacobs and Alfred Nutt (London, 1892). Leland spoke on "Etrusco-Roman Remains in Modern Tuscan Tradition" (185-200), Owen on "Among the Voodoos" (230-248), and Newell wrote on "Lady Featherflight, an inedited Folk-tale" [collected in Massachusetts] (40-64; Lang's remarks are on 65-66).

2. Published in *The International Folk-Lore Congress of the World's Columbian Exposition,* ed. Helen W. Bassett and Frederick Starr (Chicago, 1898). Abercromby, then vice-president of the English Folk-Lore Society, dealt with "The Magic-Poetry of the Finns and its Application in Practice" (26-41), MacRitchie with "The Northern Trolls" (42-55), Garnett with "Modern Greek Folk-Mythology" (182-198).

3. As in the world-ranging *Four Symposia on Folklore,* ed. Stith Thompson, Indiana University Publications, Folklore Series No. 8 (Bloomington, Indiana, 1953).

4. Articles I have written on the English folklorists are: "The Great Team of English Folklorists," *Journal of American Folklore,* LXIV (Jan.-March 1951), 1-10; "Andrew Lang's Folklore Interests as Revealed in 'At the Sign of the Ship'," *Western Folklore,* XI (Jan. 1952), 1-19; "The First Group of British Folklorists," *Journal of American Folklore,* LXVIII (Jan.-Mar. and July-Sept. 1955), 1-8, 333-340; "The Eclipse of Solar Mythology," ibid., LXVIII (Oct.-Dec. 1955), 393-416; "Hugh Miller, Pioneer Scottish Folklorist" in *Studies in Folklore,* ed. W. E. Richmond, Indiana University Publications, Folklore Series No. 9 (Bloomington, Indiana, 1957), 92-109.

5. Allan Gomme died 9 February 1955. His obituary is in *Folk-Lore,* LXVI (March 1955), 193-194. Dr. Hildburgh died 25 November 1955, and his obituary is in *Folk-Lore,* LXVII (March 1956), 49-51. A partial bibliography can be found in the list of his offprints he donated to the Society's Library (*Folk-Lore,* LXI [1950], pp. 110-111).

A number of persuasive and suggestive articles by the stalwarts of the Society have appeared in *Folk-Lore (Folklore* since 1958) in the past decade, exhorting would-be collectors, rueing the problems of a voluntary Society, surveying resources, and mapping lines of endeavor. See Allan Gomme, "The Collection of English Folklore: Ways and Means" (LXIV, 1953, pp. 321-333); M. A. Murray, "England as a Field for Folklore Research" (LXV, 1954, pp. 1-9); Peter Opie, "England, the Great Undiscovered" (LXV, 1954, pp. 149-164), and "The Present State of Folklore Studies in England" (LXVIII, 1957, pp. 466-471: three other papers in the same issue comment on folklore studies in Ireland, Scotland, and Wales, by Sean O'Sullivan, Stewart Sanderson, and Iowerth C. Peate).

New developments are discussed in Wilfred Bonser and Kenneth Garside, "The Classification of the Library of the Folk-Lore Society" (LXVI, 1955, pp. 267-281), and H. A. Lake Barnett, "The Central Register of Folklore Research in Great Britain" (LXX, 1959, pp. 289-299). Opie and Mrs. Lake Barnett speak about a grant of £14,500 to University College, London, for folklore collecting, and the refusal of the University to cooperate with the Folk-Lore Society in its use.

6. The Popular Antiquities was a cumulative work in every sense. Its history begins with Henry Bourne's *Antiquitates Vulgares; or, the Antiquities of the Common People* (Newcastle, 1725). This was incorporated by John Brand into his *Observations on Popular Antiquities: including the whole of Mr. Bourne's Antiquitates Vulgares* (Newcastle Upon Tyne, 1777). A London edition appeared in 1810. Three years later came a two-volume edition in London destined for fame: *Observations on Popular Antiquities: chiefly illustrating the origin of our Vulgar Customs, Ceremonies, and Superstitions.* By John Brand, M. A. Fellow and Secretary of the Society of Antiquaries of London: arranged and revised, with additions, by Henry Ellis, F. R. S. Sec. S. A., Keeper of the Manuscripts in the British Museum.

Much reprinted in the 19th century, Bourne-Brand-Ellis received a new editor in 1870 in W. Carew Hazlitt, who finally in 1905 brought out a completely overhauled version in dictionary form, under the title *Faiths and Folklore, A Dictionary of National Beliefs, Superstitions and Popular Customs, Past and Current, with their Classical and Foreign Analogues, Described and Illustrated.*

7. An 1856 reprinting also calls itself the "Second Edition," but the title is once more changed, now reading *The British, Roman, and Saxon Antiquities and Folk-Lore of Worcestershire*, with "Folk-Lore" in equally bold type with "Antiquities," where in the 1852 edition "Folk-Lore" was in much smaller type on the title-page. J. H. Parker, London, and J. Grainger, Worcester, are the 1852 publishers, and John Russell Smith is the 1856 publisher.

8. For instance, T. F. Thiselton-Dyer, *British Popular Customs, Present and Past* (1876); Peter H. Ditchfield, *Old English Customs Extant at the Present Time* (1896); F. J. Snell, *The Customs of Old England* (1911); George Long, *The Folklore Calendar* (1930); F. J. Drake-Carnell, *Old English Customs and Ceremonies* (1938); Christina Hole, *English Custom and Usage* (1941); Cecil Hunt, *British Customs and Ceremonies* (1954). All published in London.

9. "The Collection and Analysis of Folk-lore," in *The Study of Society, Methods and Problems*, ed. Frederic Bartlett et al. (London, 1939), pp. 328-378.

10. By contrast, anthropology is secure today. Pertinent is the comment of Wilson D. Wallis: "Until about the beginning of the century there was no organized discipline of anthropology in the British Isles; that is to say, no academic recognition of competence in this field, and no systematic training for a career in it. . . . Yet for several decades an Anthropological Society and a Folk-Lore Society had been active" ("Anthropology in England Early in the Present Century," *American Anthropologist*, LIX [Oct. 1957], 784).

11. Full references are: Nathaniel Wanley, *The Wonders of the Little World* (1678), a new edition by William Johnston (2 vols., 1806); William Turner, *A Compleat History of the Most Remarkable Providences* (1697); Thomas Pennant, "A Tour in Scotland," 1769; "A Second Tour in Scotland, and Voyage to the Hebrides in 1772" (in J. Pinkerton, ed., *A General Collection of the Best and Most Interesting Voyages and Travels in All Parts of the World*, v. 3, 1809, pp. 1-569); Reginald Scot, *The Discoverie of Witchcraft* (1584); John Stow, *The Survey of London* (1633); Joseph Strutt, *The Sports and Pastimes of the People of England* (1801). All published in London.

12. For writings by these antiquaries see Dorson, "The First Group of British Folklorists," cited in note 4.

13. Quotations are, in order, from Lover, *Legends and Stories of Ireland* (1st ser., 4th ed., London, 1837), p. viii; Cunningham, *Traditional Tales of the English and Scottish Peasantry*, vol. 1 (London, 1822), p. viii; Roby, *Traditions of Lancashire*, vol. 1 (5th ed., London and New York, 1882), p. xiii, in "Memoir of the Author." Another work belonging to this group is Mrs. Bray, *The Borders of the Tamar and the Tavy* (3 vols., 1836), whose contents are indicated in the subtitle: "Their Natural History, Manners, Customs, Superstitions, Scenery, Antiquities, Eminent Persons, etc." Actually the first field collection along modern lines was made by an Irishman, T. Crofton Croker, in *Fairy Legends and Traditions from the South of Ireland* (London, 1825).

14. Representative field materials for the later period are in James Napier, *Folk Lore: or, Superstitious Beliefs in the West of Scotland within this Century* (Paisley, 1879); Walter Gregor, *Notes on the Folk-Lore of the North-East of Scotland* (London, 1881, Publications of the Folk-Lore Society VII); Edward W. B. Nicholson, *Golspie, Contributions to its Folklore* (London, 1897); R. C. Maclagan, *Evil Eye in the Western Highlands* (London, 1902, Publications of the Folk-Lore Society XLVII).

15. Walter K. Kelly, *Curiosities of Indo-European Tradition and Folk-Lore* (1863); Sir John Lubbock, *Pre-Historic Times, as illustrated by Ancient Remains, and the Manners and Customs of Modern Savages* (1865, 2nd ed. 1869), James A. Farrer, *Primitive Manners and Customs* (1879); Charles F. Keary, *Outlines of Primitive Belief among the Indo-European Races* (1882). All published in London. The enormous impact of Tylor on the English folklorists is still to be evaluated. Margaret T. Hodgen has discussed historically *The Doctrine of Survivals* (London, 1936).

16. See "The Great Team of English Folklorists" and other articles cited in note 4. Sona R. Burstein has written on "Moses Gaster and Folklore," "George Laurence Gomme and the Science of Folklore," and "Eighty Years of Folklore: Evaluations and Revaluations" (*Folk-Lore*, LXVIII, 1957, pp. 288-290, 321-338; LXIX, 1958, pp. 73-92). The latter two papers view the present situation of the Folklore Society in the light of its origins and past achievements.

17. The works mentioned are Charlotte Burne, *Shropshire Folk-Lore* (1883); Charles Hardwick, *Traditions, Superstitions, and Folk-Lore, (chiefly Lancashire and the north of England:)* (1872); John Harland and T. T. Wilkinson, *Lancashire Legends* (1873); William Henderson, *Notes on the Folk Lore of the Northern Counties of England and the Borders*, with an Appendix on Household Stories by S. Baring-Gould (1866); Ella Mary Leather, *The Folk-Lore of Herefordshire* (1912); Edgar MacCulloch, *Guernsey Folk Lore* (1903). All published in London. The Folk-Lore Society also issued a series of county folklore volumes, based however on printed extracts.

18. Baring-Gould's best known folklore work is his *Curious Myths of the Middle Ages* (1st

series, 1866, 2nd series, 1868). See also his *Songs and Ballads of the West; a collection made from the mouths of the people* (London, 1891); and his slight *A Book of Folk-Lore* (London & Glasgow, 1894). Thiselton-Dyer wrote *English Folk-Lore* (1878), *Domestic Folk-Lore* (1881), *Folk lore of Shakespeare* (1883), *The Folk-Lore of Plants* (1889), *The Ghost World* (1893), *Folk-Lore of Women as Illustrated by Legendary and Traditionary Tales, Folk-Rhymes, Proverbial Sayings, Superstitions, etc.* (1905). All published in London.

19. Thus the revealing statement by Canon Callaway: "What Sir George Grey felt was requisite for the rightful government of the people of New Zealand,—not only a thorough knowledge of their language, but also of their traditional lore,—the earnest and intelligent missionary will feel in a tenfold degree as necessary for himself. . . ." (Preface to his translation of *Nursery Tales, Traditions, and Histories of the Zulus, in Their Own Words* [1868]).

Other works referred to (all published in London) are Rachel Busk, *Sagas from the Far East, or, Kalmouk and Mongolian Traditionary Tales* (1873), *The Folk-Lore of Rome; collected by word of mouth from the people* (1874), and *The Folk-Songs of Italy* (1887); William A. Craigie, *Scandinavian Folk-Lore* (1896); William Crooke, *An Introduction to the Popular Religion and Folklore of Northern India* (1893); Sir George W. Dasent, *Popular Tales from the Norse* (1858); Rev. William Wyatt Gill, *Myths and Songs from the South Pacific* (1876); Sir George Grey, *Polynesian Mythology, and Ancient Traditional History of the New Zealand Race* (1855); Rev. J. Hinton Knowles, *Folk-Tales of Kashmir* (1887); Mrs. K. Langloh Parker, *Australian Legendary Tales* (1896) and *More Australian Legendary Tales* (1898); William R. S. Ralston, *The Songs of the Russian People, as Illustrative of Slavonic Mythology and Russian Social Life* (1872), and *Russian Folk-Tales* (1873); Rennell Rodd, *The Customs and Lore of Modern Greece* (1892); Benjamin Thorpe, *Northern Mythology, comprising the principal Popular Traditions and Superstitions of Scandinavia, North Germany, and the Netherlands* (3 vols., 1851-52).

Indiana University
Bloomington, Indiana

STITH THOMPSON

FOLKLORE TRENDS IN SCANDINAVIA

FOLKLORE activities in Scandinavia have a long history. They began when Gustavus Adolphus of Sweden, who died in 1632, sent out instructions to all of the parish
priests that they were to collect what we would call folklore. They collected customs,
interesting beliefs that were not approved by the church, and other kinds of traditional
material, and also information about any peculiar methods the people had of farming,
dairying, and so on. Thus the Swedes think of folklore studies as definitely beginning
about 1630. And, as a matter of fact, their national academy, which is concerned with
folklore, The Gustavus Adolphus Academy, was founded in 1932 in direct recognition
of the activities of Gustavus Adolphus in starting folklore research in Sweden.

The collecting initiated in the seventeenth century does not mean, of course, that
there has been assiduous research for all these three hundred years, for there have been
long periods when no one was especially interested in folklore in Sweden. There was,
however, a very decided revival of interest in Swedish folklore in the 1830's and
toward the middle of the nineteenth century. Interest of this kind was directed into
several different areas.

The great folktale collector, G. O. Hyltén-Cavallius, did his work in the forties and
fifties. He was primarily a collector and since he needed someone to help him process
the material correctly, he enlisted the assistance of George Stephens, a transplanted
Englishman in Stockholm. A folktale collection was published jointly by them in the
1840's,[1] but Hyltén-Cavallius collected much more than he published at that time. His
additional material remained unpublished until our own generation. I recall that
when I was in Uppsala in 1935 I met and had a lengthy conversation with K. G. West-
mann, who combined jobs in a unique way. He was a folklorist and a former Prime
Minister of Sweden. When I asked him about the unpublished Hyltén-Cavallius material, he said that he had discussed the matter with the Prime Minister during the
previous week, and it had been decided that the material would be published. As a
matter of fact, the Gustavus Adolphus Academy has since published it as part of the
Academy's large series in six or eight volumes.[2]

Hyltén-Cavallius was, in a way, the beginner of the more recent movement in the
collecting of Swedish folktales. He also did studies of everything folkloristic in the
local communities. A good example is his two-volume work called *Wärend och
Wirdarne* (Stockholm, 1921-22), which describes two small Swedish communities
which he had studied intensively—their traditions, their customs, and so on.

It was in the 1870's that the folklore organizations we now have in Sweden began,
because it was then that the Nordiska Museet (Northern Museum) in Stockholm and
the outdoor museum in Skansen opened. Both museums call for some remarks. The
Nordiska Museet began its existence on a very small scale, in much the same manner
as we might proceed to establish a folk museum in the United States. It has taken
forty or fifty years to develop it into the large affair that it is at present. It would not
be to our purpose to go through the various stages in the Northern Museum's growth,

but it is worth while to mention the kinds of things that are to be found there. In a museum appear only items that are tangible; folktales, folksongs, and much else that can only be approached through hearing thus are obviously excluded. A museum is confined to seeing, and so it is filled, obviously, with objects.

Some people would say that the Nordiska Museet is an historical museum, because it is interested in the life of Sweden, not only now, but as it has been through the centuries. Its concern is with the life not only of the common people, but of all the various strata of society. Thus the Museum conducts studies of the eighteenth century aristocracy, of the merchant classes, and so on. In short, it is a center for "folklivs-forskning," the term used in Sweden for folklife research. On display are objects of all kinds brought in from every part of Sweden. Many of these objects would be placed in an historical museum in the United States.

Still the Nordiska Museet does differ from an historical museum. While the latter is interested in the house that George Washington slept in or in the coach in which Daniel Webster rode, that is, in specific and definite things, the Nordiska Museet is interested in the typical. It is trying to obtain a typical coach of the 1830's, but it is unimportant whether a Swedish counterpart to Daniel Webster rode in it or not. The Nordiska Museet is in many ways the most important folk museum anywhere, though there are other good folk museums in Oslo and Copenhagen.

With the passage of time, however, the Nordiska Museet has taken over other aspects of folklore not usually associated with a museum. Its officials have, for instance, gradually developed a folklore archive, with large files of customs and superstitions. I am unaware of how extensively they have indexed folksongs, though I suspect that they have not done so very much. On the other hand, the Museum has a large collection of folktales which I have found of great interest.

In all of the Scandinavian countries, there are also outdoor museums. These are a special development originating in Scandinavia. The one at Skansen in Stockholm is perhaps the most elaborate. In a good downtown location, the museum authorities took over a large park which is hilly and very picturesque. Into that park, in the 1880's and 1890's, buildings from all parts of Sweden were brought and grouped. For example, from Dalecarlia there is a farmhouse and its outbuildings. The whole farmstead, forming a large quadrangle, was brought to Stockholm and reconstructed along with all the various kinds of outbuildings—barns, pig houses, a place for sheep, and so on, as well as places to store food of various kinds.

Nearly every province in Sweden is represented at Skansen by its own particular section and by its own festive occasions. On a certain day in the year, for example, there is a Dalecarlia day, and crowds from Dalecarlia come down to Skansen to celebrate. They perform proper dances, sing Dalecarlia songs, eat Dalecarlia food, and generally have a good time. Skansen is an excellent combination of the serious and the amusing. It is a pretty park that sustains itself. Its small admission fee, perhaps four or five cents, is enough to keep it going. It has a fine restaurant which attracts people from the city, and which helps to make it self-sustaining. In the course of a year a great number of these special days occur, and the place is crowded on such occasions. Whenever a provincial celebration takes place, the park is a great attraction to casual tourists.

In Norway there is an outdoor museum at Bygdøy in Oslo, which is much like the one in Stockholm. Outdoor museums in Norway are a little more scattered than in Sweden, for in Norway, in addition to the one in Bygdøy, very good outdoor museums are maintained at Lillehammer (about a hundred miles from Oslo) and at Molde up in the Bjørnsen country. The most surprising thing about these Scandinavian outdoor museums is the extreme age of the buildings. In the United States, if we find a log cabin that is one hundred and fifty years old, we are likely to make some remark about it. But in Scandinavia, guides will frequently say, "Oh, this is a fourteenth century log cabin." Some of them in Molde, I remember, dated from the 1200's. These old buildings are remarkably well preserved. Equally old and well-preserved buildings are found at the excellent outdoor museum in Copenhagen.

So much for folk museums. I should now like to turn to archives, because archives are more relevant to the kinds of folklore activities practiced in the United States. American folklorists work with songs, tales, beliefs, and the like, the assembling of which is the folklore archives' essential work. The Finns were the first people to develop a first-rate archive, which they began as early as the 1830's. But there are good archives in all of the Scandinavian countries, including a small one in Iceland.

Denmark and Norway each have a central national archive of their own. In Sweden, however, there are four archives, and their efforts, unfortunately, are well scattered. They are not definitely arranged geographically, and thus there is a certain amount of conflict over which archive is responsible for a particular place or a particular area. Theoretically, Stockholm receives material from the entire nation; Uppsala only from northern Sweden; Lund from southern Sweden; and Göteborg from western Sweden. The situation, therefore, is comparable to what would happen in the United States if we had an archive responsible for the East, another for the West, another for the North, and one for the South. At the boundaries many localities would thus be claimed by more than one archive or by no archive at all. This is precisely what has happened in Sweden.

What are the Scandinavian archives like, especially those that are operating fully and successfully? Let us consider one of them in detail. The archive at Uppsala concerns itself with every aspect of folklife. It has a division, for example, on folksongs, another on folktales, still another on legends, and others on superstitions, customs, and dialect. The Uppsala Archive began as a dialect archive and only later grew into a general folklore archive. Though Uppsala is a model folklore archive, American archivists, unfortunately, have never gone to study it or any of the other comparable Scandinavian institutions.

Material is sent to Uppsala from all parts of northern Sweden. None of it is sent in casually, though, for the work of the archive is continuous and active. The archive staff is working hard to collect folklore material in Sweden, as well as to take care of it after it has been collected. Thus, they employ various people in each Swedish province who serve as correspondents in return for a small salary. Their relationship with the Uppsala Archive is much like that of small-town correspondents with a great newspaper. Serving as correspondents for the great Uppsala Archive, they maintain a certain local standing, almost like that of the local priest or doctor.

The prospective correspondent must go through a period of probation. When someone wants to act as correspondent for the archive, the staff must first find out what he is interested in collecting. He may, for example, be a folktale raconteur; he may sing; or he may merely be interested in folksong or in old practices. As a further part of his probation, he is required to send in some of his material, with no pay being given. If the material looks good, if it is faithfully taken down, and has not been tampered with, then he is put on the payroll. Thenceforth, he can send in

material and receive a certain sum for each item that is acceptable. The archive re-
tains the right to reject material that fails to meet the standard.

Folklore material is received, then, from all parts of Sweden and directed to the
proper division of the Uppsala Archive. The folktale archivist, for instance, looks
through each manuscript received for folktales. Then he goes through the stories
located to decide whether they should go into the section for folktales or into the one
for other kinds of narrative tradition. If they belong in the folktale section, then they
have to be classified according to the Aarne-Thompson Type-Index system. After a
proper card is made for each tale, it becomes part of the great card-index, so that
when, let us say, a scholar begins to study Type 769, eventually he will run across
the version that has been sent in from Smaaland.

These are the general ways in which an archive like the one at Uppsala works.
But if this were all, archives would consist only of books and catalogues. This, however, is not quite all, because the Scandinavian archives wish to make their materials
available and consequently sponsor several series of publications. The Swedish
archives publish a good deal of their own material, and more of it appears in *Arv,*
the standard Swedish journal of folklore. Various other publication series appear in
large volumes, especially material from the Uppsala Archive.[3] Another development
there, and in some of the other archives in the last few years, has been the production
of a considerable number of radio shows, and, in even more recent times, television
programs. There is close cooperation between Radio Stockholm and both the Nordiska Museet and the Uppsala Archive. Some of the directors of these new folklore
institutions do active work in preparing programs to be broadcast. In *Four Symposia
on Folklore,* Åke Campbell discusses in some detail what has been done in Stockholm in the way of radio presentation of folklore and how the producers try to keep
the entire program series close to the Swedish people.[4]

The archives in Scandinavia always have made considerable use of questionnaires.
The Uppsala Archive has prepared a series of about a hundred and fifty of them, of
which I have a fairly complete set. These are mimeographed on long sheets of paper.
Each one is not a general questionnaire—a book such as the Irish send out—but
devoted instead to a particular subject. In one questionnaire the archive requests information especially on customs that have to do with fishing, in another on those
concerned with haymaking, and the like. About every month a new questionnaire
is sent out to the correspondents.

Although collecting and archiving flourish in all of the Scandinavian countries, I
have focused on Sweden because of the excellence of these activities there. Something
should be added, however, about the older, less institutionalized collecting of folklore
in such countries as Denmark and Norway. Comparable to Hyltén-Cavallius for
Sweden, the great collector for Denmark, whose name is mentioned in the United
States especially in ballad courses, is Svend Hersleb Grundtvig. He published his first
incidental collections of Danish ballads in the 1850's[5] and continued collecting them
during the rest of his life. Those who know of Child's *The English and Scottish Popular Ballads* (5 vols., Boston and New York, 1882-98) do not always realize that
Child was in continual correspondence with Grundtvig about the entire matter, and
that Grundtvig's *Danmarks gamle Folkeviser (Denmark's Old Ballads)* (10 vols.,
Copenhagen, 1853-58) was the model for Child's work.[6] Grundtvig was also a
great collector of folktales, of which he published a good two-volume collection.[7] Unfortunately, a great deal of his collected material remains unpublished and in an

obsolete Danish script. I have been through this material in Copenhagen and am using it in the forthcoming revised edition of *The Types of the Folktale*.

Grundtvig was the great Danish collector for the mid-nineteenth century. After him came a series of good collectors. The most picturesque of these men was Evald Tang Kristensen. His is the largest collection of tales, but his manuscripts also include songs, riddles, and local legends. In addition, he left a beautifully-worked-out volume of jokes about preachers, with a very pleasing title, *Vore Fædres Kirketjeneste (Our Father's Church Service)* (Aarhus, 1899). Some of these jokes about preachers are not too churchly. Kristensen lived at Aarhus and published all of his books on a little country press. When I was in Denmark, I inquired how I could obtain his books and was told that it was necessary to write to him personally. "But," I said, "isn't he extremely old?" The answer was, "He's only ninety-one." When I returned home, I wrote to him and requested his works; and in the course of time the Indiana University Library received a large box and an inventory written out by the old man in a very shaky longhand. The librarian gave me the letter as a souvenir. Tang Kristensen was the Vance Randolph of Denmark, especially for the Jutland Peninsula. He has become a legend, quite as much so as have his own books. Though he represents a typical stage of collecting at the turn of the century, he was engaged in field-work as early as 1870 and was still gathering a few items as late as 1920. In 1927, though ninety, Kristensen still was very much alive and vigorous.[8]

The next generation in Denmark is typified by Axel Olrik. Olrik was not the same kind of person as Kristensen. By the time he came on the scene, the Danish folklore archives had been established on the general lines of those in Sweden. Olrik went ahead and put his efforts primarily into the archive. He stayed in Copenhagen. He was a scholar in his study, rather than a collector who went out among the people. His important work is theoretical. His best and most important contribution is the book he wrote on epic laws—the laws of oral narrative.[9] Olrik's most active period of scholarship was in the first twenty years of this century, when he made the Dansk Folkemindesamling (the Danish Folklore Archives) the equal of any archive in the world, including those in Stockholm and Helsinki.

The folklore archive in Norway—the Norsk Folkeminnesamling—is located in the University Library and has independent support from the state. The word *Folkeminne* means literally "folk memory," and is used in all three Scandinavian countries with very slight variations. The first great collectors of Norwegian folktales were Peter Christen Asbjørnsen and Jørgen Ingebrektsen Moe. Asbjørnsen was a forester and lived, much as an American forest ranger would, in all parts of Norway. He was an extraordinarily good collector and had the help of a scholar in Moe. Together they published the first edition of Norwegian folktales in the 1840's.[10] As one enters the present Norsk Folkeminnesamling, he is confronted by a full-sized statue of Asbjørnsen.

Following in his father's footsteps, Jørgen Moe's son, Moltke Moe, was a folklorist of the academic type. It was due to him that the archive was established in Oslo. In fact, the nucleus of the archive was his own library. Among those who were directing the archive at the time when W. Edson Richmond and I first became acquainted with it, one of them at least had been a pupil of Moltke Moe. In other words, there has been a direct line of descent.

The Norwegians engage in some organized collecting throughout their country, but perhaps they do not collect as systematically as do the Swedes. The Norwegian archivists, for example, are more dependent on material that just happens to be sent in. Yet to run a good national archive, it is necessary not only to have active collectors in the field scattered over as many areas of the country as possible, but also to have a good idea of what is coming in and its relationship to the potentialities of each location. The Swedes make considerable use of spot maps so that they know not only how many legends they have received from each particular little square on a map, but also how many more are likely to be found.

Moltke Moe was a precursor of the fine academicians in folklore that Norway has continued to produce. He was, however, more an inspiring teacher than a scholar in his own right,[11] and thus people like Knut Liestøl and Axel Olrik remembered him with not only a great deal of respect, but also with great affection.

At the turn of the century, Knut Liestøl was Norway's leading folklorist. He was interested primarily in ballads and carried on the same kind of activity with ballads in Norway that Grundtvig had carried on in Denmark. He was ready to complete his definitive edition of Norwegian ballads after his retirement, but he did not live to finish the task. It is to be hoped that this potentially great work will be carried on. Liestøl always was interested not just in ballads, but also in legends and especially in the relation of Norwegian folklore to the Icelandic sagas.[12]

For folklorists in America and especially at Indiana University, much better known is Reidar Th. Christiansen, who was here in 1956-57 as visiting professor. For many years he was the head of the archives in Oslo, and became professor of folklore at Oslo University after Liestøl's retirement in 1951. Christiansen also served in Dublin in 1958-59 as advisor for the Irish Folklore Commission.

Christiansen, first of all, is an excellent classifier and archivist. Very soon after the initial classification of folktales was made by Aarne, Christiansen published his survey, a classification of the Norwegian folktales.[13] This work was done with a thoroughness and a system that no one had ever dreamed of before. He took absolutely every tale and analyzed it in rather algebraic fashion. He was able to divide the stories up into their component parts so well that one can almost reconstruct every tale simply by taking his formulas and expanding them. Christiansen's technique of analysis has given folklorists an insight into how first-rate tale surveys should be made.

An often-neglected aspect of folklore that the Swedes have developed very extensively is the study of place names; in Sweden there is a society and a large journal devoted exclusively to this subject.[14] But even though place-name research has been carried on the most vigorously in Sweden, especially at the Uppsala Archive, it also exists in Denmark and Norway. This is one aspect of folklore that we have neglected in America, regardless of some interesting place-name possibilities. One possible reason for this neglect, however, is that our relatively short history precludes extensive linguistic treatment of the subject. In contrast, scholars in Sweden are dealing with two or three thousand years of history. Thus quite often they find it possible to establish the history of a place name for as many as fifteen hundred years, and to speculate on the changes which it has undergone over that period of time. Of course, distinctions between folklore and history become increasingly fuzzy at the earlier stages of such a span.

In my own specialty, the folktale, more theoretical work recently has been done in Sweden than anywhere else. Sweden's fine scholars do not hesitate to disagree with each other, and often through such disagreement advances are made. One of the outstanding Swedish folklorists is Waldemar Liungman, whose great work is the three-volume edition of Swedish folktales, arranged by types, with excellent comparative notes. He has written a number of theoretical articles, many of them good. Unfortunately, it seems to me that he is pugnacious and unwilling to recede from any opinion he has formed.[15]

One of the greatest of the Swedish scholars, C. W. von Sydow, began studying the folktale as a young man, and he continued these studies all the rest of his life. He was one of those authorities who knew a great deal, who had excellent students, who wrote hundreds of articles, who was recognized by everyone who came in contact with him as being one of the great men in his field, but who produced no *magnum opus*. There is no one work of his about which one can say, as one can of Grundtvig, that here is *Danmarks gamle Folkeviser*. But he was always esteemed as the man to whom one wrote for advice about any problem in the field. He was one of the kindest men who ever lived. His greatest temptation was old bookshops. Once, according to his close friend James Delargy, he entered a Leipzig bookstore and ordered almost everything, even though it occurred to him only later that the books had to be paid for! Fortunately, Mrs. von Sydow, who worked on her own, was able to pay for them. Von Sydow was an improvident person and, even to his last years, a little like an overgrown child in his attitudes. But he was lovable, and once having been in close contact with him, one always thinks of him in personal terms.

Von Sydow was very critical of the Finnish method of studying folktales.[16] It has to be borne in mind, however, that all of his students, when he set them to work studying individual tales, sooner or later found themselves using the Finnish method, because it was, and still is, the only method they could use. Yet about every fifty pages his students will write a disclaimer which states that they are not employing the Finnish method after all. This has happened over and over again, so that I think von Sydow really led some of his pupils—such as Sven Liljeblad, who has admitted it—a bit astray.[17]

Two important works done under von Sydow by his pupils have been published rather recently. One of them is Anna Birgitta Rooth's study of the Cinderella story in world tradition, which actually but unadmittedly employs the Finnish method. The other is Jan Öjvind Swahn's monumental study of Cupid and Psyche.[18] Rooth and Swahn both are in Lund where they are carrying on von Sydow's work. I will conclude on von Sydow, the Swedish folklorist whom I have known the best.

NOTES

1. G. O. Hyltén-Cavallius and G. Stephens, *Svenska Folk-sagor och Äfventyr* (*Swedish Folk-legends and Tales*) (Stockholm, 1844).

2. *Svenska Sagor och Sägner* (*Swedish Legends and Traditions*) (Stockholm, 1937—).

3. Series B of the Folkminnesarkivet in Uppsala includes the following publications: E. Odstedt, *Varulven i Svensk Folktradition* (*The Werewolf in Swedish Tradition*) (1943); L. Johannsson, *Bebyggelse och Folkliv i det gamla Frostviken* (*Settlement and Folklife in Old Frostvik*) (1947); L. Linnarsson, *Bygd, By och Gård, gammal Bygd och Folkkultur i Gäsene* (*District, Village, and Farm: Old Settlement Folk Culture in Gäsene*) (2 vols., 1948-50); Å. Campbell, *Från Vilmark till Bygd* (*From Wild Field to Town*) (1948); and L. Levander, *Alvdalskt Arbetsliv under Årtiondena Omkring 1800-talets mitt* (*Work Life in Alvdals through the Decades around the mid-19th Century*) (1953).

4. *Four Symposia on Folklore*, ed. Stith Thompson (Bloomington, Ind., 1953), pp. 149-151.

5. *Gamle Danske Minder i Folkemunde: Folkeæventyr, Folkeviser, Folkesagn og andere Rester af Fortidens Digtning og Tro, som de Endnu leve i det Danske Folks Erindring* (*Old Danish Memories in the Folk-Mouth: Folktales, Folksongs, Folk Legends and other Remnants of Early Compositions and Belief, as they still live in the Danish Folk Memory*) (3 parts, Kjøbenhavn, 1854, 1857, 1861).

6. See the chapters on Grundtvig and Child in Sigurd B. Hustvedt, *Ballad Books and Ballad Men* (Cambridge, Mass., 1930), chs. VII and VIII, esp. pp. 218-220.

7. *Danske Folkesagn*, 1839-83 (2 vols., Kjøbenhavn, 1944-48); see also, Grundtvig's *Danische Volksmärchen* (Leipsig, 1878).

8. Kristensen's major works are *Danske Sagn, som de har lydt i Folkemunde (Danish Legends, as they sound in the Folk Mouth)* (6 vols. in 7, Århus og Silkeborg, 1892-1901), and *Jyske Folkeminder (Jyske Folklore)* (13 vols., Kjøbenhavn, 1871-97).

9. *Nogle Grundsætninger for Sagnforskning (Some Foundations for Folktale Study)* (Kjøbenhavn, 1921). See also "Folkedigtningens Episke Love" ("Epic Laws of Folk Compositions") in Olrik's earlier *Folkelige Afhandlinger (Collected Papers on Folklore)* (Kjøbenhavn, 1919), pp. 177 ff.

10. Asbjørnsen and Moe, *Norske Folkeeventyr* (Kristiania, 1843).

11. On the other hand, Moe did publish a considerable number of items. Among them are *Aeventyri paa Vandring; eit Fyredrag (Tales of Wandering; a Lecture)* (Kristiania, 1895); *Eventyrlige Sagn i den aeldre Historie* (Kristiania, 1906); *Episke Grundlove (Basic Epic Laws)* (Kristiania, 1914); *Folkeminne frå Bøherad etter Upskrifter av Moltke Moe (Folklore from Bøherad from the Manuscripts of Moltke Moe)* (Oslo, 1925); *Moltke Moes Samlede skrifter; utgitt ved Knut Liestøl (Moltke Moe's Collected Writings, edited by Knut Liestøl)* (3 vols., Oslo and Cambridge, Mass., 1925-27); and *Folke-eventyr frå Flatdal etter Uppskrifter av Moltke Moe (Folktales from Flatdal from the Manuscripts of Moltke Moe)* (Oslo, 1929).

12. Liestøl's publications include *Norske Trollvisor og Norrøne Sogor (Norwegian Magic Ballads and Northern Legends)* (Kristiania, 1915); his edition of M. B. *Landstad's Folkeviser fra Telemarken (Folksongs from Telemark)* (Oslo, 1925); *The Origin of the Icelandic Family Sagas*, trans. A. G. Jayne (Oslo and Cambridge, Mass., 1930); *Folkevisor, utgjeven av Knut Liestøl* (Stockholm, 1931); *Folkesagn* (Oslo, 1942); *P. Chr. Asbjørnsen, Mannen og Livsverket (The Man and His Work)* (Oslo, 1947); and *Knut Liestøl in Memoriam*, ed. R. T. Christiansen (Oslo, 1955), which contains ballads, folktales, and legends collected by Liestøl, as well as two of his previously published articles. See also, Liestøl and Moltke Moe, *Utval av Norske Folkevisor til Skulebruk (Selection of Norwegian Ballads for School Use)* (Oslo, 1928); and *Folkeviser* (Oslo, 1958).

13. Antti Aarne, *Finnische Märchenvarianten*, FF Communications, Nos. 5 and 33 (Helsinki, 1911, 1920); Reidar Th. Christiansen, *Norske Eventyr* (Kristiania, 1921). An abstract of Christiansen's survey appeared as *The Norwegian Fairytales, A Short Summary*, FF Communications, No. 46 (Helsinki, 1922).

14. *Namn och Bygd (Names and Places)* (1913—), edited by Joran Sahlgren, is the journal of the Swedish Place Name Society. Published at Uppsala from 1913-16, its two to three numbers per year have been published at Lund from 1917 to date.

15. In addition to *Sveriges Samtliga Folksagor (Sweden's Collected Tales)* (3 vols., Stockholm, 1949-52) Liungman's works include: *En Traditionsstudie: Sagan om Prinsessan i Jordkulan (A Study of Tradition: the Tale of the Princess in the Earthmound)* (2 vols. in 1, Göteborg, 1925); *Två Folkminnes-undersökningar: Brud icke mö och Liten Åsa Gåsapiga samt Kung Ingewalls Dotter (Two Folklore Studies: A Bride but not a Virgin, and Little Osa the Goosegirl together with King Ingewall's Daughter)* (Gothenburg, 1925); *Traditions wanderungen Euphrat-Rhein, Studien zur Geschichte der Volksbräuche*, FF Communications, Nos. 118-119 (Helsinki, 1937-38); *Der Kampf zwischen Sommer und Winter*, FF Communications, No. 130 (Helsinki, 1941); *Traditions wanderungen Rhein-Jenissei; eine Untersuchung uber das Winter-und Todaustragen und einige hierhergehorige Brauche*, FF Communications, Nos. 129, 131 (Helsinki, 1941, 1945); and *Das wahrscheinliche Alter des Volksmärchens in Schweden*, FF Communications, No. 156 (Helsinki, 1955).

16. For a full-length monograph that reveals von Sydow's own approach to the study of individual folktales, see his *Två Spinnsagor: en Studie i Jämförande Folksagoforskning (Two Spinning Stories: A Study in Comparative Folktale Research)* (Stockholm, 1909). A selection of his theoretical essays is gathered in *Selected Papers on Folklore*, ed. Laurits Bødker (Copenhagen, 1948).

17. Lilejeblad has since renounced many of the conclusions in his *Die Tobiasgeschichte und andere Märchen von toten Helfern* (Lund, 1927).

18. Rooth, *The Cinderella Cycle* (Lund, 1951); Swahn, *The Tale of Cupid and Psyche* (Lund, 1955).

Indiana University
Bloomington, Indiana

WARREN E. ROBERTS

FOLKLORE IN NORWAY: ADDENDUM

THE FOLLOWING notes on folklore study and institutions in Norway are intended to supplement the remarks of Thompson and Richmond in two ways. One purpose is to give somewhat more detailed information about Norwegian folklore scholarship than it was possible for Thompson to give in his general survey of all of Scandinavia. Since my stay in Norway was in 1959 and 1960, another purpose is to supply in some cases more recent information.

Norsk Folkeminnesamling

The present director of the Norsk Folkeminnesamling and Professor of Folklore at the University of Oslo is Svale Solheim. The chief archivist is Olav Bø. Since 1960 they have been assisted by Brynjulf Alver, who was previously associated with the archive in Bergen. Reidar Th. Christiansen, though officially retired, still works frequently at the Folkeminnesamling and is available for consultation and advice.

The Folkeminnesamling is located at present in somewhat cramped quarters in the University Library not far from the center of Oslo and a few blocks from the main buildings of the University itself. In a few years, however, a new building to house the Folkeminnesamling and other university institutes is to be constructed in an area more on the outskirts of the city where other new university buildings are now placed. When the new structure is ready, the Folkeminnesamling will move from its present quarters, which have been its home since its founding in 1913. The new quarters will, of course, make available much additional and badly needed space, but I am sure that all those who have been connected with the Folkeminnesamling will feel a nostalgic twinge when they leave the old location and especially when they are forced to discontinue their daily walk to the Bon Mot for coffee, a traditional rite nearly as old as the Folkeminnesamling itself.

It is impossible in this short report to describe the actual archive of unprinted collections in any detail. Suffice it to say that it is large and still growing, though the rate of growth has slowed considerably in recent years. There are reasonably useful indexes available in print,[1] and at the Folkeminnesamling there are some unprinted indexes. The staff, moreover, is always ready to assist in locating material not covered by the indexes. Most of the manuscripts added in recent years are typewritten, but some of the older handwritten ones are nearly illegible. A prize specimen is a summary of a folktale which Jørgen Moe tried to write down while riding on horseback. Only about one word in ten is decipherable. The folktale student who works with the manuscript collections is fortunate because typewritten copies of nearly all the folktale texts have been prepared. A similar project is now under way to copy out all the riddles.

In addition to the unprinted collections, the Folkeminnesamling has its own library of printed works, many of them books which were originally owned by Asbjørnsen and by Jørgen and Moltke Moe. I remember at one time finding in the regular stacks presentation copies of several books of Hans Christian Andersen's *Eventyr,* on the title pages of which the author had inscribed messages to either Jørgen Moe or Asbjørnsen; such books, I am sure, would be kept under lock and key in most libraries. The library is strong in two fields, Norwegian folklore and nineteenth-century publications. In addition, there is a good general collection of folklore periodicals, but many important modern folklore works are missing. Fortunately, these works can usually be obtained from the University Library.

The Folkeminnesamling publishes two series of monographs. Research studies appear in *Studia Norvegica.* Collections of folklore material appear in *Norsk Folkeminnelags Skrifter,* of which over eighty volumes have been published. Nearly all of these collections have been assembled by interested amateurs, and thus the material is usually published with little or no annotation.

In addition to being a research institute, the Folkeminnesamling, through its staff, also has teaching duties. The following courses were offered as part of the University of Oslo curriculum in the fall of 1959 (other courses of lectures offered at the University in the general field of folklife research will be mentioned below): Solheim, "Basic Course in Folklore Science: Selected Texts and Subjects in Folk Literature and Methods," and "Comic Ballads and Parodies"; Bø, "Selected Topics on Norwegian Folk Belief." Because of a change made a few years ago in the general curriculum of the University, it is now possible for students to include folklore as one of their general fields of study. I am glad to be able to report that there is now an impressive number of students working in folklore. I would estimate that there were about a dozen students at the Folkeminnesamling in 1959.

Avdeling for Språk-og Folkeminnegransking, Institutt for Nordisk Filologi, Bergen

The archive at the University of Bergen which Richmond mentions is directed by Professor Per Thorson. This archive restricts its research mainly to western Norway and has an extensive collection of dialect and place-name materials. Its general folklore collections are largely the manuscripts left by the founder of the archive, Torliev Hannaas. An excellent index of the folklore material in the archive has been prepared by Brynjulf Alver (*Torliev Hannaas og hans Arbeid med Folkedikting,* Bergen, 1954).

Instituttet for Folkelivsgransking ved Oslo Universitet

The post of Professor of Ethnology and Director of the Institute for Folklife Research, held by Nils Lid until his death in 1958, has recently been filled by two scholars, Hilmar Stigum and Knut Kolsrud. In the fall of 1959 Stigum and Kolsrud were jointly offering a course at the University of Oslo in Norwegian Ethnology which included such topics as General Ethnology, Rural Society, The Sea as a Source of Livelihood, House and Farm, Cultivation of the Earth, and Household Arts (Arts and Handicrafts). A journal, *Norveg (Journal of Norwegian Ethnology),* is edited at the Institute, which has its offices in the University Library. A description of the fieldwork techniques used and the questionnaires sent out by the Institute is given in *Midwest Folklore.*[2]

Norsk Etnologisk Gransking—Norsk Folkemuseum

Another ethnological institute in Oslo connected not with the University but with the Folk Museum is the Institute for Norwegian Ethnological Studies. The present director is Hilmar Stigum, who is assisted by Lily Weiser Aall and Andreas Ropeid. In addition to supporting some fieldwork, the Institute has an extensive number of informants or correspondents scattered around the country to whom it sends questionnaires. It has its own special publication, *Småskrifter fra Norsk Etnologisk Gransking,* but much research by members of its staff is printed in other publications of the Folk Museum and elsewhere. To give some notion of the type of research carried on at this institute, I might mention that while I was in Norway one member of the staff was investigating the use of bark as winter fodder for farm animals, while another was studying the snowshoes worn by men and horses in Norway.

Instituttet for Sammenlignende Kulturforskning

The Institute for Comparative Research in Human Culture, with headquarters in Oslo, is primarily a foundation which supports research in many fields. Among others it has a Folklore Committee of which Reidar Th. Christiansen is the present chairman. The Institute is interested in promoting investigations in three folklore areas: *seter* (summer dairy) life and tradition; witchcraft and witch trials; and traces of Catholicism in post-Reformation popular tradition. Over the years the Institute has published a number of major folklore works, such as P. O. Bodding's *Santal Folk Tales* (Oslo and Cambridge, Mass., 1925-29), J. Qvigstad's *Lappiske Eventyr og Sagn* (*Lapp Folktales and Legends,* Oslo and Cambridge, Mass., 1927-29), and Svale Solheim's *Norsk Sætertradisjon* (*Norwegian Summer Dairy Tradition,* Oslo, 1952).

Folk Museums

I can make no additions to Thompson's account of folk, or open-air, museums in Norway except to emphasize the amazingly large number of these museums in a country whose total population is about equal to that of the state of Indiana. Practically every *fylke*—and there are eighteen—has its own folk museum, and many other smaller districts also support their own. Some of these are small, of course, consisting of only a few buildings, but at least two museums I visited, the Sandvik Collection at Lillehammer and the Glomdals Museum at Elverum, impressed me as being nearly as large as the national museum at Bygdøy. I should also mention that there is a national organization of museums, Norske Museets Landsforbund, which secures cooperation among the many museums to distribute funds which come in and to assist the member museums with advice and technical knowledge.

Folk Music Archives

The Norsk Folkeminnesamling has a large number of folksong texts but relatively little music. In the same building which at present houses the Folkeminnesamling, namely the University Library, there is, however, also a large archive of folk music. This is the Music Section of the University Library directed by Øystein Gaukstad. On file are about 20,000 transcribed folksongs, for an arrangement has been made whereby every person who receives a grant from the government or from the University to collect folksongs must deposit copies in this archive. There is also connected with the University the Norsk Folkemusikkinstitut headed by Professor Olav Gurvin.

A large archive consisting mostly of folk music on tapes is maintained at the Norsk Rikskringkasting (Norwegian National Broadcasting) in Oslo. This archive is under the direction of Rolf Myklebust, who is currently engaged in collecting activities, so that the archive continues to grow. Programs of folk music from this archive and from other sources are broadcast over the radio every Sunday afternoon and at other times as well. In this connection I might also mention that there are presented other programs dealing with folklore topics prepared by Odd Nordland, a folklorist and ethnologist at present on the Norwegian National Broadcasting staff.

As part of the Music Collection at the University Library in Bergen (Musikk-samlinga, Universitetsbiblioteket, Bergen), which is under the directorship of Halvard S. Bakken, there is an archive of folk music from western Norway with some material on tape.

I cannot close this brief survey without making a few general comments on my impressions concerning the noteworthy vitality I found in folklore studies in Norway. There is, first of all, an awareness of an interest in folklore in many circles as evidenced, for example, by the broadcasting of programs of the kind just mentioned. There is a substantial number of students working in folklore, thus guaranteeing a continued interest in the subject. The collecting of folk tradition is continuing in many areas. There are many publications in this field of scholarship. And, not by any means the least important, there is the large number of enthusiastic and dedicated scholars, only some of whom have been mentioned by name, devoted to the cause of folklore in Norway.

NOTES

1. R. Th. Christiansen, *Norske Eventyr* (Kristiania, 1921), is an index of folktale types in the archive as well as in printed sources. R. Th. Christiansen, *The Migratory Legends* (FF Communications, No. 175, Helsinki, 1958) is a catalogue of the Norwegian versions of this kind of folktale. Unprinted indexes at the Folkeminnesamling cover the other types of legends, proverbs, riddles, and the like.

2. Brita Gjerdalen Skre, "Folk Life Research in Norway," *Midwest Folklore*, II (1952), 221-228.

Indiana University
Bloomington, Indiana

W. EDSON RICHMOND

THE STUDY OF FOLKLORE IN FINLAND

I

THE STUDY of folklore in Finland is older than the country itself and of considerable importance for its development as a nation. Though in their search for antique origins there are scholars who will point to Michael Agricola's comments about runic songs in his sixteenth-century vernacular Psalter as the genesis of Finnish folklore studies, no true scholarship of any importance existed before the last half of the eighteenth century. At that time, however, ideas conceived as a result of the influence of Bishop Thomas Percy's *Reliques of Ancient English Poetry* and James Macpherson's Ossianic writings were to bear immediate fruit in semiliterary works, and these, in turn, were to serve as the seed for the flowering of romantic nationalism and true folkloristic studies in the next century.

Driven to chauvinism through the unwise administration of their land and its peasant population by Sweden and Russia and following the lead of equally nationalistic Englishmen and Germans, certain scholars in Turku (Åbo) and later in Helsinki (Helsingfors) determined to show the genius of the Finnish people. This genius they found in the oral literature, the customs, and the beliefs of a peasantry remarkably uninfluenced by exterior forces. On the foundation of this oral literature, of these customs and beliefs, expressed as they were in a language remote from that of administrating officials and neighboring countries, patriotic scholars built so strong an idea of a nation that it was able to take advantage of the disruption of world affairs in 1917 and come into actual existence. And even as the Finnish nation was conceived of and born in folklore, so Finnish scholars, in spite of the fact that their language is little known, have from the very first exerted a significant influence upon folklore studies throughout western Europe, parts of Asia, and those portions of the world influenced in turn by Europe and eastern Asia.

The history of Finnish folklore scholarship can be divided into three periods: the period before 1835 when Elias Lönnrot published the *Kalevala,* the period of *Kalevala* studies, and the post-*Kalevala* period. The first was an age of foreign influence and national discovery, the second was a period of romantic nationalism and introspection, and the last has been a period of expanding interest and broadening influence.

The work of Elias Lönnrot, which brought the folklore of Finland to the eyes of the world, would have been far slower in development had it not been for the studies published by four scholars connected directly or indirectly with the city of Turku which until 1828 was the seat of the national university. The earliest book about any element of Finnish folklore in the Finnish language appears to have been *Wanhain Suomalaisten Tawaliset ja Suloiset Sanan-lascut (Ordinary and Charming Proverbs of the Old Finns)* which was published by Henricus Matthiae Florinus in 1702; but it was not until the years 1766 to 1778 that folklore achieved respectability with the appearance of *Dissertationis de Poesi Fennica* by Henrik Gabriel Porthan, the "father of Finnish history."

Coming as it did from a highly respected scholar known for his work in accepted academic disciplines, Porthan's *Study of Finnish Poetry* had immediate influence. In a general way it brought to light a world of imaginative literature in the Finnish vernacular, and more specifically it made possible further studies by less well-known scholars. The most important of these men were Erik Lencqvist, Christfried Ganander, and Zachris Topelius the elder. Depending almost entirely upon written records, many of which had themselves undergone considerable rewriting by educated and semieducated people, Lencqvist conducted a series of studies culminating in *Superstitions of the Ancient Finns* in 1782; Ganander published his pioneering *Mythologia Fennica,* which, in spite of its Latin title, was written in Swedish, in 1789; and the elder Topelius brought out five booklets of folk poetry called *Suomen Kansan Vanhoja Runoja (Ancient Poetry of the Finnish People)* in 1822-31. Few countries can boast of so much of their oral literature having been brought to public attention so early as this, and though the work of Porthan, Lencqvist, Ganander, and Topelius was primarily library work, it was the kind of work necessary to give the subject dignity and to serve as a foundation for the field collecting and subsequent editing to be done in the next few years by Elias Lönnrot and Eero Salmelainen (Erik Rudbeck).

It was Elias Lönnrot, of course, who was to initiate the second period of folklore studies in Finland and whose creative imagination when applied to the oral literature and traditions of his native land was to bring these materials to the attention of the world. Indeed, until fairly recent years, all study of Finnish folklore has been conditioned by the work of this man who looked to the people themselves for his material even though he gave it a form that it probably had never known before. No one today doubts that the pattern of Lönnrot's most influential work was designed by the man himself rather than by the genius of the Finnish people as a whole. But when in 1835-36 he published the two volumes whose full title is *Kalevala taikka Vanhoja Karjalan Runoja Suomen kansan muinosista ajoista (Kalevala or Ancient Poems of Carelia Relating to the Antiquity of the Finnish People),* it was felt, perhaps even by Lönnrot himself, that he had restored a national epic by the judicious arrangement of folk materials.

Unlike his predecessors, who had worked in libraries, Lönnrot had gone directly to the peasantry, among whom he lived as a district health officer, for his materials. Because he was an educated man and because he lived in an age which was highly romantic and in a part of the world which had a strong desire for national identity, he presented these materials to the public as a piece of literature. And for a long time afterwards, the most vigorous study of folklore in Finland consisted of research on the *Kalevala* which was held to reflect the ancient poetry of the people exactly.[1] The problem was whether or not Lönnrot's "version" was valid or whether, perhaps, some other arrangement of the poems and incantations of which the *Kalevala* was composed would be closer to the original form. In other words, Lönnrot's work inspired collectors to go into the field, but they looked upon the materials which they found merely as fragments of a broken-down epic and regarded testing the validity of Lönnrot's archetype as their *raison d'être* as collectors.

The work of Lönnrot and his fellow collectors was greatly assisted by the formation in 1831 of the Suomalaisen Kirjallisuuden Seura, the Finnish Literary Society, which was eventually to create an archives, Suomalaisen Kirjallisuuden Seuran Runosarkisto (The Poetry Archives of the Finnish Literary Society) to accommodate the vast collections sent in from the field. It is perhaps significant that the word *runosarkisto* 'poetry archives' was used instead of *kansantietousarkisto* 'folklore archives' to describe the institution. In view of its origins, however, this was to be expected. Moreover, though Lönnrot himself in subsequent collecting trips gathered proverbs, riddles, and tales which he later edited and published, he continued to center his interest upon poetry. Aside from the *Kalevala,* his two most significant and influential volumes were to be the *Kanteletar,* a collection of lyric verse published in 1840, and his *Suomen kansan muinaisia loitsurunoja (Ancient Magic Verse of the Finnish People)* published in 1880.

In many ways, the work of Eero Salmelainen (Erik Rudbeck) with folktales complements Lönnrot's work with poetry. Indeed, because of the nature of his materials, his *Suomen kansan Satuja ja Tarinoita (Folk Tales and Legends of the Finnish People)* which was published in four volumes in the years 1852-66 comes somewhat closer to original field records than does the *Kalevala,* but no more so than does the *Kanteletar.* But though the later publications of Lönnrot and the volumes by Salmelainen give evidence of a dawning interest in all forms of folk literature, none of their books is an accurate reproduction of source materials in the modern sense.

The third and scientifically oriented period of folklore studies in Finland was not to begin until 1886. The intervening years showed a gradual development from inward examinations of the *Kalevala* itself to outward investigations of parallel materials and their cultural milieu. The evolutionary pattern of the scholarship can be seen in the following titles: Julius Krohn, *Wirolaiset ja ylimalkaan Länsisuomalaiset aineet Kalevalassa (Estonian and Western Finnish Elements in General in the Kalevala),* 1872; A. A. Borenius, *Missä Kalevala on syntynyt (Where the Kalevala Originated),* 1873; and Eliel Aspelin-Haapkylä, *Kalevala tutkimuksia (Kalevala Studies),* 1882. This last book attempted to apply the evolutionary theories of Darwin to folk literature, and, in doing so, it broke windows in the walls erected by the *Kalevala* and brought whole new fields and paths to those fields into view.

The breakthrough was dramatic and important not only to folklore scholars in Finland but to others throughout the rest of the world. It led first to the publication in 1886 of *Suomalaisia kansansatuja: 1 osa: Eläinsatuja (Finnish Folktales: Part 1: Animal Tales)* by Kaarle Krohn, and in 1893 of its second part, *Kuninkaallisia satuja: 1 vihko (Royal Tales: 1st installment)* by Kaarle Krohn and Lilli Lilius. Here were materials taken directly from tradition and edited in terms of what they were, not in terms of what someone thought they ought to be. Only a realization that the Finnish language presented too many obstacles for the nonnative scholar prevented publication of further volumes in the series. Even more important for the non-Finnish scholar, however, was the publication in 1897 of Julius Krohn's *Suomalaisen Kirjallisuuden Historia (A History of Finnish Literature)* in which the basis for the historic-geographic method of folkloristic research and analysis was outlined for the first time.

It would be possible to argue both that Julius Krohn was the last of the scholars from the middle period of Finnish folklore studies and that he was the first of the moderns. There is no doubt, however, that his son, Kaarle Krohn, was to take the lead in developing the methods and attitudes which condition most of folklore research in Finland and western Europe today. Appointed Docent of Finnish and Comparative Folklore at Helsinki University in 1888, he became Professor of the same subjects ten years later and thus became the first man in the world to hold such a chair at an established university. Unlike his scholarly predecessors, he was to emphasize comparative folklore and the technique for studying it. Abandoning for the most part the Finnish language publication of purely Finnish materials, he emphasized his concept of the international nature of folklore with his publication of *Bär (Wolf) und Fuchs, eine nordische Tiermärchenkette* in 1889 and *Mann und Fuchs, drei vergleichende Märchenstudien* in 1891, and stressed the necessity for an established technique with his elaboration of his father's theories in *Die folkloristische Arbeitsmethode* in 1926. But he was still Finnish enough and nationalistic enough that he looked upon his volumes of *Kalevalastudien* as his best work. These volumes were published as numbers 53, 67, 71-72, and 75-76 of the *Folklore Fellows Communications* in the years 1924-28. In the *Kalevalastudien* he attempted to show by means of the historic-geographic method that the Kalevala poems were a reflection of ancient history rather than, as earlier scholars had maintained, remnants of either mythology or an epic.

The same conclusion was reached by Kaarle Krohn's contemporary, Antti Aarne. Just how much each of these men owes to the other is impossible to say. A secondary schoolteacher and in ill health for most of his life, Aarne was to develop theory on the basis of studies of individual folktales and folksongs and to publish both the individual studies and explications of his theories. His 1908 monograph entitled *Vergleichende Märchenforschungen* complements Krohn's *Die folkloristische Arbeitsmethode,* as does his expansion of his theories in *Leitfaden der vergleichenden Märchenforschung,* which was published in 1913. Without any doubt, however, his most important contribution to folklore studies is his *Verzeichnis der Märchentypen,* first published as item number 3 in *Folklore Fellows Communications* in 1910. Expanded in 1928 by Stith Thompson, this volume became the basis for most subsequent folktale research in all parts of the world, and it serves even today as a model for the indexing of many other kinds of folklore.

Unfortunately, national pride which contributed significantly to the development of Finnish folklore studies, especially in the nineteenth century, was tied closely to the Finnish language, and this has had an adverse effect upon one area of folklore studies. A most conservative estimate would show that at least ten per cent of the people living on the south and west coasts of the country are either native speakers of Swedish or no more than one generation removed from a family which employed Swedish as its basic means of communication. Though the folklore of these people has been sporadically collected and large portions of the collected materials have been published, it is certainly true that the folklore of the Swedish-speaking population of Finland has never received the concerted and serious attention that Finnish-language folklore has received.

In the middle years of the nineteenth century when nationalism was a guiding principle and when the eyes of folklorists were turned upon the *Kalevala,* upon the Finnish language, and upon the peasantry of Carelia, it was easy and sometimes expedient to forget that in Ostrobothnia and along the south coast of Finland there was a Swedish-speaking peasantry generations removed from those who had brought them the language and set them linguistically apart from their cousins. But these people were Finns too, and most were as patriotic and as proud of the fact as were their Finnish-speaking neighbors. Some of their lore—songs, tales, beliefs, and customs —came, it is true, by means of oral tradition from the Swedes themselves, but much of it was as purely Finnish as the folklore of any area can be pure unto itself.

Little or no attention was paid to Swedish-language folklore in Finland until after Lönnrot's publication of the *Kalevala*. The tremendous impression which this poem made upon the population of the country as a whole brought about a kind of defensive reaction from the Swedo-Finns, who first turned their attention to the problem of dialects. In the years 1845 to 1847, J. O. I. Rancken and A. J. Hipping made the first experimental investigations of Swedish dialects in Nyland, and in 1848 the first of these men conducted a moderately successful attempt to gather Swedish-language folklore in Vaasa (Vasa).

For the next twenty years, Rancken and his disciples, especially Jakob Edvard Wefvar, Otto Reinhold Sjöberg, and his sons H. R. A. and Vilhelm Sjöberg, were to spend much time in the field and to publish some of their material in *Nyland*, a journal which might be said to have been founded in 1884 for this express purpose. The work gained further impetus when in 1870 the "Finska fornminnesforeningen" and in 1882 the "Svenska litteratursällskapet i Finland" gave support to the preservation and study of Swedish-language materials. Lacking, however, the incentive of attempting to justify their existence as a nation on linguistic grounds, the eighteenth-century scholars moved forward far more slowly than did their Finnish-language colleagues, and not until the first decades of the twentieth century was the bulk of their collected material to be made generally available to the rest of the world. The great and significant names in Swedo-Finnish folklore are names from the twentieth century rather than from the nineteenth and thus a subject for the second portion of this paper: Folklore Studies in Finland Today.

II

The literacy rate in Finland today is 98.2 per cent, but literacy has not erased folklore. When in 1935 the Kalevalan riemuvuoden kilpakeräys (The Kalevala Jubilee Collection Contest) was held, over 133,000 items, mostly legends and *memorats,* were delivered to the folklore archives of the Finnish Literary Society. Even as recently as 1953, a contest sponsored jointly by the Finnish Broadcasting Company and the folklore archives brought to light nearly 20,000 folksongs and popular melodies. Moreover, a large portion of the materials collected in both contests came from the western portion of Finland, an area which until the time of the contests had been largely unexplored by folklorists interested in Finnish-language materials.

Because of such activities the Suomalaisen Kirjallisuuden Seuran Runosarkisto (The Folklore Archives of the Finnish Literary Society) is a living institution. The collecting program which began shortly after the Society's founding in 1831, and which was once *Kalevala*-centered and relatively informal, now makes use of both part- and full-time collectors, questionnaires, and all such modern devices as tape- and disc-recorders. At the archives, which occupies one wing of a large building at Hallituskatu 1 in the center of Helsinki, materials are received daily, some of which are random and miscellaneous bits and fragments, but most of which are the result of a carefully planned program centered upon a particular project or type of folklore. Once in the rooms of the archives, these materials are classified, indexed according to a simple and easily grasped system, and filed by a staff of about ten clerk-scholars who work under the direction of Dr. Jouko Hautala, who has been the archivist since 1948.

But though the materials are classified, indexed, and filed, they are not buried. Both the members of the regular staff and other scholars make constant use of them. For example, the archives conducts its own publications program and assists scholars and students in the preparation of books, monographs, articles, and theses. Moreover, the foreign scholar who visits the Runosarkisto is made graciously welcome and assisted in all possible ways. Yet, he should remember that this is an archives of Finnish folklore supported at least in part by the government of the country. Its library, though magnificent for Finnish materials, is not as extensive as its directors wish, for a depreciated finmark has made the purchase of foreign books and periodicals very difficult. For the foreigner, though, there is a more serious problem than this: because the archives is above all a collection of folklore from the far reaches of the Finnish language area, no one unfamiliar with the most subtle nuances of Finnish can hope to do effective work upon the materials. If, however, one unfamiliar with the language has a specific problem involving, say, a particular tale, a song, or the like, he will find a visit well worth his time. A person knowing any one of the major European languages and the international methods of folklore classification can find his way easily through the indices; in addition, once material is located, one can easily find a clerk who can translate into German if not into English.

Unfortunately, the Finnish Folklore Archives' sister institution, Svenska litteratursällskapets folkloristika och etnografiska arkiv, is not nearly so vital a place. For the most part, its files are stored in Porthania, the newest building of the University of Helsinki, in the care of Professor Olav Ahlbäck, whose principal interests are Swedish literature and Swedish dialects in Finland. Except in the field of language study, no planned collecting program appears to be in progress, and most of the manuscript collection has seen publication already in the various volumes which form a part of the series *Finlands svenska Folkdiktning,* about which more will be said later.

The Folklore Archives of the Swedish Literary Society is not, however, the only archives of Swedish language material in Finland. In 1906, Professor Otto Andersson —the really vital force in Swedish-language folklore studies in Finland—founded "Brage, förening för vård av svensk folkdiktning." This society, which at present has rooms at Kaserngatan 28 in Helsinki, corresponds in many ways to the English Folk Dance and Song Society. Among other things, it maintains a magnificent clipping service; every item of or about folklore which appears in a Swedish-language newspaper in Finland is indexed and filed, and these materials are available to scholars upon request. In addition, Brage serves as a means of perpetuating traditional customs among the Swedo-Finns, holding occasional meetings to this end. Finally, because of Professor Otto Andersson's long association with Åbo Akademi, the Swedish-language university in Turku, valuable collections of Swedo-Finnish folksongs and music as well as a fine collection of kantele and other folk-music instruments are housed in the Akademi Library and in the Sibelius Museum which is located on Akademi grounds nearby.

The Sibelius Museum is not, however, a folk museum despite the fact that the principal interest of its present intendant, Miss Alfhild Forslin, is folksong and the ballad. The folk instruments form but an incidental part of a collection which otherwise centers upon Sibelius himself. For other elements of surviving material culture one must visit the open-air museums.

In the south of Finland there are three open-air museums, each of which obviously owes a great deal in its planning to the more elaborate museums in other parts of Scandinavia, especially to Maihaugen at Lillehammer in Norway and to Skansen in Stockholm. Indeed, Sagalund, located on Kimito, an island about forty miles south-east of Turku but reachable by car or bus, was created in direct imitation of Skansen. This open-air museum is in the heart of Swedish-speaking Finland today, and the baker's dozen of buildings which it displays are all from the same general area, thus reflecting primarily the Swedo-Finnish culture rather than the culture of Finland as a whole. As a result, the museum has an admirable unity which is further emphasized by the facts that few of the houses and outbuildings are older than the eighteenth century, and that they have been carefully selected with an eye toward representing the principal elements of the culture which produced them. In at least one of the houses the early nineteenth-century furniture has been kept intact. Other buildings are furnished as appropriately as possible with materials collected within the area.

Like Sagalund, a second museum, Seurasaari, is also on an island, but the island lies within the city limits of Helsinki less than fifteen minutes by bus or automobile from the center of town. Unlike Sagalund, however, Seurasaari has commercial buildings, churches, cabins, and outbuildings which have been brought from all over Finland. Of considerable antiquity, most of these buildings have been carefully taken down timber by timber and board by board, transported to Helsinki, and reconstructed. Buildings from particular areas are gathered together and placed in a topographical setting similar to that whence they came.

The best that can be said for both Sagalund and Seurasaari is that each gives the impression of a recently deserted area whose inhabitants expect to return soon to their daily activities. But neither is a truly living museum. In contrast, Luostarinmäki, the artisans' open-air museum which is surrounded by the modern city of Turku, is not only unusual in that its thirty-odd buildings stand on the original sites which they occupied at the end of the eighteenth century, but also in that people live in them and practice the occupations followed by their ancestors. The continuity, of course, is only physical. With the exception of the wooden houses on Luostarinmäki (the word means "cloister hill" and refers to a medieval monastery once located there), all of Turku was destroyed by fire in 1827, but the present museum was not opened until 1940. During the intervening years the houses were lived in by a variety of people; nevertheless, a minimum of work was necessary to restore the buildings to their original forms and to reestablish in them such nineteenth-century shops as those of joiners, tinsmiths, clockmakers, hatmakers, and the like. Unique among open-air museums in the picture which it gives of town life, Luostarinmäki conducts its own research program as well as serving as a tourist attraction and reminder of the older city.

That so small a country as Finland with a population approximately the same as that of the state of Indiana adequately supports three major open-air museums can be explained at least in part by a continuing sense of nationalism. All Finns appear to be proud of their heritage: whether Swedish- or Finnish-speaking, socially elite or proletariat, there are few homes without a copy of the *Kalevala*. Children are raised on the short stories and tales written by Zachris Topelius the younger, a Finn whose writing techniques parallel those of his contemporary, Denmark's Hans Christian Andersen. This pride is further encouraged by the regular educational curriculum. In the elementary and secondary schools, the study of folklore forms a regular part of the Finnish language and literature course required of all students, and this requirement extends to college and university work. Since 1888 when Kaarle Krohn became docent, the University of Helsinki has had research in Finnish and comparative folklore as a requisite for students planning to teach the Finnish language at any level.

Invariably the Professor of Finnish and Comparative Folklore at the University of Helsinki is also director of the nearby Suomalaisen Kirjallisuuden Seuran Runosarkisto, and his teaching assistants are officials of the archives. As a result, even teachers in elementary schools have been exposed to actual field materials rather than simply to literary treatments of folklore. All members of the Finnish population are thus exposed to folklore not only as carriers of tradition but also in the classroom as part of their formal education.

Unfortunately, however, the situation at the Swedish-language university in Finland, Åbo Akademi, is not nearly so vital. Though this university is in all other ways the equal of its sister institutions, the University of Helsinki and Turku University, for obvious reasons there is less emphasis upon Finnish language and literature. At various times in its history, different aspects of folklore have formed a part of the curriculum taught by the Faculty of Humanities, but since the retirement of Professor Otto Andersson from active teaching in the early 1950's, the only formal instruction in folklore either has been incidental to sociological research or has been conducted by foreigners. The latter was the case in 1959-60 when the author of this paper conducted a seminar in ballad literature.

An inevitable result of both popular and scholarly interest in folklore has been an intensive and active publication program which, though it has frequently and appropriately emphasized the folklore found in Finland, has also evidenced interest in comparative folklore. From an international point of view, by far the most important serial publication is the prestigious *FF Communications.* Organ of the loosely organized Folklore Fellows, a name which has the abbreviation *FF* in three languages besides English—Folkloristischer Forscherbund, Folkeminde Forskere, and Fédération des Folklorists—the series is now edited by Academician Martti Haavio and published by the Suomalainen Tiedeakatemia (The Finnish Academy of Sciences), the offices of which are located at Snellmaninkatu 9-11 in Helsinki. In 1907, Kaarle Krohn, along with Johannes Bolte, Axel Olrik, and C. W. von Sydow, founded the Folklore Fellows in order to make the folklore of countries all over the world available for comparative study and to publish catalogues of collections and studies of materials in the commonly read western European languages. As of 1960, one hundred and eighty-one monographs have been published, including such basic items as Walter Anderson's *Kaiser und Abt: Die Geschichte eines Schwanks* (No. 42), Stith Thompson's revision of Antti Aarne's work, *The Types of the Folk-Tale* (No. 74) as well as the first edition of Thompson's *Motif-Index of Folk-Literature* (Nos. 106-109, 116-117), Elsa Enäjärvi-Haavio's *The Game of Rich and Poor* (No. 100), and Holger Olof Nygard's *The Ballad of Heer Halewijn* (No. 169).[2]

Such a series would be a credit to any country, but there are other serial publications as well. Unfortunately, the little-known *Kansantieto* (*Folklore*) which began under the direction of Martti Haavio in 1936 was brought to an end by the Winter War in 1939 and was not reborn despite the valuable service it performed in publishing items concerned with Finnish folklore. On the other hand, *Virittäjä,* which is also Finnish-centered, began in the last decade of the nineteenth century and is still vigorous today. Published by the Kotikielen Seuran Aikakauslehti (Society for the Study of the Mother Tongue) which is located in the same building as the Runosarkisto at Hallituskatu 1, Helsinki, the journal is edited today by Dr. Lauri Hakulinen.

Though primarily linguistic in its approach, *Virittäjä* publishes occasional articles on such subjects as riddles, popular etymologies, and place-name legends. Finally, the Suomalaisen Kirjallisuuden Seura publishes a review of Finnish language and ethnology entitled *Studia Fennica* which at present is edited by Martti Haavio, Lauri Hakulinen, and Jouko Hautala. Volume VII, which appeared in 1957, is especially valuable in that it describes the history of literary and folklore studies in Finland in a series of related articles, four in English and three in German.[3]

Proportionally, Swedish-language folklore in Finland is equally well represented by periodical publication, even though the representation consists of but one journal. Published by Brages sektion för Folklivsforskning and Institutet för nordisk entnologi vid Åbo Akademi and edited by Sven Andersson, *Budkavlen* averages five or six articles each issue, most of which are concerned with various aspects of Swedish-language folklore and ethnology, though occasional articles on international subjects are printed as well. Along with its editor, Sven Andersson, the moving spirits of the journal are Professors Otto Andersson and K. Rob. V. Wikman, but virtually every scholar concerned with Swedo-Finnish folklore has published in *Budkavlen* at one time or another in its forty years of existence.

Neither the Swedish- nor the Finnish-language folklorists in Finland have neglected book publication. Two major collections, one Swedish and one Finnish, have been published in such a way that they offer to those unable to visit the archives themselves sufficient material for accurate if limited research. The ten volumes with the general title *Finlands svenska Folkdiktning,* published, beginning in 1917, by Svenska Litteratursällskapet i Finland, present an almost complete coverage of the collections found in the society's archives. Each of the ten volumes is devoted to a particular area of folklore and is edited by the principal authority in the field. For the most part, however, the material in the volumes is merely classified and arranged logically; there are few comparative notes. Similarly, the magnificent thirty-three volumes entitled *Suomen Kansat Vanhat Runot (Ancient Finnish Popular Poetry),* published by the Finnish Literary Society during the years 1908 to 1950, contain in their 26,477 pages over 85,000 poetic variants in the *Kalevala* meter. In both series the raw materials are thus available to those who wish to do further work.

It is difficult to choose the most significant volumes among the less extensive publications. For a general history of folklore studies in Finland one should turn to Jouko Hautala's *Suomalainen kansanrunoudentutkimus (History of Finnish Folklore Research)* which, since it was published as recently as 1954, is nearly up to date. Other books of great importance besides those mentioned earlier are *Suomen kansan arvoituskirja (The Finnish People's Book of Riddles)* published by Martti Haavio and Jouko Hautala in 1946; Lauri Simonsuuri's two volumes, *Myytillisiä tarinoita (Mythical Legends)* and *Kotiseuden tarinoita (Local Legends),* published in 1947 and 1951 respectively; and Matti Kuusi's *Vanhan kansan sananlaskuviisaus (Proverb Wisdom of the Ancient Finns),* which was published in 1951.

That Matti Kuusi's book should be the last mentioned in this list is perhaps appropriate, for when Martii Haavio was named a member of the Finnish Academy in 1958 and thus relinquished his university duties, Professor Kuusi was appointed to the chair of Finnish and Comparative Folklore at the University of Helsinki, a position which carries with it the directorship of the folklore archives as well. Both Academician Haavio, who is a successful novelist as well as a scholar, and Professor Kuusi have strongly nationalistic tendencies and emphasize in their studies the folklore which is found in Finland itself. Yet Professor Kuusi's latest book, *Regen bei Sonnenschein* (FF Communications, No. 171, 1957) and the collection of essays written by Academician Haavio and republished as a festschrift in honor of his sixtieth birthday in 1959 ("Essais Folkloriques par Martti Haavio," ed. by Lauri Honko, *Studia Fennica,* Vol. VIII) show the broad international interests of both of these men. Similarly, as archivist of the Suomalaisen Kirjallisuuden Seuran Runosarkisto, Dr. Jouko Hautala has as his principal duty the promotion of Finnish-language folklore. But like his colleagues, Dr. Hautala, upon whose shoulders frequently falls the responsibility for helping foreign scholars, is a brilliant comparative folklorist.

Among the Swedish-language folklorists in Finland, one name stands out above all the others: Professor Otto Andersson. The extreme enthusiasm, vitality, and cordiality of Professor Andersson would more than justify the epithet "the grand old man of folklore" even had he not produced works of effective and significant scholarship for more than fifty years. Identified primarily with folk music, Professor Andersson has been the moving spirit behind most of the attempts to preserve the Swedish culture in his own country. Born over eighty years ago in the Åland Islands, he became one of Finland's leading musicologists, and he has always pointed out patriotically and correctly that, despite linguistic differences, the folklore found among the Swedish-speaking Finns belongs to Finland and not to Sweden. An inspiring teacher and once rector of Åbo Akademi, "Uncle Otto" has led many students to a lifelong study of Swedo-Finnish folk music and lore. Perhaps the most active of these students today is Alfhild Forslin, who is especially interested in international balladry and who, among other contributions, has published in collaboration with Greta Dahlström a valuable collection of Swedo-Finnish folksong for popular consumption: *Finländsk Sång och Visa* (Åbo, 1952).

Only slightly less active than Professor Andersson have been Professor K. Rob. V. Wikman, who holds the chair of sociology at Åbo Akademi, and Professor Olav Ahlbäck and his wife Ragna Ahlbäck, both of the University of Helsinki. As a sociologist, Professor Wikman's interdisciplinary cultural studies have introduced new approaches to the examination of Swedo-Finnish culture, songs, beliefs, and tales, while Professor and Mrs. Ahlbäck have concentrated their attention upon a linguistic approach to all aspects of folklore as well as to Swedo-Finnish literature as a whole.[4]

More than most people, the Finns and their national spirit can be understood by a study of their folklore and their folklorists. Their budding spirit of nationalism was brought to full flower in the middle of the nineteenth century in large part as a result of the unifying power of Elias Lönnrot's collection and reworking of the *Kalevala* poems. The work of subsequent scholars upon *Kalevala* materials kept the popular poetry constantly in front of an increasingly literate people, and this, in turn, kept them aware of their desire for independence and statehood. It is perhaps especially appropriate that statehood was finally achieved in 1917 under the leadership of a Swedo-Finnish aristocrat, Baron Carl Gustaf Emil Mannerheim, who received much of his military training in Russia and who was thus himself a product of the forces which went to create the country itself. His own *Memoirs* show that Baron Mannerheim was well aware of the words of Väinämöinen in the portion of the *Kalevala* entitled "Väinämöisen laulu" (The Song of Väinämöinen):

> Kansat katoo,
> ei katoa mahti,
> jonka on laulanut mahtaja kansansa sielun.

(The people pass on, but the song sung by the man who has mastered the soul of his people shall not pass away.)

NOTES

1. English translations of the *Kalevala* include W. F. Kirby, *Kalevala, Land of the Heroes* (2 vols., New York and London, 1907); and Aili Johnson, *Kalevala, A Prose Translation from the Finnish* (Hancock, Mich., 1950). An important study available in English is D. P. A. Comparetti, *Traditional Poetry of the Finns,* trans. I. M. Anderton (London, 1898).

2. The most recent FFC monographs published in 1960 are Stith Thompson and W. E. Roberts, *Types of Indic Oral Tales* (No. 180), and Aarne A. Koskinen, *Ariki the First-Born* (No. 181).

3. Toivo Vuorela, "The Finnish Literary Society," pp. 1-15; Jouko Hautala, "The Folklore Archives of the Finnish Literature Society," pp. 1-36; Eino Nivanka, "The Library of the Finnish Literature Society," pp. 1-13; Aimo Turunen, "Über den Unterricht des Finnischen und der mit ihm verwandten Sprachen an der Universität Helsinki und den übrigen Hochschulen Finnlands," pp. 1-30; Jouko Hautala, "Vicissitudes in Publishing the Ancient Poetry of the Finnish People," pp. 1-36; Matti Hako, "Tatigkeits bericht des Folkloristischen Seminars der Universität Helsinki," pp. 1-24; Sulo Haltsonen, "Finnische linguistische und volkskundliche Bibliographie für die Jahre 1950-1954," pp. 1-61. It will be noted that each item is numbered separately.

4. Some of the representative works of Karl Robert V. Wikman are: *Die Einleitung der Ehe* (Åbo, 1937); *Järul en utlöpare av Syd svensk varulustro* (*Järul: An Offshoot of South Swedish Werewolf Belief*) (Åbo, 1931); *Livets högtider* (*Life's Festivals*) (Stockholm, 1944?); *Die Magie des Webens und des Webstuhls im schwedischen Volksglauben* (Åbo, 1920); *Svenska Finlands folkting 1919-1920* (*Swedish Finland's Peoples Court 1919-1920*) (Åbo, 1941). The publications of Olav Ahlbäck in *Budkavlen* include "Några anteckningar om participia precentis i finlands-svenska folkmål" ("Some Notes about the Present Participle in the Swedish Dialect of Finland"), XV (1936), 147-150; "Språkprov från Dragsfjärd" ("A Linguistic Experiment from Dragsfjärd"), XVI (1937), 130-134; "Nackårder och korsårder" ("Two Types of Ploughs"), XVII (1938), 57-61; and "Nådendal, fi. Naantali," XVIII (1939), 87-90.

Indiana University
Bloomington, Indiana

FRANCES GILLMOR

FOLKLORE STUDY IN SPAIN

IN 1580 Philip the Second of Spain sent out a questionnaire to all parts of the Spanish dominions. Answers came from every town and village of the New World, the parts numbered carefully according to the questionnaire. The *Relaciones Geográficas* have provided much of our knowledge of Aztec Mexico and its tribute area as they were still known in a time when the old people could remember the Spanish conquest and the way of life before it happened. For example, Juan Bautista Pomar begins his "Relacíon de Texcoco" which he sent to His Majesty by saying that every effort had been made to get at all possible truth, "seeking out old and intelligent Indians . . . seeking ancient songs."[1] He points out that some men will know one thing, others something else. The answers that were sent back to Spain gave Filipe II a remarkable picture of the New World—its geographic features, its social organization and customs, its legends, its medicinal uses of herbs, and its oral history.

Knowing how early the questionnaire had been used in Spain by this royal folklorist, I was not too surprised to find nearly four centuries later, when I went there in 1959-60 with a fellowship from the John Simon Guggenheim Memorial Foundation, that Spain is still fond of the questionnaire, still systematic in collecting and studying folklore.

I landed early, and fortunately, at the Museo del Pueblo Español in Madrid. This folk arts museum, under the Dirección General de Bellas Artes, was in the process of remodeling, and the heat was off. But I look upon the cordial helpfulness of its staff as providing a warm and friendly center in the wind, sleet, and snow of a Madrid winter. Whenever I was in Madrid between extended periods in other parts of Spain, this Museum of the Spanish People was my base. The Señorita Nieves de Hoyos Sancho, Conservadora, and José Pérez Vidal, Conservador and Secretario, and their welcoming staff, offered me my own table beside an electric heater in one of the offices, and free use of the excellent specialized folklore library, and of the card file, constantly being worked on and expanded, and rich in information on fiestas—my particular subject of investigation. They gave a small reception and a luncheon for me so that I would meet other folklorists. They notified me of events of folklore interest elsewhere in Madrid such as meetings of the Folklore Society and lectures at the University. They gave me introductions to folklorists in other parts of Spain which led to helpful suggestions and to other letters of introduction in a happy chain reaction.

I mention these many courtesies to emphasize the warmth, openness, and cordiality with which the visiting folklorist is met in Spain. These attitudes, I found, were typical of the whole country. During my ten months in Spain, I was given help in every region without reluctance or hesitation by people engaged in the actual study of folklore, and also by informants in every walk of life. All alike prized their traditions and recognized the importance of studying them. And even the most unexpected people on trains and buses knew the term *folklore* without my having to explain it as I usually have to at home. Several times, circling up on my subject with needless indirection, I said, "I am studying the traditions, the legends, the fiestas here in Spain," and the face of the person with me would light up as he replied, "Oh, you are studying folklore." After awhile I relaxed and used the word from the beginning. Everyone studies folklore in Spain.

An excellent base for the study of Spanish folklore is the six hundred page *Manual de Folklore* by the late Luis de Hoyos Sáinz,[2] a distinguished ethnologist, and his daughter, Nieves de Hoyos Sancho, already mentioned as curator of the Museum of the Spanish People, and constantly publishing in folklore. This book gives ethnographic background on the different regions of Spain, provides lengthy and invaluable bibliographies, and sets forth problems and methods including field use of questionnaires. I was interested in the present use of questionnaires by the museum: for example, one exploring, with French folklorists, the cult of a particular saint with its ramifications in folk medicine, traditional foods, organizations of artisans, place names, songs, tales, beliefs, ex-votos, and so forth. The curators of the museum maintain contact with folklorists in other parts of Europe and in the western hemisphere through correspondence and attendance at international meetings.

A great deal of folklore investigation is organized under the Consejo Superior de Investigaciones Scientíficas. One of the many Centros of the Consejo is the Centro de Estudios de Etnología Peninsular in Madrid. Since 1944 it has published the *Revista de Dialectología y Tradiciones Populares,* probably the most important series in Spain for the folklore student. The director of this Centro is Vicente García de Diego, and its secretary is the distinguished ethnologist and folklorist Julio Caro Baroja. The Society of Ethnology and Folklore meets there, and in its membership I was delighted the night I attended to meet Don Julio himself, who spoke on the need for more emphasis on the folklore of cities. To my delight also present was the prolific writer on folk drama and on Gypsy, Moroccan, and Jewish folklore, Arcadio de Larrea Palacín. Many of his books have been published by the Consejo Superior, including his recent *El Folklore y la Escuela,* which contains chapters on integrating the study of folklore with other subjects in school, and provides questionnaires for use by teachers in collecting in their communities.[3] This stimulating little book may well extend the study of folklore in the schools. (I could not find much of this activity now going on, even though children in Andalusian villages did sing me *romances* that they had learned in school.) Like the Museo del Pueblo Español, the Centro de Estudios de Etnología Peninsular also has a specialized library useful for the folklorist. The library is presided over by the Señorita García de Diego.

In the same building are several such specialized libraries. Among them is one particularly interesting to students of the western hemisphere—the library of the Instituto de Fray Bernardino de Sahagún, which specializes in the ethnography of the Americas. A questionnaire circulated in Spain in 1901 on birth, marriage, and death is kept here: Información Promovida por la Sección de Ciencias Morales y Políticas del Ateneo de Madrid. I have not examined the 280 replies and the more than 40,000 cards of analysis, but they are described in the *Manual de Folklore* and also by George M. Foster in his *Culture and Conquest: America's Spanish Heritage.*[4] Foster says this is the most extensive questionnaire used to date by an ethnologist. The authors of the *Manual* point out, however, that this questionnaire and all later ones have had limited response because of the populace's fear of political and taxation intent.

Beside the many useful, small, specialized libraries in Madrid, the tremendous resources of the Biblioteca Nacional should be mentioned, with folklore and its various branches well catalogued. The procedures for working in the Biblioteca Nacional are more complicated than in the small libraries. One must arrange for a reading permit and provide pictures. But again one is met with every courtesy and given every assistance.

The nation-wide folklore activities of the Woman's Section of the Falange center in Madrid. I delayed my visit to their office and archive until the end of my stay in Spain, though I had seen and enjoyed in Madrid their beautiful exhibition of regional costumes and had attended in Malaga their fine program of regional dances, done simply and freshly on a bare stage with dancers brought from all over Spain. Everywhere I heard nothing but praise for their folklore activities, which were described by everyone as cultural and nonpolitical.

When I did visit their offices, the director of their folklore work, the Señorita Maruja Sampelayo, described the extent and the limits of their collection. She said honestly that they do not occupy themselves scientifically with the things they collect, nor do they collect in all fields. Instead they specialize in songs, dances, and costume, with an emphasis on giving performances. However, the data is archived with typical Spanish exactness and precision and provides a mine of information for students in these fields. In a folder, 7¼ inches by 9¾ inches in size, is contained a four-page folded and printed form on card stock. The outside folder is numbered and labeled *Costumes, Dance,* or *Song,* and spaces are provided for the name of the item contained within, its provenience, and a brief description. On the folded card inside spaces are provided for more complete information, and extra pages are added where necessary.

The *Song* card calls for the province from which the song has been sent; the province to which it originally belonged; the commonly used title or first line; the village or town in which it was collected; the collector's name; the date; information on when and where the informant first heard it and other details; the song's artistic value; its folkloric value (with a note pointing out that a song may be interesting musically and yet not be a folksong); the place of publication if it has been published; and its genre, i.e., lullaby, work song, or humorous song. The last two pages are ruled for recording the tune.

The *Dance* card provides spaces for the above items and also for details of choreography, steps and rhythm; accompanying instruments; number of dancers; reason for which the dance is performed; history of the dance; program or competition (presumably among those sponsored by the Woman's Section) in which it was first presented; description of the village where it is danced; costume used for it; data taken from documents, archives, or published sources; and accompanying words and music.

The *Costume* card includes the basic questions on provenience but adds questions about the dances in which the costume is worn; the changes which have taken place in it; the location of the particular costume being described and the possibilities of acquiring it for collection; the type of person using the costume—e.g., bride or widow; the occasions on which it is used—e.g., Sunday, fiesta, or every day; and a description of materials, colors, ornaments, and the like. Nearly all the costume folders contain a colored drawing of the costume and often samples of the material. In addition to these kinds of classified materials the archive contains photographs and moving picture films—a direction in which it is now being built up.

The program aspect of the Woman's Section is elaborately organized. Señorita Maruja Sampelayo told me that there are eight hundred groups in different parts of Spain, some groups from pueblos of only five hundred people. Each group is directed by a leader who in addition to four years in a conservatory and a bachelor's degree must have a two-year course in music at the Escuela Nacional de la Sección Feminina. These leaders go to towns all over Spain to see if there is "an old dance, a song." In these towns they give courses in music (not in folk music alone) to children and grownups. In 1942 they set up national competitions, at first annual, then biennial. "The enthusiasm was so great, and so many people came that we did not have money to do it every year," said Señorita Maruja Sampelayo.

At first the archive kept a record of the contestants but the numbers got out of hand, and no attempt is now made to keep a file on them. In the competitions 37,000 people now take part, the winning groups going from regional into national competition. Under the auspices of the Woman's Section these dance groups have traveled to many European and South American countries, to the United States, and to Canada. Each group performs only dances from its own region.

The Sección Feminina is bringing out a series of publications on the dances of different regions of Spain. The first one appeared in 1957 on Castilla la Nueva by M. García Matos of the Instituto Español de Musicología del Consejo Superior de Investigaciones Científicas.[5] Its 198 pages give music, notation of steps, and drawings. Now in press are volumes on the Extremadura and on Aragón. Other books and *folletos* have been published, and more are in the planning stage. A pleasant thirty-four page *folleto* on Spanish songs and folk dances with photographs, brief descriptions, a few tunes, and colored drawings of costumes has been published in Spanish, French, German, and English to go with the programs.

It is important to look at the folklore activities of the different regions of Spain on their own home grounds. Though many of the regional centers of study receive their support from the already mentioned Consejo Superior, they have their own individual character. Examples of these centers are the Centro de Estudios Asturianos, the Centro de Estudios Extremeños, the Centro de Estudios Montañeses, the Centro de Estudios Leoneses, and the Centro de Estudios Canarios. Cordova and Zaragosa also have their centers of study. In addition there are many regional publications; *Berceo,* the Bulletin of the Instituto de Estudios Riojanos, is one.[6]

As an example of these regional centers of the Consejo Superior I shall take one where I worked briefly, the Instituto Padre Sarmiento de Estudios Gallegos in Santiago de Compostela. The days of the great fiesta of Santiago had just ended when I entered the lovely old building and quiet library of this Institute. Taken in hand by Secretario F. R. Cordero Carrete and by a Colaborador of the Institute, Dr. Fermín Bouza-Brey Trillo, I had roads of investigation in Galicia pointed out to me which could occupy me for the rest of my life. This particular Institute, founded in 1944, numbers among its founders many of the literary men of the former Seminario de Estudios Gallegos, whose library it inherited and to which it is constantly adding. It is housed in the eighteenth-century Palacio de Fonseca, sponsors exhibitions of historical and artistic interest, issues three times a year a magazine called *Cuadernos de Estudios Gallegos,* and in addition publishes many books and monographs. Its bulletin for the decade 1944-54 includes an extensive and classified list of studies concerning Galicia in the fields of geography, prehistory, history (including a special series on Santiago de Compostela), paleography, diplomacy, art and archaeology, philology, literature, bibliography and, of special interest to us, ethnography and folklore.[7]

The people at this Instituto were careful to call attention to other organizations in Galicia, each with its own *Boletín,* whose studies and publications have folklore interest: the Real Academia Gallega in La Coruña, the Comisión de Monumentos de Lugo, the Comisión de Monumentos de Orense, and the Museo de Pontevedra. Active folklorists include Vicente Risco and Joaquín Lorenzo Fernández in Orense; Vázquez Saaijas in Luga; and José Filgueira Valverde in Pontevedra.

Sometimes in Spain an Institute of Music forms a center for regional study of folksong. It is so in Valencia, where under the direction of composer and professor Manuel Palau a large collection is being assembled at the Institución Alfonso el Magnánimo. This institution is under the patronage of the Diputación Provincial de Valencia, which sponsors institutes of prehistoric studies, geology, and other subjects, among them an Instituto de Musicología, one section of which deals with folklore investigation. Don Manuel Palau, taking time out from his duties as director of the institution, described to me its collecting activities. It works directly in the pueblos, seeking out old people, children, and players of folk instruments in Castellón de la Plana, Alicante, and Valencia—the three provinces which composed the old kingdom of Valencia. It seeks out the most isolated communities, those with least communication with the modern world, and those, said Don Manuel, "most closely linked with the traditional expressive forms of the pueblo, which in this case is truly the creative artist. We all know that a folksong has sprung from one throat, but then has passed through thousands until, although in one mold, it has taken imprints through time that would astound the original singer." He says that folklorists interested in different aspects of tradition understand each other's work. He is interested in costume, for example, but in a secondary way. "As the basic and fundamental thing we occupy ourselves with song and dance. We have game songs, for instance, of sedentary games, of running and dancing games with chorus. We have sung tales—narrations, legends, with music or without it, though generally they carry their own music. There is music for each moment of each day: a special music for each activity of a woman in her house, on the street, at church; a song to clean the house, to wash the clothes, to scrub the floor, even to heat the water. In Valencia we have gathered some three thousand examples of songs and dances. Without doubt we will double or triple this number. I believe that we give good service to the culture of our nation, for this is an inheritance worth collecting." This composer points out the inspiration in folksong for composition. He says that after studying its scales and forms we know more about a folksong than the folksinger, are more technically within it, are "more folk than the folk." In this cause, says Don Manuel, he becomes an evangelist.

It must be pointed out that this particular collection is not open to visitors until its contents are published. Publication has been proceeding regularly, however, starting in 1950 with a series of *Cuadernos de Música Folklórica Valenciana,* supported by the Diputación Provincial de Valencia. These Cuadernos include music, words, names of collectors and informants, information about the circumstances in which the music is sung, and sometimes, as in the case of Antonio Chover's *Canciones, Danzas y Pregones de Tabernes de Valldigna* (Nos. 4 and 5 in the series, 1951) photographs showing the landscapes, house types, informants, instruments, fiestas, dances, and occupations.

Valencia is not alone in giving support to folklore through municipal and provincial authorities. Cataluña, for example, a world to itself and long rich in folklore study and publication, also gives public support to folklore. Among the many cities which might be mentioned in that region, Barcelona provides some interesting examples. I have at hand a little book on *Leyendas y Tradiciones Marineras* by Juan Amades and José Tarín, prizewinners in a contest on folklore of the sea held in 1954 under the auspices of Ediciones de la Sección de Prensa de la Diputación Provincial de Barcelona.[8] The Museo Municipal de Música de Barcelona has much of interest for the folklorist. Under the cordial and helpful direction of J. Ricart Matas there is a large collection of folk instruments from all over the world as well as from the different regions of Spain. A fine general work on the folklore of Spain published in Barcelona, though not under government auspices, is the three-volume *Folklore y Costumbres de España* edited by F. Carreras y Candi (1931-34) with signed articles by a number of different authors. Many books and periodicals for this region of Cataluña, many published by municipal and provincial authorities, and all showing the vitality of folklore study, are listed in the bibliographies of the *Manual de Folklore*.

The Ayuntamiento of Valencia—the city hall—publishes some scholarly little *folletos* each year for the fiesta of Corpus Cristi. Some are documents from the Ayuntamiento archive; some are detailed histories of some aspect of the processions; some contain interesting reproductions of old engravings. Even though in this case the intent is related to tourism, the quality of these little *folletos* is high.

In Alicante I found that the Diputación Provincial had published for the Instituto de Estudios Alicantinos a running-comment bibliography on the "Moors and Christians" fiesta. It is written in Valenciano instead of Castellano by Adolf Salva I. Ballester, and its 175 pages gave me unexpected guidance to published and documentary material on one of the principal subjects of my studies in Spain.[9]

In the Extremadura the Diputación Provincial de Cáceres and the Excmo. Ayuntamiento de Cáceres have in turn sponsored the first two volumes of a series on the history of Cáceras by Antonio C. Floriano.[10] While not folklore, such historical series are important for the folklorist studying any region of Spain.

Often one finds folklorists in archival and governmental positions. I sought out the scholarly Alcalde of Jerez de la Frontera, D. Tomás García, because he had edited a series of texts of the "Moors and Christians" play.[11] I had been sent to him by Francisco Bejarano, city archivist of Malaga, who had contributed to the series.[12] D. Tomás introduced me to the city archivist, D. Hipólito Sancho de Sopranis, whose three-volume *Historia Social de Jerez de la Frontera,* one of the Publicaciones del Centro de Estudios Históricos Jerezanos, contained a mine of background information for the folklorist.[13]

Besides official agencies of research and publication the strong sense of region and of regional speech in Spain leads to much private and local publication often of great interest to the folklorist. One of the first stops for anyone seeking bibliographical background on provincial towns in Spain should be the local bookstore. I have found understanding welcome in big stores and in little ones, from the well-known J. Porter in Barcelona—a cultural center and research library in itself with a whole room and staff devoted just to bibliography—to the small stores in Andalusian towns where an old man, or his son or grandson (this always seems to be the combination), comes forward into dim light, shows you out-of-print memoirs of a doctor or a teacher,[14] or the collected feature stories of a local newspaper man, and sends you to someone of long memory and folk concern.

Ultimately one goes, of course, to the people who take part in the fiestas, who sing the songs, who tell the tales. Even then sometimes one is not yet at headquarters. I remember sitting one evening in a kitchen in Gérgal, a small town near Almería. A woman of sixty and a girl of sixteen were singing to me. I had recorded on my little battery-run Midgetape a *romance,* then a Christmas carol. The older woman left the room for a minute to attend to her sick husband.

"I have no lullaby," I said to the sixteen-year-old. "Won't you sing me a cradle song?"

She laughed in amused embarrassment.

"But I have no baby," she said.

When a woman with a baby sings a lullaby, the collector has arrived at headquarters. Yet the Spanish folklorists, like those I have gratefully mentioned and many more, help the collector view the song and its situation in scholarly perspective. And in this folklorically active country of Spain the archives, museums, institutes, and individual scholars offer help in orienting the newcomer with such warmth and openness that it must always leave him, as it did me, filled with gratitude for the resources available to him, and humbled by the realization that a lifetime would not be enough to know the Spain that her own sons and daughters, born within her rich tradition, so devotedly record.

NOTES

1. See Pomar's "Relación de Texcoco," *Nueva Colección de Documentos Para la Historia de México: Pomar, Zurita, Relaciones Antiguas* (Siglo XVI), ed. Joaquín García Icazbalceta (México, 1941), p. 3.

2. Luis de Hoyos Sáinz y Nieves de Hoyos Sancho, *Manual de Folklore: La Vida Popular Tradicional* (Madrid, 1947).

3. The solidity and scholarship of the publication going on under the auspices of the Consejo Superior through its Madrid Institutes is indicated by Arcadio de Larrea Palacín's folklore studies. His *Cancionero Judío del Norte de Marruecos* in three volumes (Vols. I and II, 1952, 345 and 377 pp., on the "Romances of Tetuán"; Vol. III, 1954, 288 pp., on the "Canciones Rituales Hispano-Judías") was published by the Instituto de Estudios Africanos. The first volume of his *Cuentos Populares de Andalucía,* "Cuentos Gaditanos" (215 pp.) was published by the Centro de Estudios de Etnología Peninsular in 1959. *El Folklore y la Escuela* (178 pp.) was published by the Instituto "San José de Calasanz" de Pedagogía in 1958.

The Instituto "Antonio de Nebrija" de Filología in 1946-47 brought out three volumes of Aurelio Macedonio Espinosa's *Cuentos Populares Españoles Recogidos de la Tradicion Oral de España,* including the volume of comparative notes not previously published by Stanford University in the earlier edition. The same institute published Ricardo del Arco Garay, *Notas de Folk-Lore Altoaragonés* in 1943 (541 pp.).

Also under the governmental entity of the Consejo Superior de Investigaciones Científicas are the regional institutes to be mentioned later.

4. *Manual de Folklore* (see n. 1), pp. 65-67; and Foster, *Culture and Conquest,* Viking Fund Publications in Anthropology, No. 27 (Chicago, 1960), p. vii.

5. *Danzas Populares de España: Castilla la Nueva,* realizado por M. García Matos (Madrid, 1957).

6. Luis de Hoyos Sáinz y Nieves de Hoyos Sancho in the *Manual de Folklore,* pp. 23-25, list regional publications and point out that the list could be expanded. Their bibliographies at the end of chapters also list many regional series.

7. *El Primer Decenio del Instituto Padre Sarmiento de Estudios Gallegos, 1944-1954* (Santiago de Compostela, 1954), pp. 43-116.

8. Premios San Jorge 1954 (Periodismo). Juan Amades is a leading folklorist of Spain, publishing extensively. One of the books I found useful was his directory (in Catalán) of the fiestas of that region: Joan Amades, *Guia de Festes Tradicionals de Catalunya* (Barcelona, 1958).

9. Adolph Salva I. Ballester, *Bosqueig Historic i Bibliografic de Les Festes de Moros i Cristians* (Alicante, 1958).

10. Antonio C. Floriano, *Estudios de Historia de Cáceres* (Oviedo, 1957-59): Vol. I, "Desde Los Orígenes a la Reconquista"; Diputación Provincial de Cáceres (Servicios Culturales), 1957; "El Fuero y la Vida Medieval," Excmo. Ayuntamiento de Cáceres, 1959.

11. This series, sponsored by the Instituto General Franco para las Investigaciónes Hispano-

Arabes, included the following by Tomás García Figueras: No. I, *Notas Sobre las Fiestas de Moros y Cristianos en Benadalid* [Málaga] (Larache, 1939); No. II, *Las Fiestas de San Jorge en Alcoy* (Larache, 1940); No. III, *Las Fiestas de Nra. Sra. de Gracia en Caudete* (Larache, 1940).

12. Francisco Bejarano Robles, *Fiestas de Moros y Cristianos en la Provincia de Málaga: Benalauria, Benamocarra, Alfarnate,* Notas sobre las Fiestas de Moros y Cristianos en España Num. IV (Tetuán), Instituto General Franco para las Investigaciones Hispano-Arabes.

This same Institute sponsored the volume of texts and analysis by Arcadio de Larrea Palacín, *El Dance Aragonas y las Representaciones de Moros y Cristianos: Contribución al Estudio del Teatro Popular* (Tetuán, 1952).

13. Hipólito Sancho de Sopranis, *Historia Social de Jerez de la Frontera al Fin de la Edad Media:* I. "La Vida Material"; II. "La Vida Espiritual"; III. "Anécdota." (Publicaciones del Centro de Estudios Históricos Jerezanos, Segunda Serie, Núms. 3, 4, 5, 1959.)

14. A. Castillo de Lucas, *Folklore Médico-Religioso: Hagiografías Paramédicas* (Madrid, 1943).

University of Arizona
Tucson, Arizona

WILLIAM E. SIMEONE

ITALIAN FOLKLORE SCHOLARS

WHILE THERE were men in Italy collecting and studying folkloristic matters before 1800, folklore as a scholarly discipline began in the nineteenth century. Its
emergence coincided with the cult of the people or the folk that spread through
Europe in the last century. Admiration for the folk led to a respect for and a curiosity
about the culture of the folk. As a result, interested students began to take a close
look at this culture, by collecting specimens of it such as folksongs and then by
writing treatises on what they collected. The work was done by learned men, some
of them aristocrats, swept up in the cult of the people. There was, for example,
Niccolò Tommaseo, who preferred the mountain folk of Tuscany to academicians in
Florence; Count Angelo de Gubernatis, who in 1893 opened a folklore meeting in
Rome in the presence of royalty; Costantino Nigra, who represented Cavour in courts
of royalty; Giuseppe Pitrè, who after a lifetime devoted to the collection and study
of the folklore of Sicily, was made a Senator of the Realm. All of these men valued
the native culture, which is a regional culture, as the rich patrimony of the Italian
people. The patrimony is as diverse as the Italian people themselves, and Italian
folklore has always reflected this diversity.

For this reason, the study of folklore in Italy has never been seriously infected
by ideas of racial exclusiveness, even in the palmiest days of the fascist regime. When
a Soviet professor attacked Italian folklore scholarship as racist, the charge was easily
refuted. To support his charge, he contended that Italian scholars generally supported
the thesis that such folk lyrics as the *strambotto* and *stornello,* found mostly in central
and south Italy, are Latin, whereas the epic-lyric songs of north Italy are Celtic. But
as Raffaele Corso correctly pointed out, these divisions were established and accepted by Italian scholars long before the fascists came to power.[1]

To some extent, folklorists have been able to show through their studies of the
diffusion of certain folksongs that this division, whatever its racial origin, is not as
great as we had once thought. Nevertheless, Italian folklore remains basically regional,
and, as we know, this regionalism means profound differences in geography, history,
and language. Though its spirit is waning, the concept of *campanilismo* is still very
strong: the culture existing within the sound of the village bell. Many collections of
Italian folklore come from such regions as Sicily, Calabria, Tuscany, and from such
cities as Bologna and Naples. Regionalism, of course, has stood in the way of an
Italian nation unified culturally as well as geographically, and the long and successful
effort to create the Italian ethnographic museum in Rome may be the symbol of a wish
to see a national spirit assimilating but not destroying ancient regional differences.

There is still another well-known division affecting Italian life and therefore its
folklore: the north-south division already cited above in connection with the Celto-
Latin origin of Italian folk music. Illustrations of this division can be heard on two
Columbia Records made by Alan Lomax and Diege Carpitella.[2] On the disc devoted
to north and central Italy, we hear music influenced by the modes of modern art

music. The common instrument is the accordion, and singing is often choral. On the disc devoted to the music of the south and the islands of Sicily and Sardinia, we hear music ordinarily much less modern. Though the accordion is played in these parts, too, we also hear the shepherd's pipe, the bagpipe, tambourine, friction drum, and in Sardinia, an instrument called the launeddas, so ancient, scholars guess it may have come with the Phoenicians. In the sounds of these ancient instruments and in the strident, falsetto voices of some of the singers, there is evidence of the south's long traffic with other parts of the Mediterranean world.

Such traffic suggests the historic depth of the folklore in the peninsula and the islands. The peoples of the Mediterranean world have traveled there, and their presence frequently lives on in the folklore of a place. Survivals of the Phoenician, Greek, and Arab heritages are present, particularly in the south and in the islands. Some of the emigrés, such as the Albanians, still live in their enclaves in Sicily and Calabria. In the north, traffic has been primarily with Germanic and Celtic peoples. But the most pervasive folkloristic legacy in the country is of course Latin. No Italian folklorist has difficulty pointing out homely specimens of the Latinity of Italian folklore: the organization of the family (especially in the south) dominated by the paterfamilias; the construction and internal arrangements of houses in Calabria, with a fireplace *(focolare)* in the middle of the foyer; the *tarantella* whose origin probably goes back to classical times.

The study of the folklore of this culture in all its layers began in the modern fashion in the last century. Today, when folklorists in Italy have constructed a tradition of scholarship and have become sufficiently self-conscious, they look for precursors among students whose work was done before the organized and disciplined study of the subject. Of these, I will mention three. First in time is Straparola *(fl.* 1540), whose collection of tales has been translated into English.[3] His tales are not considered in the same class as those in the *Pentamerone* of G. B. Basile (c. 1572-1632),[4] first published in Naples in its dialect, and said to be the equal of such collections as those of Perrault and the Grimm brothers. Among its well-known stories are versions of Puss-in-Boots, Cinderella, and the Babes in the Wood. Though Basile's style is baroque, its contortions do not conceal the authenticity of the folktales.

The third and probably the most important is G. B. Vico (1668-1744). Italian folklorists regard Vico as the scholar who made folklore a part of cultural history, and they view his work as anticipating the methodologies of modern folklorists. In his *New Science,*[5] Vico did not confine himself, as other scholars of his time usually did, to classical antiquity. Unlike his contemporaries, he was interested in the primitive peoples of the prehistoric world. Thinking of the primitive world as a world of fantasy, Vico believed its natural language to be poetic or metaphorical and its favored modes of expression to be myths and fairy tales. While myths and fairy tales appear most clearly among primitive people, they also appear among men who have remained almost children. Because Vico was able to see such a relationship, Croce says that he was the first to adopt the comparative method of folklore.

The work of Basile and Vico was a real contribution to the literature of folklore, but it was not until the nineteenth century that folklore, in acquiring the character of a discipline, gained some of its ablest scholars. It has been said that Italy was the last nation in Europe to understand the importance of folklore, but if Italians were tardy comers to the study of folklore, they came to it with a passion. Much of the energy for the first collections, primarily of folksongs, derived from the cult of the people. The feeling was ardently romantic, and if the scholarship of these collectors was faulty, the romantic collector in Italy led the way.

This feeling is evident in the work of Niccolò Tommaseo (1802-74). Inspired by his love of the common people, *il volgo profano,* Tommaseo collected folksongs in Tuscany, Corsica, Greece, and Illyria.[6] His collection from Tuscany, for example, opens with songs in praise of the beauty of men and women, and they are followed by about one hundred *stornelli* and *strambotti*. On these songs, Tommaseo made certain philological observations. On the whole, he was content to comment on the differences between the language of the people and the literary language.

In his collection of Corsican songs, Tommaseo extended his point of view to include certain ethnological observations. The majority of the Corsican songs are those about bandits and about men who, having killed an enemy, abandon their wives and hide from public justice or private vendetta. Tommaseo noticed the dominant tones of these songs: hate, faith, love, and sorrow. But most of his comment is confined to linguistic matters, such as distinguishing one dialect from another. Where he is able, he tries to establish the dates of origins of certain songs. But he would have found distasteful the idea of collecting them in the scientific spirit then becoming dominant in much of Europe. Tommaseo was too much identified personally with the life of the songs for this kind of detachment, and his commentary reflects this view. He was interested most of all in the beauty of the songs, and it was this beauty that he wanted to preserve and convey. A recent student, Toschi,[7] has said that Tommaseo had begun to see beyond the problems of collection into the problems of song interpretation. Even if this were so, Tommaseo could not have pursued historical and comparative scholarship because not enough collections were available to him in his time.

If Tommaseo represented the impulse only to collect what one admired, a folklorist such as Constantino Nigra (1828-1907) was a methodical scholar as well as an enthusiastic collector of folksongs. Nigra's work has been modified by his successors, but his principal premises about folksong are still pertinent. In his book *Canti popolari del Piemonte* (1888),[8] he called attention to a largely unnoticed form of song, *l'epico-lirica*. Nigra thought that the *epico-lirica* form was related to the history of the Piedmont, that it was in part indigenous to this region. The presence of this form in the north enabled him to say, therefore, that the *epico-lirica* belonged to northern Italy, while the well-known *strambotto* and *stornello* belonged to the south.

Nigra speculated that the *epico-lirica* type of song belonged to a Gallo-Italic tradition, derived from a substratum of Celtic myth, partly a Celto-Romanic tradition common to such regions as France, Provence, Central Italy, Catalonia and Portugal. The theory was attacked when it was published,[9] and modern Italian scholars have modified Nigra's views by studying the distribution of the *epico-lirica* song in the peninsula. They have found, for example, that a song like *La Donna Lombarda* occurs almost everywhere in the peninsula, a fact which is evidence for a narrative song tradition in the south.[10]

While Nigra was compiling his collection of Piedmontese folksongs, he was engaged in diplomatic missions which took him to a number of European cities where he exposed himself to continental folksong scholarship. As a result of this exposure, Nigra, it is said, was able to give his scholarship a breadth described as unusual in Italian folklore for his time. One of his great scholarly distinctions was that he employed a new method for the study of Italian folksong. For example, he studied the history surrounding a historic narrative, the time and place of its origin. Besides this, he searched for variants in other provinces of the peninsula and for analogues in other languages. Thus, Nigra was not only an admiring collector of the songs of his native region but an historian and philologist after the manner of Grundtvig and Child.

One name only in Italian folklore has a stature comparable to that of Child's and Grundtvig's, and that, of course, is Giuseppe Pitrè (1841-1916). A man of great energy and devotion, Pitrè was born in a fisherman's family in Sicily and grew up to study medicine. But his fame rests on his work in Sicilian folklore, most of which is in his encyclopedic *Biblioteca delle tradizioni popolari siciliane*.[11] He became interested in the island's folklore when he began collecting proverbs and folksay, primarily from his mother and other members of his family. This interest led him to Sicilian folksongs, and he published a two-volume study and collection of them, *Canti popolari siciliani,* in Palermo in 1870-71. Pitrè was animated by a belief that these songs of the people revealed the Sicilian's many and varied affections, his fervid and excited passions.

To his work on folksongs, Pitrè added four volumes of Sicilian folktales, *Fiabe novelle e racconti popolari siciliani.* In addition to these, volumes 18, 22, and 24 of his *Biblioteca* are collections of tales. Exclusive of variants, his tale collection totals about a thousand. His collection of proverbs in five volumes numbers some fourteen thousand. And to indicate further the riches of Pitrè's *Biblioteca,* I cite the twentieth volume which is a collection called *Indovinelli, dubbi, e scioglilingua del popolo siciliano. Indovinelli* are riddles; *dubbi* are usually eight alternating rimes for questions and answers, ordinarily beginning with "Tell me who." *Scioglilingue* are "tongue twisters," a series of words difficult to pronounce, such as the English "Peter Piper picked a peck."

All of this work failed to exhaust Pitrè's folkloristic enterprises. In 1882 he co-founded the first Italian folklore journal, *l'Archivio per lo studio delle tradizioni popolari,* published in thirty volumes until 1906. Its contributors were students working in every region of the country, among them such eminent men as Croce and Borgese. Besides printing their collections, contributors discussed all vital questions connected with the discipline. As a result of the publications in this journal, Italian folklorists gained a better understanding of the regions of the peninsula. At the same time, they acquired a closer knowledge of a common culture.

The importance of Pitrè's work is not limited, however, to its great range of subject matter. One of the problems he had to solve for himself was the problem of method. What he insisted upon does not seem novel today: the sanctity of the text, the collection and publication of variants, the classification of materials. Another problem was to render a dialect with no exact spelling. Pitrè believed that the history of the people is in their dialect. We learn from the dialect who our forefathers were, what they did, how and when they lived, and with what other peoples they mingled. In his discussion of the dialect, Pitrè refers often to the etymologies of words, their places of origin, and their analogues in other Romance languages.

Despite Pitrè's preoccupation with his island culture, his work escapes the limitations of provincialism. For one thing, he knew of the work of eminent folklorists in Europe and in America, and he corresponded with several of them. On another level, he was interested in the problems that perennially interest folklorists wherever and whenever they happen to live. In the poetic-communal debate over the origin of folksong, Pitrè denied the creation of folksongs by groups. Behind each song is a poet, an individual imagination. Anonymously, the song passes from mouth to mouth, from country to country, over mountains and seas. In this journey, the song loses its author but finds its singers, some of whom may alter the form, add to its imagery, and either degrade or improve it. There is nothing in Pitrè's point of view to which folklorists could take much exception. Cocchiara's statement that Pitrè's work will always be a model of research is more than an endorsement of an enthusiastic disciple.[12]

Pitrè died in 1916. He lived long enough to inspire and to teach some of the distinguished living Italian folklorists. But before I speak of these men, something must be said about the reflections of Croce (1866-1952) on folksongs in his *Poesia popolare e poesia d'arte*. An influential essay in Italy, where it was published in 1933 in Bani, it deserves to be much better known in the United States than it is. Croce's view is that poetry does not admit categories; poetry, whether folk or art, is always poetry. So-called poetic distinctions between them grow out of external considerations and are therefore invalid. The difference between folk and art poetry is not one of essence but of tendency. Folk poetry is analogous to common sense in the intellectual world or innocence in the moral world. In the same way, folk poetry is concerned with simple sentiments expressed in correspondingly simple forms. Folk poetry does not have the breadth or the amplitude of great art poetry which expresses complicated experiences, thoughts, and sentiments. Instead, folk poetry is brief, quick. Its words and rhythms are adequate to its aims. While Italian folklorists have taken exception to portions of Croce's essay, most agree that it does illuminate the difference between folk and art poetry and that it does affirm the legitimacy of folk poetry and its places in the scale of aesthetic values.[13]

With the singular exception of Croce, nearly all of the notable Italian folklorists since the First World War have held university positions. Of the several who could be mentioned, I will cite three: Raffaele Corso, Giuseppe Cocchiara, and Paolo Toschi. Corso, Emeritus Professor of Ethnography and Folklore at the Istituto Universitario Orientale at the University of Naples, has given his work an ethnological orientation. Influenced by Tylor and Frazer, Corso has discarded the idea of folklore-as-survival because the idea is usually understood to mean ancient customs imbedded in new surroundings. Such a concept of folklore he regards as insufficient. Folklore is the reflection of the life and spirit of a people in its actuality, not dead, but living. For this reason, Corso prefers his term *reviviscenza* to *sopravvizenza,* revival to survival, because his word better suggests the always living germ of beliefs, rites, legends, and customs. He compares the idea of folklore as revivals to a vegetable organism that revives after it has seemed to be spent; it revives because it has profound roots in the hearts and minds of men.[14]

Giuseppe Cocchiara is Professor of the History of Folklore at the University of Palermo and the Director of Pitrè Museum. Like Corso, he is not notable as a collector. Instead his work to date has been a number of studies of various types of folklore: legend, superstition, folksong. An example of his work is a book called *Genesi di leggende* (Palermo, 1941), now in its third edition. Cocchiara begins with an historical survey of the over-all problem of origin: the Aryan theory, the Indianist theory, the anthropological theory, the Finnish theory. There is criticism of all these points of view. The Finnish method, for example, fails to answer questions of aesthetics. The rest of the book is devoted to studies of such legends as Lot's Wife, the Sacrifice of the Younger Son, the Singing Bones, and others. In his discussion of the story of Lot's Wife, Cocchiara identifies two motifs in the Biblical tale: the rule against looking back, and the punishment for breaking the rule. The two motifs are discussed at length, beginning with the tale of Orpheus and Eurydice. Cocchiara thinks that Orpheus' instructions not to look back may be related to a taboo prohibiting a man from looking at his wife in certain moments and situations. But it is also true that Orpheus breaks his pact with the King and Queen of Death, and for this reason he must be punished. Cocchiara then examines variants of the second motif: punishment by the petrifaction of the human being. He thinks that the petrifaction tales are basically totemistic among primitives. When such stories are found among civilized peoples, divine power is substituted for the taboo.

In recent years, Cocchiara has turned his attention to the history of folklore. The *Storia degli studi delle tradizioni popolari in Italia*[15] is an historical survey of the discipline in Italy. In a more recent book, Cocchiara has written a history of the discipline in Europe. The *Storia del folklore in Europa*[16] traces folklore from its beginnings in the European "discovery of the savage," through the idea of folklore as a political and national instrument in the Romantic era, to various aspects of folklore scholarship in the last fifty years. Cocchiara's book is valuable to anyone interested in the intellectual roots of the discipline, and its bibliography is commensurate with its scope.

Italian folklorists, like those in the United States, have been and remain primarily interested in the folktale and folksong. An example of this preoccupation is the work of a third folklorist, Paolo Toschi, who holds the *Cattedra di Storia delle tradizioni popolari* (Chair of the History of Folklore) at the University of Rome. Toschi's orientation is literary, with specific attention to sacred songs and plays. For each form he has made a collection. These he followed with a study of religious poetry, *La poesia popolare religiosa in Italia,* and a study of religious folk drama, *Dal dramma liturgico alla rappresentazione sacra* (Firenze, 1935 and 1940).

During and after the Second World War, Toschi's interests shifted. For workers and students he published a handbook called *Guida allo studio delle tradizioni popolari.*[17] Since there is still discussion of possible publication of a handbook in the United States, it may be relevant here to describe Toschi's little book. It begins with a discussion of the term *folklore,* with the goals and limitations of the discipline. Also in the first chapter, Toschi discusses the relationships of folklore with such other sciences as linguistics, sociology, and psychology. From here, he goes on to give notes on the study of folklore in Italy. In all of the chapters, spaced among the paragraphs, are bibliographical references, primarily Italian, with some references to French and German scholarship. The third chapter is devoted to methods of research, and one needs to keep in mind that Toschi is interested in material art as well as in songs and tales. His instructions are specific. In the transcription of dialect, for instance, he tells the collector to transcribe, not in phonetic transcription, but in the spelling currently used in the dialect in question. For the documentation of costumes, festivals, and dances, he recommends using modern devices like photographs, motion pictures, recordings, and sound films. A footnote to this chapter includes samples of a number of questionnaires for the fieldworker. In a sample series of questions on marriage, for instance, the fieldworker is to find out what time of year is preferred for marriages and what day of the week; whether the wedding party carries real or paper flowers; whether the bride wears special jewelry; whether the bridal couple is linked together with a small chain or ribbon; and where the meals of the wedding day are eaten.

There are fifty-six queries related to marriage customs, including a query on the proverbs relating to marriage. The next chapter is devoted to instructions on the classification and organization of the materials, and the remainder of the guide deals with types of folklore and the special problems related to each with which a collector must deal. Regarding the editing of texts for publication, Toschi insists that they must be edited with as much rigor as any classical text.

Aside from the practical matters of collecting and editing, Toschi has interested himself in the theoretical problems of folklore that require periodic reassessment. Speculating on the origin and character of folksong, for example, Toschi sets his argument in historical perspective. The romantic view, that the folk create a song, sees culture as ascending; the anti-romantic view, that the folk do not create but receive, sees culture as descending. Toschi thinks that neither the ascending nor descending scales are relevant. He uses language to explain his point of view. One person creates a term, but this term does not become language until the collectivity accepts and assimilates it. This acceptance and assimilation is no less a creative act than the invention of the terms itself. What is true of a word and a language is true of folksong and of folklore generally. A word, a song, a custom is originally the creation of a person. It can begin at the top, the middle, or the bottom, but it will not become folklore until it becomes the language or the instrument of the group. Toschi believes that we cannot determine with chronological precision the origin of anything in folklore. Like a nation, folklore does not begin at a given moment.[18]

Toschi's energies have not been limited to teaching and scholarship. He is also editor of *Lares,* the journal of the Italian Ethnographical Society and of the Institute of the History of Folklore. A journal of this name was published from 1912 to 1915. It was revived again in 1930, and since that time, Toschi has been the key man in its life. During the Abyssinian War, its pages were cut by one quarter. During the Second World War, it was published until 1944. Publication began again in 1949 under the imprimatur of the Olschki publishing house of Florence.

The other major journal is *Folklore,* founded by Corso in 1925. Its publication was interrupted by the war in 1941, but it resumed publication in 1946 under Corso's editorship.[19]

Besides publishing journals, Italian folklorists have been interested in developing folk museums. Pitrè established the first one in Sicily. In 1881, Pitrè gathered a number of artifacts, namely costumes and utensils, to send to an industrial exposition in Milan. The next year the city of Palermo organized an exposition, and for it Pitrè put together an ethnographical collection which included, among other things, the dress and tools of shepherds, farmers, and hunters, and also vehicles, foods, amulets, and children's toys. But it was not until 1910 that Pitrè was able to establish a museum, Il Museo Etnografico-Siciliano. For more than thirty years after his death, the museum remained in a state of neglect. Largely through Cocchiara's efforts, the collection was housed where it is now, in the Parco della Favorita in Palermo. The museum owns more than twenty thousand items, and those on display aim to reconstruct various aspects of Sicilian folklife. The museum also has a library which makes it an important center for study and research in folklore.[20]

There are other regional folk museums, though none is equal to the Pitrè Museum. At the other end of the country, at Bolzano, there is the Museo Civico, which contains an important ethnographical collection. It includes a superb collection of costumes from the Trentino and Tirole, besides large collections of ceramics, wood carvings, and art metal work.

In addition to such regional museums, Italy now has a national museum named after Lamberto Loria, who played a large part in its creation. Loria thought that Italy had a richness of traditional art that could and should fill a museum. The national museum, or the idea of one, received some stimulus from the ethnographical display in the international exposition held in Rome in 1911. Following the exposition, its materials were taken to the Villa d'Este, and there they remained in crates. From 1911 until 1956, the state of the national ethnographic museum interested and irritated folklorists. The lack was something which pricked the national pride; Italy should have a national folklore museum! Certain things were done at the Villa d'Este; some costumes were put on mannequins; and the library annex to the museum was made usable. The collections continued to grow. Finally in April 1956, after two world wars, there was opened in one of the buildings built for the ill-fated Ezposizione universale di Roma (EUR-1940) Il Museo Nazionale delle arti e tradizioni popolari. In an article in *Lares* (1957, pp. 49ff.) Toschi relates some recent history connected with the museum. It received a boost from the postwar Italian concern with southern Italy. In 1953, a show of art in the life of the south was organized in Rome; a part of the show was to be folk art from the south. With others, including Cocchiara, Toschi went to Tivoli to select material from the collections in the Villa d'Este for the exposition. On seeing the condition of the place, Cocchiara, whose Pitrè Museum was in excellent shape, said that this neglect was a cultural crime: "Ma queste è crimine culturale!" Three years later, in 1956, the crime was expiated with the opening of the very fine National Museum in its present quarters. The exhibits there are arranged to show particular objects in their native contexts: for example, women's apparel from Puglia are on mannequins standing in replicas of houses from that part of Italy.[21] Those interested in the museum, however, are not altogether satisfied. The library must be enlarged, and the museum should have a publication.

For the American folklorist knowing no Italian, the literature available is slender. There are the translations of the books of Straparola, Basile, and Vico. In the last century, Pitrè's influence stimulated two English-speaking scholars to translate certain texts and to comment in English-language publications on Italian folklore. One was Thomas F. Crane, Professor of Romance Languages at Cornell University. In 1874, Crane has said, he read one of Pitrè's articles, and his curiosity was so greatly stimulated, it led him to a lifelong interest in Italian folklore. Over a period of years, he wrote articles and book reviews on the subject in such periodicals as the *North American Review* and *Lippincott's Magazine*.[22] Crane's work is useful because he explains a number of technical terms still common in the discipline. But his most impressive contribution was his translation of a collection of folktales, *Italian Popular Tales* (Boston, 1885). Most of these are fairy tales, but there are also "stories of Oriental origin," "legends and ghost stories," "nursery tales," and finally "stories and jests." The tales are taken from collections representing many regions of the country, but most are from Sicily. Besides the 109 tales, there are notes and bibliography. This collection is the largest and most representative that we have in English.

Pitrè's influence also affected an Englishwoman, Rachel Harriette Busk, who lived in Rome for many years. In a book called *The Folklore of Rome* (London, 1874), she presented one of the first collections of the city's folklore. Another of her books, *Folksongs of Italy* (London, 1887), is an effort to translate into English certain types of songs that come chiefly from Sicily. The Sicilian selections were made by Pitrè himself. The dialect texts are given with her translations, but an equally valuable part of the book, for the non-Italian reader, is her discussion of lyric song-types. The *rispetto,* described by Pitrè as the true and principal form of a purely Italian folksong, she describes as a song of reverence or respect for true love. Its eight lines are normally endacasyllabic, with the first four lines in alternating rime and the last four in pairs. Subdivisions of the *rispetto* include: the *mattinata,* a morning song sung by a lover; the *dispetto,* an utterance of disappointed or outraged love; the *disperati,* for the hopeless lover of either sex, containing the choicest expressions of refined and exquisite agony; the *serenata* or *inserenata,* the night song. In such song-types as the *mattinata* and the *serenata,* we may see the impact of Italian folk music on art music, especially Neopolitan *bel canto.*

To books like those of Busk and Crane may be added a translation of De Gubernatis' *Zoological Mythology* (2 vols., London, 1878). Charles Speroni has written on the Italian proverb.[23] Estelle Canziani has a series of articles in *Folk-Lore.*[24] Then there are books such as Frances Toor's *Festivals and Folkways of Italy,* which is a guidebook of interest to folklorists. More impressive is Carlo Levi's *Christ Stopped at Eboli*[25] in which folk custom and belief is worked into the writer's chronicle of exile in the mountains south of Naples where even Christ did not come.

On the transplanted Italian, the immigrant in the United States, practically no work has been done. The longest treatment of the subject has been written by a social worker in New Haven, Connecticut. She is Phyllis Williams, and her book is *South Italian Folklore in Europe and America* (New Haven, 1938). The vast area of Italian immigrant folklore in America still awaits its students.[26]

NOTES

1. The Soviet Professor was Eugene Kagaroff of Leningrad University. His article appeared in *Soviet Ethnography* (Leningrad, 1937), pp. 186-191. Corso's reply is his article "Critiche sovietche allo studio dell'Etnografia nell'Italia Fascista," *Archivio per la raccolta e lo studio delle tradizioni popolari italiane,* XIII-XIV (Naples, 1938-39), 1-11.

2. The Columbia World Library of Folk and Primitive Music. Vol. XV has the music of northern and central Italy, Vol. XVI the music of southern Italy and the islands.

3. *Le piacevoli notti di m. Giovanfrancesco Straparola* ... a cura di G. Rua (2 vols., Bologna, 1899-1908); *The Nights of Straparola,* now first translated into English by W. G. Waters (2 vols., London, 1894).

4. *Il pentamerone; ossia, La fiaba delle fiabe,* tradotta dall'antico dialetto napoletano ... da Benedetto Croce (Bari, 1957). Two translations into English are: *Il Pentamerone; or The Tale of Tales,* being a translation by Sir Richard Burton (New York, 1927). *The Pentamerone of Giambattista Basile,* translated from the Italian of B. Croce, ed. N. M. Penzer (2 vols., New York, 1932).

5. G. B. Vico, *La scienza nuova,* a cura di F. Nicolini (2 vols., Bari, 1928). The English translation is *The New Science of Giambattista Vico,* tr. T. G. Bergin and M. H. Fisch (Ithaca, 1948). Cf. Croce's study, *The Philosophy of G. B. Vico,* tr. R. G. Collingwood (New York, 1913).

6. *Canti popolari toscani, corsi, greci e illirici* (4 vols., Venezia, 1841-42).

7. Cf. Paolo Toschi, *Guida allo studio delle tradizioni popolari* (Rome, 1945), p. 146.

8. A new edition with an introduction by Giuseppe Cocchiara has been published by Giulio Einaudi (1957). Nigra's theories are in the introduction to his collection. Cf. also Vincenzo Carollo, "Costantino Nigra Folklorista," *Annali del Museo Pitrè,* II-IV (1951-53), 48-61.

9. By Gaston Paris, *Journal des Savants* (Sept.-Nov. 1889), 526-545; 611-622; 666-676.

10. Cf. V. Santoli, *I canti popolari italiani* (Firenze, 1940); G. B. Bronzini, *La canzone epicolirica nell'Italia centro-meridionale* (Roma, 1956), Vol. I.

11. There are twenty-five volumes in Pitrè's *Biblioteca:* (1) *Canti popolari siciliani raccolti e annotati,* 2 vols. (1870-71); (2) *Studi di poesia popolare* (1875); (3) *Fiabe, novelle e racconti popolari siciliani raccolti e annotati,* 4 vols. (1875); (4) *Proverbi siciliani raccolti e confrontati con quelli degli altri dialetti d'Italia,* 4 vols. (1880); (5) *Spettacoli e feste popolari siciliani* (1881); (6) *Giuochi fanciulleschi siciliani raccolti e descritti* (1883); (7) *Usi, costumi, credenze e pregiudizi del popolo siciliano,* 4 vols. (1887-88); (8) *Fiabe e leggende popolari siciliane* (1888); (9) *Medicina popolare siciliana* (1896); (10) *Indovinelli, dubb, scioglilingua del popolo siciliano* (1897); (11) *Feste patronali in Sicilia* (1900); (12) *Studi di leggende popolari siciliane e nuova*

raccolta di leggende siciliane (1904); (13) *Proverbi, motti e scongiuri del popolo siciliano* (1910); (14) *Cartelli, pasquinate, canti e leggende del popolo siciliano* (1913); (15) *La famiglia, la casa e la vita del popolo siciliano* (1913). All published in Palermo. The National Edition of Pitrè's works, authorized in 1939, includes various other writings in addition to the *Biblioteca*.

12. Cf. G. Cocchiara, *Pitrè e le tradizioni popolari* (Palermo, 1941). Cocchiara also discusses Pitrè in his *Storia degli studi delle tradizioni popolari in Italia* (Palermo, 1947), pp. 203-234.

13. Cf. Paolo Toschi's evaluation of Croce as a folklorist, *Lares*, XIX (1953), 1-7.

14. Cf. Raffaele Corso, *Reviviscenze. Studi di tradizioni popolari italiane* (Catania, 1927). An important book of Corso's is *Folklore: Storia-Obbietto-Metodo-Bibliografia* (4th ed., Napoli, 1953). See the detailed review by Charles Speroni in *Journal of American Folklore*, LXXVII (1954), 312-314. Among Corso's publications, the following may also be cited: "Paganitas," *Bilychinia* (Roma, 1923), 2nd series, no. 27; "L'Italia Etnografia," *Le Razze e i Popoli della Terra*, ed. Renato Biasutti (4 vols., Torino, 2nd ed., 1953) pp. 87-120; *Problemi di Etnografia* (Napoli, 1956); and *Studi di Tradizioni Popolari* (Napoli, 1956).

15. Cited above, n. 12. I am much indebted to this useful introduction to the study of folklore in Italy.

16. (Torino, 1954.) Among Cocchiara's publications, the following also may be cited: *Gli studi delle tradizioni popolari in Sicilia* (Palermo, 1928); *The Lore of the Folk-Song* (Oxford, 1932); *Il linguaggio della poesia popolare* (Palermo, 1942); *Popolo e letteratura in Italia* (Torino, 1959).

17. (2nd ed., Roma, 1945). Among Toschi's other publications, the following also may be cited: *Panorama della poesia popolare italiana* (Roma, 1938); *Bibliografia delle tradizioni popolari d'Italia dal 1916 al 1940* (Firenze, 1946); *Fenomenologia del canto popolare* (Roma, 1951); *Le origini del teatro italiano* (Torino, 1955); *"Fabri" del folklore, ritratti e recordi* (Roma, 1958).

18. Cf. Toschi's "Nuovi orientamenti dello studio della poesia popolare," *Lares*, XVI (1950), 1-18.

19. Vols. 1-10 (1925-35) were published under the title *Il folklore italiano;* vols. 11-16 (1936-41) under the title *Archivio per la raccolta e lo studio delle tradizioni popolari italiane;* vol. 1 (1946-) under the title *Folklore: Rivista di tradizioni popolari.*

20. Cf. Giuseppe Cocchiara, *La vita e l'arte del popolo siciliano nel Museo Pitrè* (Palermo, 1938). The Museum publishes the *Annali del Museo Pitrè*. The following numbers have been issued: vol. 1, 1950; vols. 2-4, 1951-53; vols. 5-7, 1954-56; vols. 8-10, 1957-59 (pub. 1960).

21. Toschi has edited a guide to the Museum (Roma, 1956). It is sold at the Museum.

22. See, e. g., "Sicilian Folklore," *Lippincott's* (Oct. 1876), 433-443; "Italian Fairy Tales," *St. Nicholas*, VI (Dec. 1878), 101-107; "Italian Popular Tales," *North American Review*, CXXIII (July 1876), 25-60; "Recent Italian Popular Tales," *The Academy*, XV (London, March 1879), 262-263.

23. Speroni, *Proverbs and Proverbial Phrases in Basile's "Pentamerone"* (Berkeley, 1941); *Merbury's "Proverbi Vulgari"* (Berkeley, 1946); *The Italian Wellerism to the End of the Seventeenth Century* (Berkeley, 1953).

24. Canziani, "Piedmontese Proverbs in Dispraise of Woman," *Folk-Lore*, XXIII (1912), 91-96; "Courtship, Marriage, and Folk-belief in Val d'Ossola," ibid., 457-458; "Piedmontese Folklore," ibid., XXIV (1913), 213-218; "Savoy Traditions and Folk-belief," ibid., XLII (1931), 60-67.

25. Translated by F. Frenaye (New York, 1947).

26. Besides Williams' book, two examples of what has been done are Charles Speroni, "The Observance of St. Joseph's Day among the Sicilians of Southern California," *Southern Folklore Quarterly*, IV (1940), 135-139; and M. D. Ramirez, "Italian Folklore from Tampa, Florida," ibid., V (1941), 101-106.

Southern Illinois University
Carbondale, Illinois

WILLIAM H. JANSEN

TURKISH FOLKLORE: AN INTRODUCTION

THIS essay is organized around general bibliographical data which, it is hoped, will yield simultaneously a picture of the types of folklore extant in Turkey and the direction of folkloric studies in that country.

To begin with, two general bibliographies are useful to the student who is most at ease with English. The first, and the more valuable, is by the late John Kingsley Birge, probably the greatest Turkologist of our time. Called *A Guide to Turkish Area Study* (Washington, D. C., 1949), his book presents a kind of running expository comment on both source materials and research based on these materials. In this indispensable work the folklorist will find particularly rewarding Chapters IV, VII, and XI. Though not a folklorist himself, Birge was one of the few scholars who realized that in Turkish culture there is no clear demarcation between folk and nonfolk. He perceived that an understanding of the Turkish character is only possible through a close study of Turkish folklore, and that modern Turkish culture is both a product of the conscious welding of Turkish folklore with Western "nonfolk" culture and a product of the purposeful rejection of the literate culture of prerepublican Turkey. The latter rejection is assured, for the literature of Ottoman Turkey published in Arabic characters is no longer available to the modern Turk who knows only the Romaic alphabet. The alphabet reform certainly has deprived the modern Turk of magnificent heirlooms, many of which of course have been transliterated; but this reform naturally has in no way affected the survival of the national folk heritage, dependent as it is upon oral transmission.[1]

The second general bibliographical source is Grace Hadley Fuller's mimeographed and hard-to-obtain *Turkey: A Selected List of References* (Washington, D. C., 1943). This bibliography, prepared for the Library of Congress, supplements Birge's later work, as it mentions a number of relevant periodical and journalistic articles. For the student of folklore, the three most useful subject headings in this study are Religion, Women, and Arts and Letters. That these unlikely headings yield the most rewards for the folklorist affords in itself a too-revealing commentary upon Western study of, and attitudes toward, Turkish folk culture.

Still under the general heading, I must mention three Turkish societies as well as an institution difficult to classify; all of these have contributed largely to Turkish folklore study and publication. What I take to be the oldest of these organizations is the Türkiyat Enstitüsü (The Institute of Turkology), founded at Istanbul in 1924, which is now moribund if not defunct. Under the general editorship of the nation's great senior historian, Köprülüzade Mehmed Fuad, better known to the West as a fine statesman under his later name Fuat Köprülü, the Institute began to issue in 1935 the *Türk Halk Edebiyatı Ansiklopedisi* (*The Encyclopedia of Turkish Folk Literature*). Although the published beginnings of this encyclopedia (from AA only partially through B) reflect impressive and dedicated scholarship, for reasons unknown to me the project was evidently abandoned in the same year in which it began. Under the same aegis and fine editorship, there also began to appear a series of monographs on the *sazşairleri*.[2] This series has continued under various sponsorships, including the University of Istanbul and commercial publishers, and is one of the most impressive in Turkish folklore scholarship, both because of the caliber of the research and because of the peculiar interest of the material presented.

The *sazşair* is a folk minstrel, both composer and singer, who performs and sometimes creates or adapts folk lyrics and balladlike songs of which he frequently claims to be the hero. The *saz* is a musical instrument resembling a long-necked mandolin; *şair* means singer-composer. Today only a rather sad remnant of the species may still be encountered, a remnant adulterated by the radio and popular music. While the "art" composers and poets of the Osmanlı and earlier Turkish eras (ca. 1071-1566) were imitating foreign, usually Persian, forms and often actually composing in foreign languages, the *sazşairs* were working in the vulgate Turkish and were preserving the simple but effective art forms that the Turks presumably brought with them to Asia Minor as part of their folk culture. Not only the names but rather full biographies of these folk poet-minstrels survive, even from the early centuries of the Turkish occupation of Anatolia.[3] And their poems, probably orally composed and orally circulated —though of course frequently transcribed in later times—survive orally, still ascribed to their traditional and revered composers.[4] An illustration of the effect of these minstrels upon modern Turkish culture is *Yunus Emre,* an oratorio by Turkey's greatest musicologist and current Director of the Ankara Conservatory of Music, Adnan Saygun. Written and first performed in 1946, the oratorio tells the story of Yunus Emre, an ancient *sazşair* (1280-1330), and uses the strangely moody, despondent folk lyrics (moving both in words and in music) still ascribed in the folk mind to that folk genius of long ago.

The *Türk Dil Kurumu* and the *Türk Tarih Kurumu* (the Turkish Linguistic and the Turkish Historical Societies), both founded in Ankara and in part supported by the Turkish hero Kemal Atatürk, have published extensively in folklore and have stored in their various archives of source material enormous mines for future research and publication. As an example of this resource material, I will cite one archive in the Linguistic Society's truly remarkable library. This archive contains, very systematically arranged, the material for a kind of linguistic atlas for the folk speech of each of Turkey's sixty-three provinces. For each word there are given instances of its occurrences in proverbs, riddles, and the like with these folk sayings quoted exactly as collected in the various provinces. Need I enumerate the possibilities here for the eager folklorist?[5]

The "institution difficult to classify" cited earlier is the *halkevi* (plural, *halkevleri*: folk houses). The *halkevleri* were community adult education and cultural centers founded by Atatürk and his Republican People's Party in 1932. They were government-sponsored and supported centers, located throughout the country in cities, towns, and even in small villages. Here the people could find copies of the nation's newspapers; participate in social activities such as folk dancing; learn to read and write, using the new alphabet; and perhaps be indoctrinated with political dogma. When the Democratic Party, under Celâl Bayar and Adnan Menderes, came to power in 1950 the approximately four hundred *halkevleri* were closed because of their close connections with the opposition party. And, so far as this speaker knows, they have mostly remained so. Whatever the political significance of the *halkevleri,* the folklorist must gratefully acknowledge that, strangely perhaps, a number of them sponsored and published varyingly impressive volumes of folklore collected in the specific areas where they were severally located.[6]

The total number of monographs, volumes, and journals (at least eight journals are now defunct) published by these societies and by the *halkevleri* is unknown to this writer, but it must run into the hundreds. Neither am I aware of how many occasional folklore articles have appeared in quarterlies published by the various Turkish university faculties, but once again the figure seems to be a large one. I suppose a complete collection of Turkish folklore scholarship in print may not exist outside of Turkey, though representative collections are available in the Library of Congress and at Indiana University. Oddly, neither collection is catalogued.[7]

I shall turn now to more specific matters, hoping to give simultaneously an impression of what specific scholars are doing in Turkish folklore and an over-all view of emphases peculiar to folklore in Turkey. The greatest active Turkish folklorist of today is Pertev Naili Boratav. Now living in France, Boratav nevertheless concerns himself with the Turkish folktale, a very rich branch of Turkish folklore encompassing a bewildering number of generic names. Among these terms for oral narrative are: *hikâye* (a story, novel, narrative, rather like the romance, sometimes translated in English as "minstrel tale," and in form resembling the *cante fable*); *destan* or *dasitan* (the folk epic, whose hero is frequently both a bandit and a *sazşair,* sometimes indistinguishable from the *hikâye* except in length); *masal* (sometimes apparently a synonym for *destan*); *fıkra* (the anecdote); *nükte* (an anecdote involving a witticism); and many others, including those designated by Western folklorists as *Märchen* (*peri masalı* or *masal*) and saints' legends (*evliya destanı*). This plethora of generic Turkish nouns designating overlapping types of folk narrative may explain the reluctance of Turkish folklorists to use the Thompson indexes.[8]

An excellent idea of the extent of Turkish folk narrative may be gained from Boratav and Wolfram Eberhard, *Typen Türkischer Volksmärchen* (Weisbaden, 1953). The invaluable introductory essays in this volume deserve great praise, as does Boratav's introduction to his *Contes Turcs* (Paris, 1955), an excellent sampling of the gems in his own collection, representing the types and characteristic styles described in the introductory essay. Other good small modern translations are Margery Kent's *Fairy Tales from Turkey* (London, 1946), growing incidentally out of a *halkevi* project, and Naki Tezel's *Contes Populaires Turcs* (Istanbul, 1953), distributed *gratis* by the Turkish Information Offices.

The innumerable collections and translations of collections of *Nas'r eddin Hoca* anecdotes need not be discussed here, though it is worth noting that in various cheap editions and popular adaptations they sell well in every Turkish bookstore and newsstand, as do other collections of anecdotes not so well known in the West.[9] One group of anecdotes centers around the *Bektaşi* dervish order (all such orders in Turkey were dissolved in the early days of the Republic) and glorifies a kind of worldly sophistication towards traditional religious practices and tabus.[10] As an illustration of how such folklore dominates the national culture, I remember a truly hilarious comic strip—the Turks have a long history of excelling in caricature—featuring one *Canbaba* (roughly Father John), a bumbling but lovable man of old-fashioned religious customs who is completely baffled by modern ways and who I suspect is traceable to the *Bektaşi* of anecdotal fame.

Perhaps most exciting to the few Western folklorists who know about them are the romances in *cante-fable* form, or the minstrel tales as Eberhard has termed them.

A number of these epiclike narratives exist, glorifying bandit outlaws, all of whom seem to have been also folk poets. It is usually claimed that the bandits wrote the romances in which they star or, at the very least, composed impromptu the songs contained within the narratives.[11] The heroes usually are depicted as of middle-class or humble origin, of colossal proportions, of passionate and loving nature, and frequently as having been wronged by society, the law, or the aristocracy. In some details, they and their narratives are reminiscent of British balladry's Robin Hood and, even more, of the Serbians' Marko Kralyevic.

The best study of these minstrel tales or romances is Boratav's monumental *Köroğlu Destanı* (Istanbul, 1931), the German translation of which has been predicted repeatedly. *Köroğlu* (the Blind Boy or the Blind Man's Son) is both the name of the hero and of the romance in which he appears. This narrative, the longest of its kind (its English translation, though incomplete, runs into hundreds of pages),[12] is, I suppose, the one most loved by the Turks. It tells of a young man who, in avenging an injury to his stableman father, becomes the leader of a horde of bandits and the terror of sultans and rival bandit chiefs. After a number of Herculean feats, performed frequently with the aid of his wonder horse, the hero allows himself to be killed rather than to go on fighting after his horse has been treacherously hamstrung. Eberhard reports on modern occurrences of this and other romances in a first-rate monograph of 1955, *Minstrel Tales from Southeastern Turkey.*

There are numerous indications of the continuing popularity of these romances. Like the lyrics ascribed to the various *sazşairleri* of ancient times, many of them are available in lurid, cheap-paper editions, particularly at newsstands in rural and poor urban areas. A somewhat atypical romance, *Kerem ve Aslı,* is the basis of the greatest modern Turkish opera, composed by Adnan Saygun.[13]

From folk narrative to folk drama is not a long step for the Turkish scholar, who considers the folktale's performance as one facet of the folk theater. The best work on the entire subject of Turkish folk drama is Selim Nüzhet Gerçek's *Türk Temaşası* (Istanbul, 1942). This rather rare little volume, much deserving of translation, treats Turkish folk theater under three headings: the *meddah,* the *orta oyunu,* and the *karagöz.* To define these terms will indicate the nature of folk drama in Turkey. The *meddah* was (past tense, unfortunately, except for nostalgic revivals and perhaps remote provincial survivals) the coffee-house and mosque-yard entertainer who performed folktales without using properties other than the shawl and stool which were the traditional badges of his profession. Seated on a table, on an improvised platform, or under the arch of a mosque cloister, he would recite the old tales (frequently *Märchen* or *novelle*) from memory, relying only upon his facile voice and gesticulation to bring them to life.

The *orta oyunu* (literally, "performance in the middle") was a kind of folk theater in the round. It is nonexistent today, even though there are still active performers in the nonfolk theater who served their apprenticeship therein. Each *orta oyunu* consisted of two men, one of whom acted all the female parts in the traditional pieces of their repertoire. These traveling companies would open their theater by laying a rug down in a public square, at a picnic ground, or elsewhere alfresco. Upon one corner of the rug the performers placed a three-sided dressing room for one, about the size of a phone booth; and then they staged their plays, using costumes and rough props. Their simple, slapstick productions featured dialect, conventionalized characters (the Arab, the Armenian, the Albanian, the Greek, the Westerner, the soldier, the bully, the sissy, the drug addict, and so on), and ad-libbing. The audience stood on all four sides of the rug stage and willingly suspended their ability to see into the dressing room and through the nonexistent scenery.

The *karagöz* is the shadow theater, the one type of Turkish folk drama well studied internationally, as witness Georg Jacob's *Turkische Schattentheatre* (1900) and Hellmut Ritter's *Turkische Schattenspiele* (1924). In Turkey this form of folk drama has been treated not only in Gerçek's work but also in Sabri Esat Siyavuşgil's *Karagöz* (Istanbul, 1941), translated into French (Istanbul, 1951) and into English (Ankara, 1955)—a handsomely illustrated study which vigorously attacks the psychological and sensual emphases made by the earlier German scholars of the shadow theater.

In the early spring of 1953 it was my good fortune both as a member of the audience and as a privileged backstage visitor, to see the *Karagöz* of *Küçük Ali* (Little Ali), perhaps the last great *hayali* or *karagözcü* (shadow-theatre operator) of Turkey. The stage was a translucent screen, perhaps four feet square, with projecting wings that hid the operator. The screen was set upon a table, draped so that the operator's legs were invisible to the audience seated in front. Behind the screen were placed lights, like footlights (once candles). The operator, standing behind the lights, placed several two-dimensional translucent puppets, made of brightly colored camelskin, against the screen and manipulated them by slender three-foot-long rods. The audience seated on the other side of the screen saw these figures as brightly-tinted shadows moving animately and jerkily back and forth on a white screen. There were also colored shadow props, such as a well, a ship, a tree, and a palace, that were camelskin images leaned against the back of the screen. All of the characters were manipulated by the one operator, who also spoke all of the marvelously differentiated voices. He was aided by an apprentice who kept the proper puppets in readiness to go on stage and helped to set up and take down the theater. In performances of this kind, there may also be one or more musicians who supply incidental music on traditional Turkish instruments.[14]

The shadow plays, of which several dozen exist, have characteristics and characters similar to those of the *orta oyunu* with one very important exception: in the shadow theater the two main characters are always Karagöz and Hacıvat. Karagöz, whose name means Black Eye and who is portrayed by a puppet with piercingly black eyes, is a bearded country innocent who is put upon in every way by the sly, citified, pseudo-sophisticated, and unctuous Hacıvat, whose name is a corruption of *Hacı* (Pilgrim) Ayvat. The two get into broad burlesque, sometimes ribald situations, from which Karagöz despite his naiveté somehow always emerges victorious, to the discomfiture of the clever trickster Hacıvat. Interestingly the plays all utilize conventionalized opening and closing formulae which are beautifully symbolic invocations of the proprietor disclaiming fatalistically any responsibility for the actions of the puppets.

Except for mention of the *sazşair's* poems and the lyrics imbedded in the romances, I have scarcely referred to Turkish folk music—a vast subject by itself. There have been tremendous government-sponsored field expeditions for the collecting of folk music. In the National Conservatory of Music at Ankara are stored thousands of field recordings of the *türkü* (a balladlike song), the *mani* (lyric), the *ninni* (lullaby), dance tunes, such as the *zeybek,* and the ritual song of the dervishes and of other religious groups. Among others, Adnan Saygun and Halil Yönetken have organized and led such collecting expeditions.[15] Other expeditions were sponsored, less scientifically, by local *halkevleri.* Of all this vast collected material, almost nothing has been published, though some commercial recordings of genuine folk music are available.

Much has been done with folk speech, with proverbs, and with dialect vocabulary, although the full extent of such work is not quickly evident since a great deal of it has been published in regional and sometimes obscure Turkish periodicals. Sami Ergun, among others, has published collections of the *bilmece* or *mesele* (riddle or puzzle).[16] Abdülkadir İnan has written several folkloric researches of merit, including the very significant *Tarihte ve Bugün Şamanizm* (Ankara, 1954), a title which might be rendered as *Shamanism Past and Present.* This is another work which merits translation into an accessible language.

In brief, what I have said boils down to this: there is a vast amount of folklore in Turkey, and it is of great potential interest and significance to the international science of folklore; a very respectable amount of research has been done on Turkish folklore, much of it by Turks and much of that still inaccessible to international scholars; a wealth of opportunities for folklore research exists in Turkey, and for a few projects the fieldwork has already been done.

What I have left unsaid is, I fear, of staggering extent. Turkey is a country of fascinating minority groups. According to popular belief, if one stands for an hour on Istanbul's Galatasaray Bridge, he will hear all of the languages of the world—and, I would add, some no longer spoken any place else. There are hundreds of other folk cultures in Turkey beside that ordinarily thought as of Turkish. The folkloric potentialities of a community separated from its homeland for five centuries;[17] of an almost unstudied culture such as that of the Kurds; of the as yet completely unstudied Laz people of Trabzon; and of many intriguing enclaves are fascinating beyond measure.

In even briefer terms, I am saying that Turkey may well be the El Dorado of folklore.

NOTES

(The editor thanks Mrs. Daisy Crystal of Turkey, a graduate student at Indiana University in 1960-61, for assistance on this article, the author being in Indonesia.)

1. The alphabet reform, one of the many innovations made to westernize Turkey and to help it advance in all fields, was made in 1928. It is actually the complete substitution of one alphabet for another. The collected works of such well-known authors as Kadı Burhaneddin, Yunus Emre, and Hayali Bey have been transliterated. In addition to these and other great collections of Turkish literature, limited selections of religious and philosophical works, early travel accounts, and Moslem poems used at memorial services also have been transliterated. The average modern Turk has difficulty appreciating such works, however, not only because of the new alphabet but also due to the language employed. Both the untransliterated and transliterated literatures are incomprehensible to him because of the heavy Persian and Arabic borrowings, both in vocabulary and grammar. Many of these borrowings, as a matter of fact, never were part of the average person's speech. During the Ottoman era, for example, only the intelligentsia (comprised mainly of government officials and people connected with the court) were trained to write in this language.

2. The monograph series includes under the general title *Türk Sazşairlerine Ait Metinler ve Tetkikler (Texts and Analyses of Turkish Minstrels)* individual studies of minstrels, e. g., by Mehmet Fuat Köprülü, *XVII asır Sazşairlerınden Gevheri (Gevheri, One of the Seventeenth Century Minstrels)* (1929); *XIX asır Sazşairlerinden Erzurumlu Emrah (Erzurumlu Emrah, One of the Nineteenth Century Minstrels)* (1929); S. Nüzhet, *XVII asır Sazşairlerinden Pir Sultan Abdal (Pir Sultan Abdal, One of the Seventeenth Century Minstrels)* (1929); Köprülü, *XVI asır Sonuna Kadar Türk Sazşairleri (Turkish Minstrels Until the End of the Sixteenth Century)* (1930); Köprülü, *Kayıkçi Kul Mustafa ve Genç Osman Hikâyesi (Kayıkçı Kul Mustafa [a minstrel of the seventeenth century] and the Young Osman Story)* (1930); and P. Naili, *Köroğlu Destani (The Köroğlu Epic)* (1931).

3. The Ottoman Empire was founded in 1299. The Seljuk era, however, was earlier; it began in 1071 and lasted until 1244. For further information on foreign-language influences upon Turkish literature, see Agâh Sırrı Levend's *Türk Dilinde Gelişme ve Sadeleşme Safhaları* (Ankara, 1949).

4. Some biographies of the minstrels are discussed by Ilhan Basgöz in his "Turkish Folk Stories about the Lives of Minstrels," *Journal of American Folklore*, LXV (1952), 331-339.

5. The archives of the Türk Tarih Kurumu contain interviews with soldiers who were involved in the post-World-War-I fight for Turkish freedom; folk-minstrel songs about that and earlier wars; and the research of many students who have tried to prove some of Atatürk's theories about the long-range ancient history of the Turks. Articles of interest to folklorists appear in the Türk Dil Kurumu's monthly publication *Türk Dili*, e.g., Behçet Kemal Çağlar's "Folklorun Aynasında Türk Insanı I: Türküler, Töreler, Oyalar" ("The Turkish Person in the Mirror of Folklore, I: Folk Songs, Customs, Embroidery"), XCVIII, No. 76. For full-length folkloric publications of the Türk Dil Kurumu, see, e.g., Muharrem Ergin's *Dede Korkut Kitabi* (*The Dede Story Book*) (Ankara, 1960); the five-volume collection of dialect words from all parts of Turkey, *İllerimez Ağızlarından Toplamalar* (*Collections of Dialects*) (Istanbul, 1939-52); and *Türkiyede Halk Ağzından Söz Derleme Dergisi* (*Magazine of Collected Folk Sayings*), ed. Şakir Ülkütaşir and Ömer A. Aksoy (Ankara, 1952), a collection of dialect words referring to local customs, published as a supplement to the five volumes of dialect words listed above. For folkloric publications of the Türk Tarih Kurumu, see, e.g., A. Caferoğlu's *Folklorumuzda Millî Hayat ve Dil Bakiyeleri* (*National Life and Language Treasures in our Folklore*) (Ankara, 1940); and Abdülkadir İnan's *Tarihte ve Bugün Şamanizm: Materyaller ve Araştırmalar* (*Shamanism in History and Today: Materials and Investigations*) (Ankara, 1954).

6. See, e.g., the Gaziantep Halkevi's *Gaziantep Dilinin Tetkiki* (*Analysis of the Gaziantep Language*), by Omer Asim Aksoy (Gaziantep, 1933); and the Muğla Halkevi's *Türk Adları* (*Turkish Names*), by M. Cavit and O. Saffet (Mugla, 1934). For folklore journals published by the now defunct local folk houses, see, e.g., the Ankara Halkevi's *Ülkü* and *Altı Ok* (24 issues between 1933-36); and the Eminönü Halkevi's *Halk Bilgisi Haberleri* (*Communications on Folklore*). The latter was the only real Turkish folklore journal in existence when the folk houses were closed by the government in 1945. Preceded by *Halk Bilgisi Mecmuası* (*The Magazine for Folklore*), which was published in 1927 by the short-lived folklore organization, Halk Bilgisi Derneği, *Halk Bilgisi Haberleri* was published by this organization from 1928-30, and then from 1931-45 by the Eminönü Halkevi in Istanbul.

7. Journals in Turkey that publish folklore articles today include: *The Anthropological Review*, published by the Institute of Anthropology and Ethnology at the University of Ankara; the *Publications* of the Turkological Institute of the University of Istanbul; *Arkeologya, Tarih ve Etnografya*, published by the Ministry of Education, Ankara; the *Publications* of the literary and theological faculty of the University of Istanbul; *Türk Yurdu; Yeni Mecmua; Millî Tetebbular; Küçük Mecmua; Dergâh;* and *Millî Mecmua*. A new folklore journal, edited by Eflâtun Cem Güney and others, is *Türk Folklor Araştırmaları*. Volume I (Istanbul, 1949-51) contains 24 numbers, and was published by the Türk Halkbilgisi Derneği (The Turkish Folklore Society).

8. Their reluctance is discussed at greater length in my review of Wolfram Eberhard and Pertev Naili Boratav, *Typen Türkischer Volksmärchen, Journal of American Folklore*, LXVIII (1955), 231-235.

9. Collections and studies of Nas'r eddin Hoca anecdotes include Henry D. Barnham's *Tales of Nasr-ed-din Khoja* (London, 1923, also titled *The Khoja: Tales of Nasr-ed-din*, New York, 1924); Beha'i's *Letaifi-Nasreddin Hoca* (*Pleasantries of Nasreddin Hoca*) (Istanbul, 1926); F. Köprülü's *Nasreddin Hoca* (Istanbul, 1918); I. Kunos's *Naszreddin Hodsa Tréfái* (*Jests of Hoca Nasreddin*) (Budapest, 1899); and A. Wesselski's *Der Hodscha Nasreddin* (2 vols., Weimar, 1911).

10. For anecdotes about the Bektaşi order, see *Bektaşi Hikâyeleri* (Istanbul, 1918). The word *Bektaşi* designates not only a member of the Bektaşi order of dervishes, but also sometimes connotes a freethinker or a dissolute person. More important for the folklorist, however, is its common usage as the name of a generic type of character who appears in Turkish anecdotes. Just as Americans can begin a story with "Once there was a Scotchman" and thereby create a stereotype in the listeners' minds, so the Turks can say "There was a Bektaşi" and produce the same effect. The stereotype thus invoked is that of a supposedly typical member of the Bektaşi dervish order, which derives its name from Hacı Bektaş Veli, a "saint" of the Islamic faith. The Bektaşi order dates back to the sixteenth century but probably was founded much earlier than Bektaş. Members of the Bektaşi order developed numerous ceremonial and ritualistic customs, based on their attachment to the Caliph Ali and other saintly persons, but they rejected established ritual. They wove into the order's Islamic background certain Gnostic and Christian elements, including the mystical significance attributed by Gnosticism to numbers, and the Christian concept of a trinity (*Encyclopedia of Islam*, ed. M. Th. Houtsma, et al. [London, 1913], I, 691).

11. This claim is made within the romances themselves, just as it also is made in the *sazşairler's* ballads. It can safely be considered as a convention of romance style. The clichés in these minstrel tales receive further discussion in my article, "A Culture's Stereotypes and their Expression in Folk Clichés," *Southwestern Journal of Anthropology,* XIII (1957), 184-200.

12. This partial English translation comprises most of Alexander Chodzko's *Specimens of the Popular Poetry of Persia as Found in the Adventures and Improvisations of Kurroglu . . . and in the Songs of the People Inhabiting the Shores of the Caspian Sea* (London, 1842), pp. 17-344.

13. *Kerem ve Aslı* is *atypical* in that it glorifies a romance between a Turk and an Armenian. It is *somewhat* atypical in that I know of at least one other romance, "Ali Pasha," that does the same thing. See Eberhard, *Minstrel Tales from Southeastern Turkey* (Berkeley and Los Angeles, 1955), pp. 27-29.

14. The typical performance starts with a musical solo on a primitive pipelike instrument. Then, after another musician plays on a tambourine, Hacıvat, one of the two major characters, comes on stage and sings one of the many songs available for this purpose, all of which conform to a fairly definite pattern. His song concluded, the play itself begins (Selim Nüzhet Gerçek, *Türk Temaşası,* Istanbul, 1942, p. 77). The shadow play I saw, however, was an unusually gala performance which employed four musicians; but the same *hayali* occasionally staged productions which utilized only one musician or none. During my stay in Turkey (1951-53) there were other shadow-theater operators besides Küçük Ali—even some in the National Theatre. But these latter were hardly authentic folk artists.

15. Yönetkin is a composer, conductor, and professor at the National Conservatory. Each collecting expedition, led by a professor plus several students, lasts throughout the long summer holidays.

16. Other publications of Turkish riddles include Hamamizade İhsan's *Bilmeceler,* in Türk Halk Bilgisine Ait Maddeler (Materials on Turkish Folklore), No. 3 (Istanbul, 1930), which contains 800 items; and Bahaeddin Ögel's 94 "Riddles from Erzurum," *Journal of American Folklore,* LXIII (1950), 413-424.

17. The conquest of Istanbul (1453) effectively closed off a number of communities from their homelands: among others, the Genoese, the Florentines, the Maltese, and the Sephardics—all of whom still speak their medieval languages. Midway between Istanbul and the Black Sea, moreover, is an enclave of Poles who have maintained their language for at least three centuries without any contact with the homeland. Incidentally, the Sephardics no longer have a homeland which speaks their language!

University of Kentucky
Lexington, Kentucky

FELIX J. OINAS

FOLKLORE ACTIVITIES IN RUSSIA

THE PRESENT survey is more concerned with the work done in folklore in Soviet Russia than in Tsarist Russia. Since, however, some of the present trends have their roots in the past, by way of an introduction we will mention some facts about the interest in and the study of folklore in the prerevolutionary (pre-1917) period.[1]

Folklore has always been popular among all strata of the Russian population, from the tsars and noblemen to the peasants and workers. Some Russian tsars used to have storytellers around them who related fairy tales at bedtime. Rich men, suffering from insomnia, had their attendants tickle the soles of their feet and tell them stories. But especially the lower strata of the population—the peasants, fishermen, workers, and the boat haulers on the Volga—have cherished and used folklore more than anyone else. Master taletellers and singers have always been, and continue to be, highly appreciated in the villages. Skillful tellers are especially hired by the north Russian groups of lumbermen, fishermen, and hunters to beguile the hours of work and leisure.

Despite the general love of folklore in Russia, for a long time it was not written down. This is partly due to the fact that writing was mainly in the hands of the clergy, and the clergymen viewed oral poetry with hostility as unclean and containing rudiments of heathen ideology. Therefore it is not surprising that the first records of Russian folklore were made by foreigners—by the Englishmen Richard James and Samuel Collins. James, chaplain to an English diplomatic mission in Moscow, noted down several historical songs in 1619-20. Collins, who lived in Moscow as the physician to the tsar in the 1660's, recorded several Russian folktales.

At the end of the seventeenth and during the eighteenth centuries, casual records were made of Russian folklore, mainly out of curiosity. Among them, one folksong collection is significant; it was done by a cossack, Kirša Danilov, in the Ural region.[2] This collection, containing about seventy songs, was compiled evidently for the mill-owner P. A. Demidov in the second half of the eighteenth century. The texts show clear traces of being subjected to the collector's editorship and reworking.

The real interest in the collection and publication of folklore, which arose in Russia only in the first decades of the nineteenth century, was connected with the romantic movement and inspired by the German folklorists, especially the brothers Grimm. Famous Russian writers, such as Žukovskij, Puškin, and Gogol', used folklore for artistic purposes. Folklorist-mythologists of this period who deserve mention are P. V. Kireevskij, an enthusiastic collector of folksongs, the bulk of which were published only posthumously about thirty years after the collection was made; F. I. Buslaev, a noted philologist, who has been called "the first Russian scholar of folklore"; and A. N. Afanas'ev, by education a lawyer, who published Russian folktales.[3] Afanas'ev's work, which consists mainly of tales collected by others, is the biggest and most important Russian folktale collection, comparable with that of the brothers Grimm in Germany.

In the 1860's, a sudden rise of interest in folklore was noticeable in Russia. This was caused by the discovery of a flourishing byliny tradition in the Olonets region in Karelia. (Bylina, pl. byliny, is an heroic epic folksong.) Up to that time it had been believed that the byliny were almost extinct as a living form in Russia. P. N. Rybnikov, an official in the Russian civil service, who for political reasons had been sent to serve in Olonets, discovered that the byliny were there still flourishing among the singers. He collected and published 224 byliny.[4] Rybnikov's discovery was so surprising and sensational that it was first met with a scepticism similar to that which greeted MacPherson's *Ossian* in England. About ten years later, A. F. Gil'ferding set out to the same region to supplement Rybnikov's work. Gil'ferding went farther north than his predecessor and succeeded in finding much valuable new material in Olonets and Karelia (altogether 318 texts).[5] Rybnikov's and Gil'ferding's work gave a strong impetus to the systematic search for the byliny everywhere in northern Russia, a search which has lasted up to the present time. The results have been most gratifying. It turned out that the byliny survived not only in the Karelia and Olonets region, but also on the shores of the White Sea and the rivers flowing to the north (such as Pinega, Mezen', Pechora), and in northern Siberia, although none of these areas could compete with Olonets. This collecting resulted in big and valuable byliny publications by N. S. Tixonravov, V. F. Miller, A. V. Markov, A. D. Grigor'ev, N. E. Ončukov, and others, at the end of the nineteenth and the beginning of the twentieth centuries.[6] Also other genres of folklore were collected and published at the same time, such as folktales (by N. E. Ončukov, D. K. Zelenin, B. M. and Ju. M. Sokolov),[7] lyric songs (by A. I. Sobolevskij, P. V. Šejn),[8] lamentations (by E. V. Barsov),[9] proverbs (by V. I. Dal'),[10] and riddles (by D. N. Sadovnikov).[11]

In collecting and publishing folklore, one aspect was especially emphasized—the personality of the individual singers and narrators. Russian folklorists, more than those of any other country, stressed the close interrelationship between the personality of the teller and his creation. Thus, beginning with Rybnikov and Gil'ferding, biographical information about and characterizations of the informants have been gathered and published. To underline their role, the materials in the collections have been arranged according to the tellers. This principle was first followed by Gil'ferding in his byliny publication in 1873.[12] Since that time, other significant folklore collections have been arranged on the same principle.

Of the folklorists at the turn of the present century, A. N. Veselovskij and V. F. Miller deserve special mention. Veselovskij's main field was the reciprocal cultural and literary intercourse between the Slavs, Byzantium, and western Europe during the Middle Ages. His vast production gives evidence of enormous erudition and of an ability for detailed analysis and generalizing synthesis. Miller's field was the study of the Russian byliny. His aim was to link Russian folk poetry with Russian history —to explain every byliny hero and every event in the byliny on the basis of history. Under his influence, the historical school in Russian folklore was considered "the last word in scholarship" right before the October Revolution in 1917.

* * *

After the revolution, Russian folklore continued to develop at first in the spirit of the historical school. At the beginning of the 1920's, however, the formalistic trend became strongly felt not only in literature but also in folklore. The formalistic studies by A. P. Skaftymov, V. Ja. Propp, A. I. Nikiforov, V. M. Žirmunskij, and others on various genres and aspects of folklore are significant contributions in the field. Skafty-mov's *The Poetics and Genesis of Byliny*[13] emphasizes the significance of the study of structure over that of ideology; it succeeds in explaining certain disputed problems (such as the negative traits of Prince Vladimir) by the requirements of structure. Propp, in his *Morphology of the Folktale,*[14] studies the structure of the magic tales on the basis of the function of the *dramatis personae;* his conclusion is that all the fairy tales are uniform in their structure. Nikiforov, who focused his attention on the complete folktale repertoire of certain regions, was also concerned with functions of personages. Žirmunskij contributed to the study of the poetics—rhythm and met-rics—of folklore. Formalism was, however, short-lived in Russian literary scholarship. In the later 1920's, it became the object of violent attacks by official Soviet circles as "a narrow and impractical academism."

Criticism was voiced also against the so-called Finnish school, which applied the historical-geographical method for clarification of the origin and migrations of folk-tales. The most significant representative of this school was N. P. Andreev, who published several monographs and prepared a Russian edition of the Aarne-Thomp-son Type-Index.[15] Following criticism from the official side, the historical-geographical method—like formalistic trends—was abandoned. Thus, at the beginning of the thir-ties, there occurred a shift in folklore study toward stricter concentration on social problems and ideology, a trend which had already been followed by some folklorists.

The Soviet Russian folklorists have continued the traditions of their predecessors in organizing extensive collecting in the field. One group after another has left for the north and northeast to the well-known areas where flourished the byliny, folktale, and other folklore genres. The first expedition, called "In the Footsteps of Rybnikov and Gil'ferding," was organized by the State Academy of Fine Arts in Moscow in 1926-28 to go to the Olonets region under the direction of the brothers Sokolov. It has been followed, up to the present time (with a break during World War II), by numerous expeditions to Karelia, the White Sea region, the areas of the big northern rivers, and Siberia.

In this extensive fieldwork, the territory covered by earlier collectors has been revisited over and over again. The repertoires of the same singers and narrators have often been written down several times, with intervals of one or more decades between them. This has enabled the folklorists to go deeper into the nature of the changes which folklore undergoes. The expeditions have, in addition, brought to light quite a number of hitherto unknown variants of byliny, folktales, and songs. A part of this material has been published in large collections by M. K. Azadovskij, A. M. Astaxova, Ju. M. Sokolov, A. N. Nečaev, R. S. Lipec, and others.[16] A great part of the collected material is, however, still in manuscript.

The collectors in the field have, as before, carefully observed the personality of the individual singer and narrator. This has resulted in a number of studies on the narrators by B. M. Sokolov and especially by M. K. Azadovskij.[17] These works, un-like the prerevolutionary accounts on the narrators, emphasize especially the correla-tion between personal creation and the ideology of the collective. The keen interest in the individual narrators has led to the development in Soviet Russia of a new type of folklore collection, confined to the repertoire of a single person, so to speak the "collected works" of a certain master narrator. Such special collections have been devoted to the folklore of the Siberian storyteller Natal'ja O. Vinokurova, the Voronezh storyteller Kuprijanixa (Anna Kuprijanovna Baryšnikova), the White

Sea storyteller Matvej M. Korguev, the White Sea narrator Marfa S. Krjukova, and others.[18]

The studies of Soviet Russian folklorists since the twenties have stressed the social uses of folklore rather than the questions of origin and migration. The folklorists have worked most eagerly on those genres of folklore which were neglected or ignored by the prerevolutionary folklorists, such as satires on priests and noblemen, folk traditions about revolutionary movements, and the folklore of workers. The satirical stories about priests and medicine men have been extensively collected and published by Ju. M. Sokolov, E. D. Višnevskaja, and others.[19] These stories, widely disseminated in cheap popular editions, have served as a means of intensifying antireligious propaganda. Sokolov also published a collection of satires about noblemen.[20] The folk traditions about revolutionary uprisings, especially about those led by Razin and Pugačev, were collected and published by A. N. Lozanova and B. M. Blinova.[21] Of the songs of soldiers only the so-called recruits' songs attracted some interest in Tsarist Russia; now also other aspects, such as the revolutionary soldiers' songs, became the object of study (especially by I. S. Èventov). The old workers' songs, showing the hard life of the workers in factories and mines, have been collected not only by the folklorists but also by the factory workers themselves in the industrial centers of Russia.

Even the genres which were the center of study before the October Revolution, such as fairy tales, byliny, historical songs, *častuški,* have received due attention after the revolution. The Soviet folklorists have concentrated especially on the changes which these genres have undergone during the Soviet rule. In fairy tales, they have emphasized the trend from the fantastic and miraculous toward the realistic, and the introduction into the tale of details from the contemporary life. What strikes one most is the pervading antagonism toward the tsar, who appears now as merciless, cowardly, stupid, and comical. In some fairy tales, the dethroned tsar is put on trial and even taken to the gallows. Also the figure of Prince Vladimir has in some byliny acquired a strongly negative coloring.

Much interest has been manifested in Soviet Russia toward the collection and study of the entirely new creation of Russian folklore—new tales, new byliny, new laments. Such works imitate the traditional folklore, making use of its motifs and poetical features, but employing contemporary life as their subject. Their heroes are often the Soviet political and military leaders. Thus, the tale "The Most Precious Thing" describes the Nekrasov-like wandering of three collective farmers in search of truth and their ultimate discovery that "the best and most precious thing we have on earth is the word of Comrade Stalin." The tale "The Hero and the Eagle" is an allegory of Lenin's revolutionary fight: its youthful hero has devoted his life to the liberation of an epic hero who has been kept prisoner by a two-headed eagle. The White Sea narrator Marfa S. Krjukova, one of the most talented improvisers, composed several poems on Lenin. Her "Tale About Lenin" deals, in the vein of a mixture of ancient byliny, historical songs and lamentations, with the main periods of Lenin's life. Krjukova's lament for Lenin has almost an authentic popular character.

Since the second half of the twenties, biographical narratives and memoirs *(skazy)* have been objects of systematic collection. They have been collected from ordinary people about their own life, about the events they have witnessed, and about the remarkable people they have met. These narratives are concerned with wives' sufferings under their despotic and drunken husbands, the events of the revolution, the civil war, the restoration of the war-torn economy, the collectivization of agriculture, and the life in the Red Army.[22] One of the most favored themes is the contrast between the old and the new mode of life. Some of these narratives are moving and sincere, and offer interesting documents of the present era. Even the stories about military and political leaders are sometimes touching in their naiveté, such as the story by a woman relating how she sewed a button on Lenin's coat (without the latter's knowing it) and how she proudly recognized her button on the photos of Lenin afterwards. Since 1942, the so-called Great Fatherland's War has been the central theme of folklore collection and systematization.[23]

Questions have been raised by some folklorists (e.g., by Ju. M. Sokolov) concerning the inclusion of the biographical narratives and memoirs in folklore, since they are related at times "without any special pretensions to artistic merit; some of the tales are in the form of a single, solitary fact; many of them do not pass from mouth to mouth, they do not attain any permanent form."[24] They have, nevertheless, been included, according to Azadovskij, "as a kind of new phenomenon which belongs to the facts of oral creation."[25]

By eliminating the principle of traditionality and thus extending the definition of folklore, Soviet folklorists have attempted to refute the usual thesis of the decline and disappearance of folklore and popular creation. On the contrary, they maintain that "in the conditions of the socialist reality the folklore assumes new forms and becomes new both in quality and content."[26]

Folklore, like every other field of scholarship in the Soviet Union, is conceived of as a means for the realization of socialism and communism. Being close to the hearts of the masses, folklore has especially great propagandistic value, and it has been used extensively for this end. This fact has been duly emphasized by the Soviet folklorists:

Never, in all the history of Russia, has the oral poetic word served the social aims so broadly and powerfully as in the Soviet period. Soviet folkloristics has helped to reveal the agitational and propagandist significance of folklore. And thereby, Soviet folkloristics has firmly allied itself with the practical tasks of our social life.[27]

The popular tellers conceive their activity as agitational-propagandistic. They are popular agitators, people's tribunes, carrying their artistic patriotic word to the masses. Their works summon the readers and listeners to the conscious work for the glory of Fatherland.[28]

Although the Soviet folklorists had been aware of the social aspects and political significance of folklore, for some time they did not follow the specifically Soviet, i.e., Marxist-Leninist, ideology. They were "still captives of the old methodology, the roots of which are firmly entrenched in the ideology of the bourgeois society and closely connected with the processes characteristic of the bourgeois ideas in Europe and in Russia in the prerevolutionary years."[29] This appeared, among other things, in their interpretation of the role of the peasants and workers in the popular creation. B. M. Sokolov and other leading folklorists, following V. F. Miller, held that the byliny originated in the higher classes—in the singers of the princes' retinue. They thought that the byliny were taken over from them later by *skomoroxi*, the professional singers of the lower classes, and reached the peasants—through the mediation of the *skomoroxi*—only in the sixteenth and seventeenth centuries. In November, 1936, Demjan Bednyj's drama *The Epic Heroes (Bogatyri)* was, on the order of a committee at the government, removed from the repertoire of a theater in Moscow as a misinterpretation of Russian history and epic heroes, since it depicted the byliny heroes as representatives of the nobility in the traditional derogatory way. At the same time a wide folkloristic discussion about the character and origin of the epic was started. It resulted in a basic change in the attitude toward the byliny by scholars, who now denied "aristocratic origin" and insisted upon "genuine popular quality."

In the second half of the forties, a change in the Soviet policy in literature occurred which also affected the study of folklore. Then began a most intensive campaign, led by Ždanov, against all Western elements in Soviet literature and literary study. Among the literary scholars, the folklorists Propp and Azadovskij were accused of stressing the international character of folklore and following the comparativist line. Propp's book, *The Historical Roots of the Magic Tale,*[30] which contained abundant quotations from such international scholars as Frazer, Boas, Kroeber, and others, was compared to a London or Berlin telephone directory.[31] The change of trend that followed is clearly manifest in folklore studies after 1948 until the death of Stalin. The folklorists now refrained from giving any references to Western scholarship in their works. The new folklore textbook for the higher educational institutions, edited by Bogatyrev,[32] unlike Ju. M. Sokolov's well-known *Russian Folklore,* presented the development of Russian folklore from indigenous national roots and without any relationship with the West.

Folklore has become one of the very popular subjects in the Soviet Union. Since 1934-35, folklore materials have been published in local papers and magazines, and sent in by teachers, agronomists, workers of machine-tractor stations, and members of the collective farms. The materials published in these regional papers have often been termed very valuable. The popularity of folklore appears also in the founding of folklore clubs in numerous collective farms and factories. Folklore is taught as a special subject in pedagogical institutions and universities.

Notable folksingers and tellers enjoy high esteem in the Soviet Union, being surrounded by general attention and care. They are honored at home and are frequent guests in the capitals and provincial centers, at sport events, at scientific conferences, and at writers' congresses. Some of them have received high decorations. The more important singers and tellers are granted financial support by the government.

Several hundred Soviet folklorists have been actively engaged in research. Of them, A. M. Astaxova, V. Ja. Propp, M. K. Azadovskij (died 1954), and V. I. Čičerov (died 1957) are worthy of special mention. Astaxova's study *The Russian Byliny Epic in the North*[33] is perhaps the highest achievement of Russian folklore. Unlike V. F. Miller and other leading prerevolutionary folklorists, Astaxova studies the byliny not as archaic stagnant phenomena, but as living processes. Analyzing the bylina tradition of the last one hundred and fifty years, she establishes basic laws pertaining to the creative process of the folk epic, and studies the significance of the environment and the influence of written literature on the byliny.

Propp, after abandoning formalism, turned to the social aspects of folklore. His imaginative study on the historical roots of the magic tale, mentioned earlier, deals with the fairy tales as an entirety and traces their origin back to primitive initiation rites. In his extensive work *The Russian Heroic Epic,*[34] Propp, following Belinskij, endeavors to formulate the basic idea of each bylina, contending that the idea of a bylina expresses the ideals of the corresponding epoch.

Azadovskij started as an investigator of folktales and laments, with special emphasis on the role of the teller, but became more and more attracted to the history of Russian folklore and the problems of the interrelationship between literature and folklore.[35] V. I. Čičerov contributed to the study of the same interrelationship, to the theory of folklore, and to ritual poetry.[36]

In addition to those mentioned above, there are many other contemporary (or recently deceased) folklorists who have distinguished themselves in the study of Russian folklore. M. O. Skripil' (died 1957) and V. P. Adrianova-Peretc have studied folklore in Old Russian literary works; the latter's special sphere of interest has been the relationship between the styles of folk and art literature. P. B. Bogatyrev has been engaged in the study of the theory of folklore, popular theater, and the Slavic epic. V. G. Bazanov deals with all aspects of Karelian folklore. D. S. Lixačev, a scholar of great amplitude, has examined the origin and early development of byliny and historical songs. Various aspects of the byliny have been studied also by R. S. Lipec, A. P. Evgen'eva, P. D. Uxov, and M. P. Štokmar, and the historical songs have been treated by V. K. Sokolova and B. N. Putilov. The folktale has been the concern of I. V. Karnauxova, A. N. Nečaev, È. V. Pomeranceva, E. M. Meletinskij, and I. Levin. Russian lyrical songs have been studied by T. M. Akimova, N. P. Kolpakova, and V. M. Sidel'nikov; the workers' songs by P. G. Širjaeva; and the revolutionary songs by A. M. Novikova. Research on the popular theater has been carried on especially by V. N. Vsevolodskij-Gerngross, V. Ju. Krupjanskaja, and T. M. Akimova. The so-called "small genres" (riddles and proverbs) have been the object of study by A. M. Rybnikova, M. O. Šanxovič, and V. P. Anikin. This list could easily be expanded with the inclusion of many more young and promising folklorists.

Much important work has been done in the collection, publication, and study of the folklore of the various nationalities in the Soviet Union. This has followed, in general, the same line as the collection and study of Russian folklore. Special attention has been given, in recent years, to the rich and flourishing epic tradition of the nationalities, considered as being "closely linked with significant processes in the history of mankind and with the liberation of nations."[37] The study of the folklore of nationalities has been largely in the hands of scholars from the nationalities involved, although some Russian scholars (such as Žirmunskij) have occasionally contributed. This research, however, is outside the scope of the present survey.

The organizations for the collection and study of folklore in the Soviet Union have since the October Revolution passed through a considerable metamorphosis; their names and affiliations have been frequently changed. At present, the following two are most important: the Folklore Committee of the Institute of Russian Literature (Puškin House) at the Academy of Sciences in Leningrad, headed by Boris N. Putilov, and the Folklore Section of the Gor'kij Institute of World Literature in Moscow, directed by Petr G. Bogatyrev.[38]

The Institute of Russian Literature (Puškin House) and the Institute of World Literature have cooperated in sponsoring several large-scale conferences on folklore in Leningrad. The conference held in November 1953 was, for instance, devoted to the discussion of two problems—Soviet folklore (its nature, characteristic features, tasks, and methods of its study) and the history of Russian folklore and its periodization. In this conference there were 250 participants, all invited. The conference in May 1956 was dedicated to the project of the publication of the "Collection of Russian Folklore" ("Svod russkogo fol'klora") in as many as one hundred volumes. It was decided that this gigantic work would embrace the republication of the classical collections, along with the publication of manuscript collections and of materials still to be collected. This program is actually the revival of an idea which arose in the 1930's and was approved in 1940, but was interrupted by the war. The conference of folklorists in November 1958, with 240 participants, centered around the problems of contemporary folklore. In addition to the all-Union conferences, meetings of regional folklorists are arranged frequently for the discussion of special problems. Thus, a regional conference was held in Petrozavodsk (Karelian SSR) in 1957 on the collection and study of the folklore in the north, and another one in Ulan-Ude (Buryat-Mongol ASSR) in 1959 on the study of folklore in Siberia and the Far East.

The future direction of folklore study in the Soviet Union has been outlined by V. E. Gusev in the following way:

Further research will doubtless proceed in two directions. Two really urgent tasks are the concentration of the folklore history of various peoples and work on genres at various stages of historical development. Such works are being planned by the Institute of Russian Literature of the USSR Academy of Sciences. Systematization of the various histories will in turn enable scholars to develop a general Marxist history of folklore, tracing the objective process of its development at successive stages in the history of human society.[39]

NOTES

1. The data on the history of Russian folklore can be found in the following works: A. N. Pypin, *Istorija russkoj ètnografii,* 4 vols. (St. Petersburg, 1890-92); M. K. Azadovskij, "Sovetskaja fol'kloristika za 20 let," *Sovetskij fol'klor,* VI (Moscow-Leningrad, 1939), 3-53; Ju. M. Sokolov, *Russkij fol'klor* (Moscow, 1941), pp. 54-121, tr. Catherine R. Smith as *Russian Folklore* (New York, 1950), pp. 40-155; Margaret Schlauch, "Folklore in the Soviet Union," *Science and Society,* VIII (1944), 205-222; Roman Jakobson, "On Russian Fairy Tales," in *Russian Fairy Tales,* tr. N. Guterman (New York, 1945), pp. 631-656; E. V. Gippius and V. I. Čičerov, "Sovetskaja fol'kloristika za 30 let," *Sovetskaja ètnografija,* No. 4 (Leningrad, 1947), 29-51; A. M. Astaxova et al., *Očerki russkogo narodnopoèticeskogo tvorčestva sovetskoj èpoxi* (Moscow-Leningrad, 1952); V. P. Adrianova-Peretc et al., *Russkoe narodnoe poèticeskoe tvorčestvo,* 3 vols. (Moscow-Leningrad, 1953-56); V. K. Sokolova, "Sovetskaja fol'kloristika k 40-letiju Oktjabrja," *Sovetskaja ètnografija,* No. 5 (1957), 72-85; M. K. Azadovskij, *Istorija russkoj fol'kloristiki* (Moscow, 1958); V. E. Gusev, "Aktual'nye voprosy izučenija fol'klora," *Vestnik Akademii Nauk SSSR,* XXX, No. 7 (Moscow, 1960), 39-44, tr. as "Folklore Research in the USSR," *Soviet Review,* II (Jan. 1961), 51-58.

2. *Drevnie rossijskie stixotvorenija, sobrannye Kiršej Danilovym* (St. Petersburg, 1818). A part of it was published, without the collector's name, in Moscow, 1804; latest edition, Moscow-Leningrad, 1958, ed. A. P. Evgen'eva and B. N. Putilov.

3. A. N. Afanas'ev, *Narodnye russkie skazki,* 8 parts (Moscow, 1855-64). It has been republished in Russia so far in 6 editions; the latest one in 3 vols. (Moscow, 1957), ed. V. Ja. Propp, contains excellent notes, comments, and indexes.

4. *Pesni, sobrannye P. N. Rybnikovym,* 4 vols. (Moscow, 1861-67); 2nd edition in 3 vols., ed. A. E. Gruzinskij (1909-10).

5. A. F. Gil'ferding, *Onežskie byliny* (St. Petersburg, 1873; 4th ed., in 3 vols., Moscow-Leningrad, 1949-51).

6. N. S. Tixonravov and V. F. Miller, *Russkie byliny staroj i novoj zapisi* (Moscow, 1894); A. V. Markov, *Belomorskie byliny* (Moscow, 1901); A. D. Grigor'ev, *Arxangel'skie byliny,* I (Moscow, 1904), II (Prague, 1939), III (St. Petersburg, 1910); N. E. Ončukov, *Pečorskie byliny* (St. Petersburg, 1904); V. F. Miller, *Byliny novoj i novejšej zapisi* (Moscow, 1908).

7. N. E. Ončukov, *Severnye skazki* (1909); D. K. Zelenin, *Velikorusskie skazki Permskoj gubernii* (1914); D. K. Zelenin, *Velikorusskie skazki Vjatskoj gubernii* (1915); B. M. and Ju. M. Sokolov, *Skazki i pesni Belozerskogo kraja* (1915). All published in St. Petersburg.

8. A. I. Sobolevskij, *Velikorusskie narodnye pesni,* 7 vols. (St. Petersburg, 1895-1902); P. V. Šejn, *Velikoruss v svoix pesnjax, obrjadax, obyčajax, verovanijax, skazkax, legendax i t.p.,* 2 parts (St. Petersburg, 1898-1900).

9. E. V. Barsov, *Pričitanija Severnogo kraja,* 3 vols. (Moscow, 1872-86).

10. V. I. Dal', *Poslovicy russkogo naroda* (Moscow, 1861-62; 4th ed., Moscow, 1957).

11. D. N. Sadovnikov, *Zagadki russkogo naroda* (St. Petersburg, 1876; 3rd ed. [with omissions], Moscow, 1959, ed. V. P. Anikin).

12. The principle of arranging materials in collections according to the tellers was first suggested by P. N. Rybnikov, but was discarded by the first editor of his byliny. Not until the second edition (1909) were Rybnikov's byliny arranged in cycles according to the tellers.

13. A. P. Skaftymov, *Poètika i genezis bylin* (Moscow-Saratov, 1924). The central portion of

this work has been republished in Skaftymov's *Stat'i o russkoj literature* (Saratov, 1958), pp. 3-76.

14. V. Ja. Propp, *Morfologija skazki* (Leningrad, 1928); tr. Lawrence Scott as *Morphology of the Folktale* (Bloomington, Ind., 1958).

15. N. P. Andreev, *Ukazatel' skazočnyx sjužetov po sisteme Aarne* (Leningrad, 1929).

16. M. K. Azadovskij, ed., *Skazki iz raznyx mest Sibiri* (1925); A. M. Astaxova, *Byliny Severa*, 2 vols. (Moscow-Leningrad, 1938-51); Ju. M. Sokolov, *Onežskie byliny*, ed. V. Čičerov, *Letopisi Gosud. literaturnogo muzeja*, XIII (Moscow, 1948). See also works listed under n. 18.

17. B. M. Sokolov, *Skaziteli* (Moscow, 1924); Mark Asadowskij, "Eine sibirische Märchenerzählerin," FF Communications, No. 68 (Helsinki, 1926); È. V. Gofman, "K voprosu ob individual'nom stile skazočnika," *Xudožestvennyj fol'klor*, IV-V (Moscow, 1929); M. Azadovskij, *Russkaja skazka: Izbrannye mastera*, 2 vols. (Moscow-Leningrad, 1932).

18. M. Azadovskij, *Skazki Verxnelenskogo kraja* (Irkutsk, 1924; on cover: 1925); the majority of these tales have been republished in Azadovskij's *Verxnelenskie skazki* (Irkutsk, 1938); A. M. Novikova and I. A. Ossoveckij, *Skazki Kuprijanixi* (Voronezh, 1937); A. N. Nečaev, *Skazki Karel'skogo Belomor'ja*, 2 parts (Petrozavodsk, 1939); È. Borodina and R. Lipec, ed., *Byliny M. S. Krjukovoj*, 2 vols., *Letopisi Gosud. literaturnogo muzeja*, VI and VIII (Moscow, 1939-41); M. K. Azadovskij, ed., *Skazki F. P. Gospodareva* (Petrozavodsk, 1941).

19. Ju. M. Sokolov, *Pop i mužik* (Moscow-Leningrad, 1931); E. D. Višnevskaja, *Antireligioznye skazki narodov SSSR* (Moscow, 1939).

20. Ju. M. Sokolov, *Barin i mužik* (Moscow, 1932).

21. A. N. Lozanova, *Pesni i skazanija o Razine i Pugačeve* (Moscow-Leningrad, 1935); E. M. Blinova, *Skazy, pesni, častuški* (Chelyabinsk, 1937).

22. Some collections of the narratives are: S. Mirer and V. Borovik, *Rasskazy rabočix o Lenine* (Moscow, 1934); V. M. Sidel'nikov, *Krasnoarmejskij fol'klor* (Moscow, 1938).

23. Two collections concerning this war are: V. Tonkov, *Narodnoe tvorčestvo v dni Velikoj Otečestvennoj vojny* (Voronezh, 1945); V. Ju. Krupjanskaja and S. I. Minc, *Materialy po istorii pesni Velikoj Otečestvennoj vojny* (Moscow, 1953).

24. Ju. M. Sokolov (n. 1, Engl. tr.), p. 682.

25. M. K. Azadovskij (n. 1), p 18.

26. E. V. Gippius and V. I. Čičerov (n. 1), p. 49.

27. Ju. M. Sokolov (n. 1, Engl. tr.), p. 141.

28. A. M. Astaxova et al. (n. 1), p. 523.

29. M. K. Azadovskij (n. 1), p. 38.

30. V. Ja. Propp, *Istoričeskie korni volšebnoj skazki* (Leningrad, 1946); Italian tr.: *Le radici storiche dei racconti di fate* (n.p., 1949).

31. Gleb Struve, *Soviet Russian Literature 1917-50* (Norman, 1951), p. 342.

32. P. G. Bogatyrev, ed., *Russkoe narodnoe poètičeskoe tvorčestvo* (Moscow, 1954; 2nd ed., 1956).

33. A. M. Astaxova, *Russkij bylinnyj èpos na Severe* (Petrozavodsk, 1948).

34. V. Ja. Propp, *Russkij geroičeskij èpos* (Leningrad, 1955; 2nd ed., Moscow, 1958).

35. M. K. Azadovskij, *Literatura i fol'klor* (Leningrad, 1935); *Stat'i o literature i fol'klore* (Moscow-Leningrad, 1960).

36. V. I. Čičerov, *Zimnij period russkogo zemledel'českogo kalendarja XVI-XIX vekov, Trudy Inst. Etnografii im. N. N. Mikluxo-Maklaja*, Vol. 40. (Moscow, 1957); *Voprosy teorii i istorii narodnogo tvorčestva* (Moscow, 1959); *Russkoe narodnoe tvorčestvo* (Moscow, 1959).

37. V. E. Gusev (n. 1, Engl. tr.), p. 54.

38. The most important periodical publications of folklore (and ethnography) in the Soviet Union are: *Siberian Living Antiquity (Sibirskaja živaja starina)*, Vols. I-VIII/IX (Irkutsk, 1923-29); *Artistic Folklore (Xudožestvennyj fol'klor)*, Vols. I-V (Moscow, 1926-29); *Ethnography (Ètnografija)*, Vols. I-V (Moscow-Leningrad, 1926-30), superseded by *Soviet Ethnography (Sovetskaja ètnografija)* (Leningrad, since 1931).

Nonperiodical publications and yearbooks include: *Soviet Folklore (Sovetskij fol'klor)*, Vols. I-VII (Moscow-Leningrad, 1934-41); *Russian Folklore (Russkij fol'klor)* (Moscow-Leningrad, since 1956; 5 vols. so far published). Recently a new important series was established: *Monuments of Russian Folklore (Pamjatniki russkogo fol'klora)* (Moscow-Leningrad, since 1960), of which two volumes have been published so far—a collection of the byliny of the eighteenth and nineteenth centuries, and a collection of the historical songs of the thirteenth to the sixteenth centuries.

39. V. E. Gusev (n. 1, Engl. tr.), p. 53.

Indiana University
Bloomington, Indiana

NORTH
AND
SOUTH AMERICA

LUC LACOURCIÈRE

THE PRESENT STATE OF FRENCH-CANADIAN FOLKLORE STUDIES

THIS paper surveys the origin and development of French-Canadian folklore scholar-ship, and discusses the folklorists who have done the collecting, archiving, analyzing, interpreting, and publishing in this field.

What is French Canada? Let us look at a Canadian map.[1] Even though there is only one province with a predominance of French inhabitants, Canada has no official linguistic and folkloric frontiers within its limits. The French-speaking group consti-tutes one third of the nation's entire population, and in varying proportions there are some French elements in each of the ten provinces. In the valley of the St. Lawrence and in the Province of Quebec the French constitute eighty-two per cent of the popula-tion; in Ontario they constitute ten and four-tenths per cent; in Prince Edward Is-land, sixteen per cent; and in New Brunswick the figure reaches thirty-nine per cent. In the other provinces French-speaking citizens represent less than twelve per cent of the total. From a folkloric point of view, the French-speaking groups that were the most isolated are of greatest importance, for they have best maintained their cus-toms and oral traditions. Such is the case for the Acadians of southern Nova Scotia at La Baie Sainte Marie, the French of Cape Breton, the groups in the western part of Prince Edward Island, and even those of the region of Baie-St-Georges in New-foundland. As for the French population in the West, it is still more scattered. In Ontario, for instance, the French total five hundred thousand, but proportionately this figure is lower than in New Brunswick, for the French comprise only one-tenth of Ontario's total population.[2]

There are two distinct and yet similar groups in French-speaking Canada: the French Canadians and the Acadians. The difference between these two ethnic groups stems from their places of origin in the provinces of France, and from the history and social conditions of their new-found home. The population of Quebec Province now congregated in the St. Lawrence Valley came from the northwestern provinces of France—Normandy, Poitou, and the Parisian region—while the Acadians migrated from the Loire Valley. Another factor distinguishing the linguistic traditions is the absence among the Acadian immigrants of "les filles du roi," the orphan girls edu-cated in the convents of Normandy and of Paris. These girls spoke not provincial but urban French, a fact which exercised an important influence on the evolution of the St. Lawrence Valley French, among whom the orphans were numerous in the period of colonization. The largest contingent of the population arrived and settled before 1700. The tragic history of the Acadians is well known to everybody and I will not dwell upon it, but what happened after the period of wandering is of great interest from the folkloric point of view. Of the original Acadians, two thirds were dispersed and one third was driven back into the woods toward La Baie de Chaleurs and Gas-pésie. Some of those dispersed returned to form many little Acadias that lived and grew without much contact with each other, in Nova Scotia, Prince Edward Island,

New Brunswick, and also in Gaspésie and les Iles-de-la-Madeleine in the Province of Quebec. The people of Quebec did not experience the same turbulence because the Indian wars, the Seven Years War, and the attendant political strife passed them by.

There are two interesting traits that characterize the Quebec group, traits observable not only in one family but also in one and the same individual. These characteristics are, first, the attachment of the sedentary peasant to his soil and, second, the adventurous spirit of the *coureurs de bois* and *voyageurs* who discovered the American continent and who left so many traces in the place names of the United States. This spirit of adventure manifested in the early history of the New World has persisted until our day in the modern lumberman. Parenthetically we may notice that the *coureurs de bois* and *voyageurs* were instrumental in creating a third language. Many of them married Indian women, whose descendants live today in Manitoba along the Red River and speak a *metis* which is analogous to the Negro creole French of Louisiana. This small ethnic group has been very well studied by historians, but unfortunately, with the exception of a few recordings, no folkloric investigation has been conducted among them.

Historical and social phenomena influenced the folklore of Quebec. The territories along the St. Lawrence were colonized under the seigneurial regime, which was subsequently abolished in 1854. Its influence appears not only in the topographical divisions of the territory of the older parishes but also in the customs and architecture which have persisted until today. After 1830, all the new lands were occupied under the English tenure system which divided them into townships of ten square miles.

From the beginning of Canadian history to the middle of the nineteenth century, folklore and oral tradition were in what we could call *"un âge d'or."* They continued developing naturally and spontaneously. Even the Seven Years War and the cession of Canada to the English offered no obstacles; quite to the contrary, these important historical events created a new climate in which the peasant's attachment to the soil became more pronounced and his French traditions more deeply rooted.

Because of the attitude of the king of France, who never allowed the establishment of a press in New France, and of the English Government which consistently, after the conquest of Canada, used English as an instrument of propaganda for introducing that language and Protestantism, there was a complete lack of publication in French and a scarcity of French schools. This period, which appears to some historians as a new dark ages, was truly the golden age of oral literature. During the nineteenth century, however, the situation changed little by little. In addition to the illiterate peasant masses there emerged an intellectual elite, composed mostly of clergy and professionals, but also including journalists and statesmen, which became increasingly powerful. To this group belonged the first writers of French Canada. Some, without knowing the word "folklore" (which was coined only in 1846), tried to create a Canadian literature based on their traditions, under the influence of French romantic writers who were directing attention for the first time toward peasant life. Moved by nationalistic ambitions, they exploited traditional themes, chiefly mores and legends rather than tales and songs. For example, these writers emphasized popular ceremonies like the May Day *(plantation du mai)* before the seigneurial manor, and *les feux de la Saint-Jean* on St. John the Baptist's Day, the 24th of June. This last holiday is still celebrated as the national fête of the French Canadians, with *défilés*, parades with allegoric and historic pageants, banquets and patriotic speeches. The aim of these writers was literary creation and not the recording of the oral expression of the people. To this group of Quebec authors we owe the most characteristic works of the old Canadian literature. Two of the foremost writers were Philippe Aubert de Gaspé and Joseph Charles Taché. While the former describes with great understanding the seigneurial and peasant life of *Les Anciens Canadiens*[3] (1864), the latter depicts in his *Forestiers et Voyageurs*[4] (1863) the life and legends of the lumberman. He also reserves a prominent place in his writings for the voyageur and the coureur de bois, who first disseminated folklore in Canada. These two writers, however, should be considered rather litterateurs than folklorists.

In the same period appears the first true folklorist in the person of Ernest Gagnon. Born in 1839, he had the opportunity to complete his musical studies in France at a time when France was organizing its first collections of folksongs by the decree of Napoleon III under the leadership of Jean Jacques Ampère. Upon his return to Canada, Gagnon collected and published in 1865 his book, *Chansons populaires du Canada,* containing one hundred songs. This collection is of capital importance in the studies of folklore, for three important reasons. (1) Being a fine musician Gagnon noted his melodies with great precision and without changing them. (2) He included data on his informants and the regions where he collected. (3) He published the first songbook of its kind. Consequently he is as important for folksong study in Canada as is Child for ballad scholarship in the United States.

Unfortunately, Gagnon was an isolated case in the nineteenth century. He did not have disciples to follow in his footsteps, and no one else did any collecting for many years after him. Meanwhile elements of folklore continued to appear in several literary works of the period.[5]

In 1892, a branch of the American Folklore Society for Canada and French Canada was established under the influence of Alcée Fortier, the prominent Louisiana writer and folklorist, who came especially to Montreal to stimulate folklore studies. At that time, he succeeded only in gathering together a group of literati from both the French as well as the English groups: men like Louis Fréchette, Honoré Beaugrand, and Dr. William Henry Drummond. The accomplishments of this branch society were meager. Fortier recruited people who were too old and who could not, upon their death, be replaced by younger students of folklore. In the years following the organization of the society, its work was limited to literary endeavors, which did nevertheless direct attention and interest toward folklore.[6]

A more important development than these literary attempts at folklore was the interest in folk speech manifested by an alert group of scholars, including several professors at Laval University under the leadership of Adjutor Rivard. This group is responsible for founding in 1902 the *Société du Parler français au Canada,* still in existence. The important contribution of this society was the publication, for sixteen years (1902-18) of the review, *Bulletin du Parler français,* and of the *Glossaire du Parler français au Canada* (1930) in both of which the folklorist can find valuable items pertaining to folk traditions. Presently the Society is engaged in preparing a revised glossary and a linguistic atlas covering Canadian and Acadian French speech.

In the last quarter of the nineteenth century, folklore studies in France were developed by philologists, dialectologists, and romanists who became interested in medieval texts of folk literature. For this reason, the earliest French folklore publications are to be found in the linguistic and medieval journals of the latter part of the nineteenth century. During this period, two important folklore reviews flourished in France: *Les Traditions Populaires* (1886-1918) which counted among its contributors prominent names like Paul Sébillot, and *Mélusine* (1877-1912) whose editors were Eugène Rolland and Henri Gaidoz.

In 1900, on the occasion of the Universal Exposition in Paris, the first international congress of folklore was held there. Honoré Beaugrand was sent to this congress as a representative from Canada. In Paris he met Paul Sébillot who persuaded him to undertake research on the folktale upon his return to Canada. Beaugrand returned home full of enthusiasm and plans for work, but unfortunately he died almost immediately upon his arrival. No folkloristic investigation of importance was undertaken thenceforth until the time of Marius Barbeau, with the exception of the dissertation by Cyrus MacMillan written at Harvard in 1909 under the direction of Professor Kittredge. MacMillan, a Canadian from Prince Edward Island, made a compilation of songs already published by Gagnon and lesser collectors, and added song texts he himself had collected in an area extending from the province of Quebec to Prince Edward Island. Each song and group of songs are preceded by a discussion of the genre and parallels with French songs. But since only a few persons have read this unpublished dissertation, it never has exercised any real influence.[7]

The turning point of folklore studies in Canada came with the appearance on the scene of Marius Barbeau, a young anthropologist who had returned to Canada in 1911, after three years of university study in England and France, to work for the National Museum of Canada. His early research dealt with Huron and Wyandot mythology. At a joint meeting of the American Anthropological Association and the American Folklore Society, in 1914, he met Franz Boas, who in an informal discussion asked him some questions about the existence of popular tales in French Canada. Barbeau had no answer at the moment, but after thinking it over he remembered that while collecting Indian material among the Hurons at Lorette, near Quebec, he had rejected stories which had no relation to Indian mythology as being decidedly too French. Upon his return to Canada, Barbeau at once reactivated the Canadian Folklore Society with new members. Strongly supported by the National Museum, the revived society achieved a much higher prestige than the old.

Barbeau then started collecting French folklore among the Hurons and in his own family, especially from his father. Subsequently financed by the National Museum, he continued to collect in the Province of Quebec. Between 1915 and 1935, he successively and intensively gathered tales and songs in the Beauce Region, Kamouraska, Charlevoix, Saguenay, and on the Gaspé Peninsula. He presented his findings to the Royal Society of Canada, and through this channel he was fortunate to recruit his best collector in the field of folklore, and especially folksongs, E. Z. Massicotte. Among others of the group whom he attracted were Evelyn Bolduc, Gustave Lanctôt, and Adélard Lambert, who collected, on their own, folktales, legends, and songs. The major portion of their collections appeared in eight French numbers of the JOURNAL OF AMERICAN FOLKLORE, between 1916 and 1950, but much of their material still remains unpublished in the files of the National Museum in Ottawa.

Throughout his long life, Marius Barbeau has never stopped exploring new fields of research and collecting. To the fields already mentioned he added studies in folk art, sculpture, architecture, embroidery, cooking, and all the crafts, both in French Canada as well as among the Indians of the Northwest coast. His Indian studies include linguistics, social organization, and arts and crafts. He is well known for his books on totem poles and other Indian subjects. His bibliography included 578 titles in 1946 and is nearing a thousand today.

The group gathered around Marius Barbeau at the beginning of his career worked successfully together until the thirties, when their time gradually became occupied by other duties. In the late thirties Barbeau attracted another group of followers, including Joseph-Thomas Leblanc, François Brassard, and myself. In 1937 Leblanc, who was a journalist, read Barbeau's *Romancero du Canada,* which had just come off the press, and became so interested in folksongs that, before his untimely death in 1943 at the age of forty-three, he had collected twelve hundred Acadian folksongs through the correspondents of his paper, l'*Evangeline,* published in Moncton, New Brunswick. François Brassard, organist and composer in the town of Jonquière, collected close to one thousand songs in the Saguenay region and in northern Ontario. As for myself, I became interested in folklore studies in 1939 through Miss Evelyn Bolduc, who directed me toward Mr. Barbeau. I was further stimulated in continuing my studies by a Guggenheim fellowship in 1943. A year after my return to Laval University I was asked to offer folklore courses and to organize *Les Archives de Folklore.*

The basic course in the folklore program at Laval University is usually a general introductory course in international and Canadian folklore and in the evolution of the discipline. It includes a discussion of methods of collecting folklore in the field and an initiation into library research. There follow specialized courses in the folktale, folksong, place names, traditional costume, and folk arts. Within the framework of the program related courses are offered intermittently, such as the folklore of regional groups (Acadians of New Brunswick, Nova Scotia, Prince Edward Island, and so on), and occupational folklore pertaining to forestry, farming, and domestic acts. In addition, literature courses related to folklore are offered yearly. These include "Popular traditions in the works of Rabelais and other authors of the sixteenth century" (who, by the way, are very important for French folklore studies), "Folklore of La Fontaine, Molière, Perrault," and others. A few years ago we offered a course in "Literary forms of popular tales," and this past year I lectured on "Les Contes de Voltaire," attempting to separate the traditional from the creative elements in the *contes.*

The practical side of our folklore program includes initiation into collecting and practice in transcribing, identifying, and classifying the recorded materials. Experience in collecting is introduced in two ways: either we take small groups of students, two or three at a time, into the homes of informants where the students observe and note how a scholarly collection is compiled, or we bring good informants, whom we know very well, to the classroom where we give a demonstration session of collecting. After the collection, the students learn to transcribe the tape and to identify the genre of the material, dividing it into tales, legends, local anecdotes, songs, and so on, after which comes the classification and indexing on special cards. In addition, the students may transcribe tapes of already collected materials available in the Archives. Every folklore student is responsible for the transcription of a minimum of one hour of recorded material.

For specialists, a master's or doctor's thesis in folklore is required. The twenty theses already completed at Laval represent a diversity of subjects and a valuable addition to our manuscript collections.[8] The main kinds of dissertations written so far are (1) exhaustive studies of folklife in individual parishes, such as Sister Marie-Ursule's study of a Canadian parish, and ones by Corinne Saucier and Elizabeth Brandon on specific parishes in Louisiana; (2) Nora Dawson's examination of material culture in St. Pierre, Isle d'Orléans; (3) James La Follette's linguistic study of folktales; and

(4) collections of songs with musical and linguistic commentaries, by Alfred Poui-
nard, Russell Scott Young, and Claude Prey. At present, there is in preparation a
dissertation on 350 variants of one song (220 from Canada, 130 from France), "La
Fille à la Fontaine." We also have had bibliographical theses on the works of Canadian collectors such as Joseph-Thomas Leblanc and Adélard Lambert, theses on
folklore in literature, and some on more specialized subjects including children's folklore and individual customs such as the "Quête de la Chandeleur" in Cape Breton.
Last but not least, some doctoral candidates have written comparative monographs on
individual folktales which they first collected and then studied. Father Germain
Lemieux from Sudbury studied Aarne-Thompson Type 938, "*Placidas* (Eustacius),"
and Sister Ste-Hélène currently is writing a thesis on Types 706 and 712.[9]

In the Archives at Laval, our aim is to gather all the information possible on the
folklore of French Canada. We first concentrated on building a folklore library of
Canadian and international reference books and reviews. We also started a collection
of records. Presently we have a library of about four thousand volumes. From the beginning we have been compiling a complete bibliography of Canadiana, printed and
in manuscript, which we subsequently classify and file. By now we have a considerable bibliography of works on Canadian folklore produced in Canada as well as in
other countries. In compiling this work we patterned ourselves on the *Manuel Bibli-
ographique du Folklore Français* of Arnold Van Gennep.

Collecting is a very important activity of the Archives. It is done mostly in the
summer, but also during weekends of the school year, both by the regular staff and
by students and associated folklorists, who deposit the originals or copies of their collections in the Archives. Presently we have more than 17,000 items on 800 tapes, in
other words 1600 hours of recording. Some of these collections were made possible by
special grants from the National Museum of Canada, from the Provincial Government, or from private foundations. I shall mention the names of a few of our collaborators whose collections (in manuscript or on tapes) are of particular interest.
Madeleine Doyon, for ten years secretary of the Archives, assembled the material on
folk costume covering the entire Province of Quebec. She has deposited 1500 drawings of items of original apparel, accompanied by detailed descriptions. Simonne
Voyer, professor of physical education and folk dance specialist, collected about 200
folk dance figures, from Montreal to Acadia and the Magdalene Islands. Dominique
Gauthier from Shippagan, New Brunswick, a country doctor, became interested in
collecting oral traditions as a hobby after seeing us work in his territory. His collection now amounts to 700 items, including tales and songs. Father Anselme, a Capucin
priest, returned to his place of birth in Cape Breton in Cheticamp, where he amassed
300 songs and a few tales from his relatives. Russell Scott Young, instructor at Groton
School, Massachusetts, collected 700 songs in the region of Quebec and the Magdalene
Islands. He has already published a book of songs and has two others in preparation.
(He is the folklorist who is studying the 350 variants of the "Fille à la fontaine.")
Father Germain Lemieux, professor at Sudbury University, collects tales and songs in
Ontario, some of which were published by the *Société Historique du Nouvel-Ontario*.[10]
He has already started local archives, and is active in recruiting student fieldworkers
in his province.

The permanent staff of the Archives, comprising Monseigneur Félix-Antoine
Savard, Conrad Laforte, Roger Matton, and myself, has collected 6500 items of oral
tradition, mostly tales and songs. Our research has covered all French Canada,

including Acadia which had not previously been explored by the National Museum. These collections, as well as those on which dissertations have been written, are deposited in the Archives, where they have been transcribed, analyzed, and classified. The items of each collection are numbered from "1" ad infinitum, and all pertinent information is entered in a special "topographic" file.

For each card of this file, four of five other cards are made for a cross-filing system regarding informants, places of collection, and types for tales, legends, and songs. For tales we use the Aarne-Thompson *Types of the Folk-Tale,* with the addition of Paul Delarue's new types and others that we created ourselves. For legends and local history we have a classification which we initiated, patterning ourselves on Stith Thompson's *Motif-Index of Folk-Literature.* Proverbs, place names, riddles, games, folk remedies, and lesser items are filed alphabetically.

The classification of French folksongs has from the beginning created an almost insurmountable problem for collectors, because of the variety and number of traditional, semi-literary and literary songs found in oral circulation. Neither the French nor the Canadian folklorists were ever able to arrive at a satisfactory system of classification. The printed collections were limited to too small a number of songs, and they used in the same classification elements of identification that did not permit establishment of the variants of the same song. By this I mean that confusion stemmed from classifying the song by *subject:* love songs, military songs, "complaintes," and the like; by *social functions:* work songs, dance songs, ceremonial songs, and so on; by the *form* or *prosody;* or again by the *age* of the song.

Let us take, for instance, a song like "La Chanson du Moine Blanc" that was published by Christophe Ballard in 1723 as a dance *ronde.* The same song was classified in Switzerland by Rossat as a *chanson de carnaval;* in Canada it has neither one nor the other of these characteristics, but is considered a gay, satirical song.[11] Thus, the song overlaps different types, and any editor can classify it according to his own whim. At the Archives we were confronted with this difficulty. We have a catalogue of all the French-Canadian songs that have been printed in books, pamphlets, and reviews; we have all the songs collected since 1942; and recently we acquired copies of those collected for the National Museum by Barbeau, Massicotte, Carmen Roy and others. Our complete collection amounts to 38,000 variants. The problem was to recognize these variants and to group them together, a task not always easy when stanzas are lacking, when the first line of the same song differs, or when two different songs have the same opening line. Thus there was no other way but to define a type under a common title for each song and to group variants accordingly in alphabetical order. In this way, the common title resembles a number in the Aarne-Thompson index. For a song that is published, a reference to a very well-known songbook suffices to identify it; if it is unpublished and has only a few variants, then we are forced to reproduce the first stanza and sometimes the refrain and a summary of the contents under the common title on the filing card. Secondary titles are also included, with cross references referring to the common title.

With this system we realized that the 38,000 known variants of French-Canadian folksongs represented 2,600 common titles or types. My assistant, Conrad Laforte, has been working with this catalogue since 1952. During these years we did not intend to publish our classification system, but since the National Museum staff also had the problem of classifying their songs, the director of the Museum, Jacques Rousseau, sent to our Archives the head of the folklore department, Carmen Roy, already well known for her research and thesis on the *Littérature orale en Gaspesie,* to study our system of classifying songs as well as our system of filing other materials. As a result of the discussions during her visit, the National Museum decided to adopt our classification system for the folksong. It then became clear to us that the publication of our system would be useful to all the collectors of French folksong in France, Belgium, Switzerland, and Louisiana. We started to prepare the volume for publication without delay, and 125 copies of our catalogue of the 2,600 common titles was published in 1958.[12] Specialists in the French folksong have made many suggestions for the revised edition that we have in our plans.

Let me finish by briefly discussing the publications of our organization. Between 1946 and 1960, eight numbers of *Les Archives de Folklore* appeared. Three of these numbers are special monographs prepared as dissertations. Sister Marie-Ursule's *Civilisation traditionelle des Lavalois* (numbers 5 and 6) describes the complete folklife and folklore of a single parish in the vicinity of Quebec. It contains a large collection of oral texts: games, riddles, proverbs, omens, songs, legends, and tales. These last two divisions are analyzed according to the Aarne-Thompson Type-Index and Thompson's *Motif-Index of Folk-Literature*. Sister Marie-Ursule's book was so well received in France that Paul Delarue, her leading folklorist, wrote that "no other monograph so completely presenting the folklore of a French-speaking village has ever been written."[13] The second monograph (number 7) is by Russell Scott Young, an American musician and teacher specializing in French folk music. This is a *recueil* of 50 songs, entitled *Vieilles Chansons de Nouvelle-France.*

The first four volumes of *Les Archives de Folklore* contained a series of studies and documents concerning different aspects of French folklore in America, written or assembled by leading men in this field. A few articles were contributed in English by American collaborators. I should like to mention one study in particular, the Bio-Bibliography of Marius Barbeau, which is a key reference for his work in French-Canadian as well as in Indian folklore up to 1946.

The publication of these *cahiers,* well illustrated with photographs and drawings, some of them in color, was very expensive. We were forced to discontinue or at least to space the publication of the issues after 1951. However, we started again in 1960, since Les Presses Universitaires Laval have assumed the expense of publication that at first I assumed personally. Moreover, Les Presses have since received the support of the Canada Council of Arts and the Provincial Secretariat.

During the interval, we accumulated in the Archives many valuable works worthy of publication, such as the dissertations mentioned above. And our files are overflowing with new, well-classified documents based on fieldwork. For example, the "Type Index of French Folktales in North America," still on cards, contains more than five thousand versions identified and summarized from printed, manuscript, and recorded sources. It is probably the most important collection of folktales in any language in North America.

We also wish to publish a "Bibliographie raisonnée du folklore français d'Amerique," on which I have been working for two years with a special grant from the Rockefeller Foundation. This exhaustive bibliography will probably require two volumes, the first one devoted to oral traditions and the second to customs and material lore. For the moment we are concentrating on the first part, which is divided into speech, personal names, place names, proverbs, riddles, games and rhymes, superstitions, legends, tales, songs, music, and dance.[14] It will be more than a simple list of references, since every item receives a commentary. The work claims to be at the same time a history of research in oral lore, because references are given chronologically and geographically according to the principal French areas in North America. In the commentary for each item, we give a brief summary of the publication's contents and try to point out the originality of every contribution, separating the authentic and properly documented folk tradition from all the derived forms of applied folklore which too often refer to secondary sources.

In assuming this task, we are conscious of the difficulty of presenting final judgments. But in the introductions to each of the main divisions of the bibliography, we discuss the criteria which permit an exact appreciation of every contribution. A general index of authors referring to each entry by number will permit an easy access to a surprising amount of information on French folklore in North America, gathered in Canada, and in other countries as well, by authors ranging from the early travelers to modern fieldworkers, and from literary authors to journalists. To our mind, this cumulative bibliography is not an end in itself, but an indispensable tool for further research in a complex field that deserves the attention of linguists, historians, sociologists, ethnomusicologists, and anthropologists as well as folklorists.

NOTES

1. Map insert entitled "Distribution de la population d'origine française en 1941" in *Études sur le Parler français au Canada,* by La Société du Parler français au Canada 1902-1952 (Quebec, Les Presses Universitaires Laval, 1955), following p. 56. As indicated on this map, each black point represents one thousand French inhabitants.

2. In this paper, I do not mention in detail the French groups of the United States in New England, Missouri, Louisiana, and elsewhere.

3. Philippe Aubert de Gaspé, *Les Anciens Canadiens* (Quebec, 1864). This book had several editions and is still very popular. There are three English translations with different titles: *Canadians of Old,* tr. Georgiana M. Pennee (Quebec, 1864); *Seigneur d'Haberville (The Canadians of Old), A Romance of the Fall of New France,* tr. Georgiana M. Pennee, introd. by T. G. Marquis (Toronto, 1929); *Cameron of Loheil,* by Charles G. D. Roberts (Boston, 1905). See also by P. A. de Gaspé, *Mémoires* (Ottawa, 1866).

4. *Forestiers et Voyageurs, étude de moeurs* was first published in *Les Soirées canadiennes* (Quebec, 1863), vol. 3, pp. 13-260. The latest edition, with a preface by Luc Lacourcière, appeared in Montreal, Éditions Fides, 1946 (Collection du Nénuphar, No. 3).

5. One can find such literary pieces utilizing folklore in that period in the three following publications: *Les Soirées canadiennes,* 5 vols. (Québec, 1861-65); *Le Foyer canadien,* 8 vols. (Québec, 1863-66); and *Les Nouvelles Soirées canadiennes,* 7 vols. (Montreal, 1882-86).

6. See Marius Barbeau, "The Folklore Movement in Canada," *Journal of American Folklore,* LVI (1943), 166-168.

7. Cyrus MacMillan, "The Folk-Songs of Canada" (doctoral diss., 2 vols., Harvard University, 1909).

8. The following folklore dissertations at Laval have been published:

    A. Doctoral dissertations: Soeur Marie Ursule, *La Civilisation traditionelle des Lavalois* (Quebec, Les Presses Universitaires Laval, 1951). 403 pp., ill. musique (*Les Archives de Folklore,* 5 and 6).

    Nora Dawson, *La Vie traditionnelle à Saint-Pierre (Ile d'Orléans)* (Quebec, Les Presses Universitaires Laval, 1960). 190 pp., ill. (*Les Archives de Folklore,* 8).

    Corinne Lelia Saucier, *Histoire et Traditions de la paroisse des Avoyelles en Louisiane.* Part of this dissertation appeared under the title of *Traditions de la paroisse des Avoyelles en Louisiane* (Philadelphia, American Folklore Society, 1956). 162 pp. (Memoirs of AFS, Volume 47).

    Elizabeth Brandon, *Moeurs et Langue de la paroisse Vermillon en Louisiane.* Parts of this dissertation have been published under the title of *La Paroisse de Vermillon* in *Le Bayou,* University of Houston, Texas: (No. 64, winter 1955, pp. 449-468; No. 65, spring 1956, pp. 64-86; No. 66, winter 1956, pp. 164-180; No. 68, winter 1956, pp. 269-281; No. 69, spring 1957, pp. 358-367; No. 70, summer 1957, pp. 420-431).

    B. Master's thesis: Russell Scott Young, *Vieilles Chansons de Nouvelle France* (Quebec,

Les Presses Universitaires Laval, 1956). 129 pp., ill., musique (*Les Archives de Folklore, 7*).

9. The tale-types mentioned appear in Stith Thompson's *The Types of the Folk-Tale* (FF Communications, No. 74, Helsinki, 1928), which is a revision and translation of Antti Aarne's *Verzeichnis der Märchentypen* (FF Communications, No. 3, Helsinki, 1910).

10. Germain Lemieux, S.J., *Folklore franco-ontarien; Chansons* (1949); *Folklore franco-ontarien; Chansons II* (1950); *Contes populaires franco-ontariens* (1953); *Contes populaires franco-ontariens II* (1958). See also his *Index analytique des 35 Documents de la Societé historique du Nouvel-Ontario* (1959). These are all published in Sudbury, Ontario, by La Societé historique du Nouvel-Ontario, and are 40 to 60 pages long. They appear in the series "Documents historiques" as nos. 17, 20, 25, 35, and 36.

11. J.-B. Christophe Ballard, *Le Moine Blanc,* cited by Eugene Rolland, *Recueil de Chansons populaires,* vol. I (Paris, 1883), 149-152, and vol. II (Paris, 1886), 104-105; Arthur Rossat and Edgar Piguet, *Les Chansons populaires recueillies dans la Suisse romande,* vol. II, first part (Basel, Societé suisse des Traditions populaires, 1930), 56-60. For a complete discussion of this song see Luc Lacourcière, "Les Transformations d'une chanson folklorique: Du Moine tremblant au Rapide-Blanc" in *Recherches sociographiques,* I (Quebec, Les Presses Universitaires Laval, Oct.-Dec. 1960), 401-434.

12. Conrad Laforte, *Le Catalogue de la Chanson folklorique française.* Preface by Luc Lacourcière (Quebec, 1958).

13. Paul Delarue, *Le Mois d'Ethnographie française* (Paris, Musée National des Arts et Traditions Populaires, vol. V, no. 9, Nov. 1951), 103-104.

14. One section of the Bibliography has been published: Luc Lacourcière, "Bibliographie raisonnée de l'Anthroponymie canadienne," in *Mémoires de la Societé généalogique canadienne-française* (Montreal, vol. IX, nos. 3-4, July-Oct. 1958), 153-174.

Laval University
Quebec, Canada

FRANCES GILLMOR

ORGANIZATION OF FOLKLORE STUDY IN MEXICO

THE INTERESTS of a number of scholarly organizations in Mexico touch on folklore to a greater or lesser degree. The Sociedad Folklórica de México, as its name indicates, is primarily concerned with folklore. Other groups have folklore as a secondary interest, and in their investigations and publications a folklorist is likely to find material of great value to him.

The Sociedad Folklórica de México is a society that my friends in Mexico used to refer to as my "secret society" because when I first started going down to Mexico twenty years ago I had to hunt each year for its current place of meeting. It was always moving around. But whether it was meeting in a music college, a university building, or a private home, it was always a working society, publishing the *Anuario de la Sociedad Folklórica de México*[1] under the editorial direction of the president, Vicente T. Mendoza, and the secretary, Virginia Rodríguez Rivera de Mendoza.[2]

These two distinguished folklorists have made many studies both individually and in collaboration. Virginia Rodríguez Rivera, who has usually written under her maiden name, likes to work, she says, with little things. She has worked on particular beliefs and their distribution in Mexico, such as *Nagualismo* and witches. Her articles and detailed tabulations of these studies in the *Anuario* show her careful workmanship.[3] Vicente Mendoza, a composer himself, has worked especially with folk music. His many publications include books on the *romance* and the *corrido,* and on children's folksongs.[4]

The *Anuario,* as one will discover by looking at its classified table of contents, deals with the main types of folklore in Mexico. I find it particularly valuable in providing texts of folk dramas; for a long time it was the only publication that frequently contained texts of folk plays. When I published my little group of texts of "Moors and Christians" and their variants at the University of Arizona,[5] I hoped that we might be establishing a series, but Arizona did not continue publishing in that direction. Now the University of California is producing a folklore series which has already included two excellent volumes on folk dramas: one of them, by George C. Barker, with a translation in English; the other, by Stanley L. Robe, with only Spanish texts.[6] But up to this time the *Anuario de la Sociedad Folklórica de México* had been the publication which placed most emphasis on this very important genre of folklore.

The *Anuario* deals with folk custom too. I found it useful when I was asked about the making of *pulque,* a drink with much preconquest religious and mythological background, whose popularity still continues. At dusk, all over central Mexico, one sees the *tlachiqueros* going out to the maguey fields with an interesting contraption on their shoulders—a skin container and sucking apparatus in which the honeywater of the maguey is sucked up. It is later fermented very quickly and sold. *Pulque* has about the same intoxicating quality as a mild beer, is pale white in color and a little sour, and tastes somewhat like buttermilk, cool and refreshing. It has some interesting aspects of fermentation which a chemist at the University of Arizona wanted to study. On the spur of the moment, when he asked me for information, I was able to produce for him from the *Anuario* a detailed account of that particular centuries-old procedure in Mexico when he could not find it described in any other source.[7] This is an example of the odd bits of information one can get from the *Anuario*. It is a good solid publication, one that is always written and edited conscientiously.

The Society as such has been careful to study modern methods of folklore. It arranged in 1945 to have Ralph Steele Boggs down to give a course in folklore technique at the National University. His own *Bibliografía del Folklore Mexicano* (Mexico, 1939) is, of course, one of the students' main entries into Mexican folklore.

The *Anuario* was supported during the first ten years of its existence (1938-48) by the National University of Mexico, but the Society itself is not a University society, although there are University people in it. The first issue contained a statement by the then Rector of the University saying that University support for such a publication had been requested by the Pan American Circle of Folklore. Its founder in Brazil had sent a memorial to the National University through its delegate in Mexico, who was, of course, Professor Vicente Mendoza. The intention was that Mexico, by means of the *Anuario's* publication, should be the first American country to contribute to the coordination of folklore investigation which the Pan American Circle had undertaken. This relationship indicates something of the complicated structures which build up in Latin American countries into national and international organizations. Due to lack of funds, however, the support of the University was withdrawn from the *Anuario* after 1954. In 1955 Volume 10 was backed by two men, one of whom was the *secretario* and the other *oficial mayor* de la Secretaría de Hacienda de México. Hope now is pinned to such private sponsorship for single issues.

A number of publications other than the *Anuario* have come forth from the Sociedad Folklórica. Under its auspices valuable short studies emphasizing methods have appeared in two small volumes in 1953 and 1958: *Aportaciones a la Investigación Folklórica de México* and *Nuevas Aportaciones a la Investigación Folklórica de México*. Julio Sánchez García has compiled the first volume of a *Calendario Folklórico de Fiestas de la República Mexicana* (Mexico, 1956), dealing with fiestas of fixed dates, with further publication planned on fiestas of movable dates and fiestas of special occasions.

Several institutes, though folklore is not their primary concern, in one way or another, either through investigations that they carry on or through publications they maintain, aid and abet folklore studies in Mexico. These institutes are research and publication units within the University structure. The people on their staff may or may not be teaching classes in the University. Often their whole time is spent in research. The Instituto de Investigaciones Estéticas has issued distinguished publications. It is there that Professor Mendoza has his office, and, as has been pointed out, the Instituto has published some of his books. People seek him out at the Instituto to consult with him on folklore and often to use his personal library, which contains important folklore series from all over the world, and a great deal, of course, on Latin American and Mexican folklore in particular.

The director of this Institute of Aesthetic Investigations is Justino Fernández. His interest is in art criticism rather than in folklore, but folklore comes into his concerns.

For example, he has written an outstanding work on Coatlicue, the Goddess with the Skirt of Serpents, whose massive statue stands in the Museo Nacional of Mexico. He analyzes the whole sculpture from the standpoint of the religious backgrounds of the Aztecs and the aesthetic forms of that culture, in an anthropological, artistic, and folkloristic study that is very exciting. From this study one can see that he sympathizes with interdisciplinary research. He reaches into many creative and scholarly fields—a catholicity appropriate for a director of aesthetic studies. His book, *Coatlicue: Estética del Arte Indígena Antiguo* (1954), was not, however, published by his own institute but by the Centro de Estudios Filosóficos, which is also connected with the National University and is publishing a great deal of interesting material.

The Instituto de Historia at the University, like the other institutes, reaches out to that interdisciplinary area in which folklore finds its concerns. I might mention its recent publication of one of Sahagún's many manuscripts.[8] Fray Bernardino de Sahagún, as is well known, came to Mexico as a young man, only a few years after Cortés, and died at an advanced age, after devoting his full life to studies of the Aztec culture which was, of course, still alive and flourishing when the Spaniards arrived, and which to an extraordinary degree lives on in present-day Mexico. His work was praised for its scientific completeness by Ruth Benedict in her presidential address to the American Anthropological Association a few years ago which dealt with the contribution of the humanities to scientific method.[9] Sahagún provides important background data for the student of Mexican folklore.

Another publication of the Instituto de Historia is of special interest from the standpoint of international publishing arrangements. The *Códice Xolotl,* one of the Texcoco group of picture manuscripts, with commentary by Charles Dibble of the University of Utah, was published by the University of Utah and the Universidad Nacional Autónoma de México through the Instituto de Historia.[10] It is an historical rather than a calendrical codex, and shows the details even to conversation which can be given by pictures. Dibble opened up interesting considerations in pointing out that Ixtlilxochitl, a late sixteenth and early seventeenth century chronicler of Texcoco,[11] writing as was customary among the chroniclers of the period with long quoted conversations, includes some conversations which were also pictured between the speech scrolls of this codex.[12]

The institutes mentioned so far are all related to the Universidad Nacional Autónoma de México, which also offers folklore courses. Some are given during summer school to Americans; Frances Toor gave one for a long time until her death. Her *Treasury of Mexican Folkways* (New York, 1947), in English, gives a useful survey of Mexican folklore. From 1925 to 1937 she published *Mexican Folkways* (after 1933 with irregular special issues). This magazine, in parallel English and Spanish, is a valuable source on Mexican folklore. It has been indexed by Ralph Steele Boggs.[13] Patricia Fent Ross, who writes pleasant accounts of folklife in Mexico,[14] has also given the summer school course in folklore, shedding human light on the great folk core of the country for the American visitor. Vicente T. Mendoza gives advanced courses, particularly in folk music.

Leaving the University with its institutes, publications and classes, let us mention other organizations which give some support to folklore study. El Colegio de México, a distinguished and scholarly institution which cooperates with the University, has had an interesting separate history. Its forerunner was the Casa de España, founded by Spanish intellectuals who were political refugees. After that aspect of its history ended, it was established in 1940 as it is now and has drawn aid from the Rockefeller Foundation, the National School of Anthropology, the Benjamin Franklin Library, and other supporting scholarship funds. It is the publisher of Vicente T. Mendoza's already mentioned *Lírica Infantil de México.*

El Colegio Nacional through lectures and publications has taken some interest in folklore—mainly, so far, through history or mythology. Its *Memorias,* beginning in 1946, contain many papers by Alfonso Caso on the preconquest material still so important in understanding modern folklore.[15] Alfonso Reyes, in a series of lectures on Greek literature, gave one in 1959 on Greek legends of the sea. El Colegio Nacional offers lecture series on all fields of the sciences and the humanities. Whenever I read the quotation on its lecture programs from Article 17 of the law which established it in 1943, I feel that it is the kind of institution about which academic persons dream. Translated, the article reads: "Attendance at the lectures shall be completely open and free. It shall not carry matriculation or registration of any type, nor shall an attendance list be passed. There shall be no tests or examinations of any kind, and no certificates, diplomas, or degrees shall be given." The motto of this institution devoted to adult education is "Liberty to Know."

The Instituto Nacional Indigenista, as its name indicates, is particularly concerned with Indian affairs. Headed by Alfonso Caso, it coordinates many of the government activities relating to Indians to avoid overlapping and duplication with services in health, education, and so on. It acts in an advisory capacity, carries on anthropological fieldwork, and issues publications, such as the *Bibliografía Indigenista de México y Centro America, 1850-1950,* done by Manuel Germán Parra and Wigberto Jiménez Moreno in 1954, with quite a long section on folklore—not all of it related to Indians. Another publication is a collection of Indian songs of Mexico, *Cantos Indígenas de México,* by Concha Michel (1951). Many of its publications on specific Indian groups contain folktales.

The Instituto Indigenista Interamericano was established in 1940 by the first Inter-American Indian Conference. It is involved with about seventeen different countries. The representatives on the Council are political appointees, not necessarily anthropologists. The directors, however, have been distinguished anthropologists. Manuel Gamio, director for many years until his death, was succeeded in 1960 by Miguel León-Portilla, whose particular concern has been with Nahuatl linguistic texts and the philosophy of the Nahuatl-speaking people.[16] The Instituto's magazine, *América Indígena,* publishes material of folkloric interest: for example, articles on survivals of the pre-Columbian intellectual culture among contemporary Indians,[17] on folk medicine,[18] and on folk art.[19]

Another organizational set-up of interest to folklorists is the Instituto Nacional de Antropología e Historia. It "depends from"—to use a phrase frequent in descriptions of institutional relationships in Mexico—the Secretaría de Educación, a division of the Cabinet. This institute has charge of all museums and all colonial monuments. One of the most important of the museums is the Museo Nacional de Antropología e Historia, which has a documents section presided over by Eulalia Guzman. It is an historical archive mainly, but Merle E. Simmons in his book on *corridos* says he found broadsides there—a whole stack of them.[20]

The Museum also is the headquarters of the Sociedad Mexicana de Antropología. In the distant past, the Sociedad Folklórica was part of the Sociedad de Antropología, and then became independent. The Sociedad Mexicana de Antropología has published since 1939 the *Revista Mexicana de Estudios Antropológicos,* which sometimes contains matters of folklore interest. Finally, the Museum houses the Escuela Nacional de Estudios Antropológicos, which gives all of the University's courses in anthropology. In its own right it confers a master's degree. A doctorate, however, comes from the University and the examining committee contains people from both institutions. Everything is closely interlocked.

Under development in Mexico is a folk arts extension of museum activities. Daniel F. Rubín de la Borbolla, who used to be director of the Museo Nacional de Antropología, has given up that position to take entire charge of a series of folk arts museums to be established throughout the nation. There is already one in Sonora at Los Alamos, which I have not seen, and one in Patzcuaro, which I have seen and which is charmingly and instructively arranged. These museums deal with contemporary folk arts and with their historical development. The central one is in Mexico City, on the Avenida Juárez, almost across from Bellas Artes.

And that brings me to Bellas Artes. The Instituto de Bellas Artes is under the Secretaría de Educación. It is doing a tremendous amount in all areas of folklore. The Mendozas have worked with the Instituto Nacional de Bellas Artes on various projects. For example, they travelled across the state of Pueblo, studying the folklore in a succession of villages in a straight line. This required a considerable period of full-time work. Apparently the results will mean a tremendous publishing job, before which even Bellas Artes quails. But it is hoped that Bellas Artes will publish the work. The Instituto did publish in 1952 their huge book on a single community in Zacatecas—*Folklore de San Pedro Piedra Gorda, Zacatecas.* Stith Thompson once remarked that he did not think such a costly and beautiful book on folklore could find a publisher in the United States.

This book suggests another type of activity in Mexico of importance to folklore studies. Though published by Bellas Artes, it was a contribution to the Ninth Session of the Congreso Mexicano de Historia. Congresses and round tables take place frequently in Mexico. Practically all of them include one or two folklore papers, and most of them publish their proceedings later on. The Congress of History meets once in two years, always in a different place, and centers on the history and folklore of the section of Mexico where it is meeting.

The Archive of the Instituto Nacional de Bellas Artes offers treasure to the folklorist. Merle Simmons used it for his study on *corridos,* a book I consider one of the finest guides available for opening up leads to Mexican public archives and private collections. The extensive resources available in Mexico are shown in his main bibliography and the many short bibliographies given in his notes. The Bellas Artes archive in particular is also described in some detail by Vicente T. Medoza in "Cincuenta Años de Investigaciones Folklóricas en México"[21]—an account which is invaluable in giving perspective on the growth of folklore studies in Mexico through the first half of this century.

A brief but useful survey, not mentioning folklore in particular, but conveying much practical information on the location and rules of a number of different historical archives, many of which might be of interest to the folklorist, was done by Paul and Greta Ezell under the title "Research in the Archives of Mexico, D.F."[22]

There are also church archives. I had a most happy experience when through a professor of history I was given an introduction to Father Garibay, a Nahuatl scholar and folklorist, and he in turn gave me an introduction to the *Mitra,* the diocesan officers at the Cathedral. There the person in charge of church archives can provide entree to the various monastic libraries and church parochial archives, which often have interesting and unexpected material in them. I have seen parish records going back to the time when they were kept in the Nahuatl language and were sometimes illustrated in codex style.

Mention should be made of the extensive course work in folklore offered by Virginia Rodríguez Rivera at three institutions in Mexico: the National Conservatory of Music, the Academy of the Mexican Dance, and the Mexican Institute of Social Security. In her paper on "The Teaching of Folklore in Mexico," presented at the meeting of the American Folklore Society in Mexico City in 1959, she described the content of these courses, the growth of folklore courses in Mexico during recent years, and the publications resulting from them. The students in her classes do not approach folklore as material for performances, but work with many aspects of collecting, bibliography, mapping, and so on.

Courses of a more introductory nature, and designed for foreigners, are given at summer schools all over Mexico. Besides the ones already mentioned in the summer session of the Universidad Nacional Autónoma de México, one might mention, as examples, those listed in the summer offerings of the Universidad de Guanajuato, the Universidad Michoacana de San Nicolás de Hidalgo at Morelia, Mexico City College, the Universidad Veracruzana at Jalapa, the Universidad Autónoma del Estado de México at Toluca, and the University of Arizona Guadalajara Summer School, now independent, but at different times in the past associated with the Universidad de Guadalajara and the Universidad Autónoma de Guadalajara. Often these courses are directed toward learning folksongs and folk dances, but sometimes they are related more closely to the study of Mexican culture and historical background. The course in Mexican Culture in the University of Arizona Guadalajara Summer School emphasizes folklore and uses Frances Toor's book as its text. In all the summer schools the study of folklore is looked upon as an avenue to understanding Mexican life.

This outline of the present state of folklore studies in Mexico reveals a complicated picture, one that is overorganized, interorganized, and replete with overlapping personnel. Yet it makes apparent a concern with folklore in many related disciplines, a concern which results in extensive collecting, archiving, publishing, and teaching. There is a distinction in emphasis, and no doubt an enrichment through the variety of perspectives. And the recognition of folklore as a discipline in itself is not lacking.

If the visiting folklorist will seek direction from any one of the groups mentioned, he will find everyone most cordial. One often notices in Mexico how remote the average city man is from the village, how little he knows of what goes on at rural fiestas, for example. Yet this is not true of the folklore-minded scholar in these groups. He will point one directly to the village. Once near Guadalajara, I ran into a *La Conquista,* a version of the *Moros y Cristianos* in which the fighting men are Aztecs and Spaniards at the time of the conquest. Remembering that a *La Conquista* had already appeared in the *Anuario de la Sociedad Folklórica,*[23] I thought it might be wise to look it up to be sure that I was not duplicating a job already done if I embarked on the two- or three-day task of taking down the text at the dictation of the *Maestro,* who in this case had no written script—only cue lines and his memory. I went into the library in Guadalajara to find the *Anuario.* When the girls at the desk could not find the particular issue, though all the others seemed to be there, they sent me in to the head librarian, Sr. José Cornejo Franco. He picked it up and passed it to me from his own desk. He himself was the man who had sent the script in to the *Anuario*—a different one, it turned out, from the version I was about to copy. I still had a job to do—and he promptly and generously pointed me to a second.

"Out in Tonalá," he said, "you will find a fighting play—*Los Tastoanes*—a much more primitive form of fighting play than *La Conquista.* There are animal characters and masks. It shows the mixing of two cultures. Why don't you go out to Tonalá and see what you can find?"

So, in quest of the *Anuario* of the Sociedad Folklórica I had gone to a librarian in Guadalajara, and from him I went out to Tonalá in a bus on market day, to a nice old lady who was selling pottery on the plaza. (I always go to old people first, those with the right kind of wrinkles. They have the confidence of age. They can judge you; they can judge your motives. A young person is a little afraid of you. A young person is very conservative. And so I approach the old.)

My old lady with the pottery was quite willing to talk about fiestas—even about *Los Tastoanes.* She said, "The mask maker is right over there on that bench." I left her little pottery *puesto* and went over and talked to the mask maker, who took me down the street to the *maestro,* who showed me his script.

In short, one goes from this intricately organized superstructure of Mexican educational institutions and scholarly societies sometimes in a rather straight line to the informant in his little Mexican village. Then one is at headquarters, and that is where the real fun begins.

NOTES

1. Affiliated in 1942 with the Círculo Panamericano de Folklore, Natal, Rio Grande do Norte, Brasil, the *Anuario* was printed till 1954 by the Imprenta Universitaria, México. Since 1954 only occasional, privately supported issues have appeared.

2. Though they later resigned these offices, they still continue their interest in the Society and its publications.

3. See, e.g., her "El Nahuatl en el Folklore de México," *Anuario de la Sociedad Folklórica de México,* VII (1951), 123-137, and her "Las Brujas, Análisis y Cuadro," ibid., VI (1950), 457-483.

4. See, e.g., Mendoza's *El Romance Español y el Corrido Mexicano: Estudio Comparativo,* Universidad Nacional Autónoma de México, Instituto de Investigaciones Estéticas (México, 1939); *Panoramas de la Música Tradicional de México,* idem (México, 1956); and *Lírica Infantil de México,* El Colegio de México (México, 1951), all well known to students of folk music.

5. *Spanish Texts of Three Dance Dramas from Mexican Villages,* University of Arizona, Humanities Bulletin No. 4 (Tucson, 1942).

6. Barker, *The Shepherds' Play of the Prodigal Son (Coloquio de Pastores del Hijo Pródigo),* University of California, Folklore Studies No. 2 (Berkeley and Los Angeles, 1953); and Robe, *Coloquios de Pastores from Jalisco, México,* University of California, Folklore Studies No. 4 (Berkeley and Los Angeles, 1954).

7. Roberto García Conde, "Los Tinacales, el Maguey y sus Productos," *Anuario de la Sociedad Folklórica de México,* V (1944), 331-352.

8. Bernardino de Sahagún, *Ritos, Sacerdotes y Atavíos de los Dioses,* Introd., Paleografía, Versión y Notas de Miguel León-Portilla (México, 1958).

9. See Benedict's "Anthropology and the Humanities," *American Anthropologist,* L (1948), esp. 587.

10. Charles E. Dibble, *Códice Xolotl,* Editado en Colaboración por las Universidades de Utah y de México, Publicaciones del Instituto de Historia, primera serie, No. 22 (México, 1951).

11. Fernando de Alva Ixtlilxóchitl, *Obras Históricas* (2 vols., México, 1891-92). Written ca. 1611.

12. E.g., on p. 105 of *Códice Xolotl* Dibble relates the conversation pictures on Sheet 8 of the codex to the conversation recounted by Ixtlilxóchitl in his *Obras Históricas,* I, 201.

13. See Boggs's *Bibliografía Completa, Clasificada y Comentada, de los Artículos de Mexican Folkways (MF), con Indice* (México, 1945), originally in the *Boletin Bibliográfico de Antropología Americana* (México), Instituto Panamericano de Geografía e Historia, Vol. VI, Enero a Diciembre (1942), pp. 221-265.

14. See, e.g., her *Made in Mexico* (New York, 1952).

15. See, e.g., Caso's "Explicación del Reverso del Codex Vindobonensis," *Memoria de El Colegio Nacional,* II: 5 (1950), 9-46, and his "Lienzo de Yolotepec," ibid. II: 4 (1957), 41-55. (Note: Tomo II, Núm. 5, was misnumbered Tomo VI, Núm. 5, and corrected in Tomo II, Núm. 8, 1953.)

16. See León-Portilla's *La Filosofía Náhuatl, Estudiada en sus Fuentes* (México, 1956; 2nd ed., México, 1959).

17. See, e.g., Angel Ma. Garibay K., "Supervivencias Religiosas Precolombinas de los Otomíes de Huizquilucan, Estado de México," *América Indígena,* XVII (Julio 1957), 207-219, and (Octubre 1957), 319-333; and Rudolf van Zantwijk, "Supervivencias Intelectuales de la Cultura Náhuatl en el Municipio de Milpa Alta, D.F.," ibid., XVIII (Abril 1958), 119-128.

18. See, e.g., Cornelia Mak, "Mixtec Medical Beliefs and Practices," *América Indígena,* XIX, (Abril 1959), 125-157.

19. See Daniel F. Rubín de la Borbolla, "Las Artes Populares Indígenas de América: Supervivencia y Formento," *América Indígena,* XIX (Enero 1959), 5-42.

20. Simmons, *The Mexican Corrido as a Source for Interpretive Study of Modern Mexico (1870-1950)* (Bloomington, Indiana, 1957), p. 615, under "Folklore."

21. In *Aportaciones a la Investigación Folklórica de México* (México, 1953), pp. 81-115.

22. In the *Arizona Quarterly,* XI (1955), 251-255.

23. "La Danza de la Conquista," Adquerida por el Sr. José Cornejo Franco, *Anuario de la Sociedad Folklórica,* IV (1943), 155-186.

University of Arizona
Tucson, Arizona

STITH THOMPSON

VISITS TO SOUTH AMERICAN FOLKLORISTS

DURING THE past fourteen years I have had the opportunity to make several trips to South America to find what our South American neighbors are doing with folklore studies and to establish a cordial relationship with them. Our first trip, in 1947, came as a result of an invitation from the Venezuelan Government to act for some months as technical advisor to the Ministry of Education in the establishment of a Service for National Folklore Investigations, in Caracas. Taking advantage of a half year of sabbatical leave, my daughter, Mrs. Thompson and I first traveled to Colombia, where, with the help of John Campbell, the Cultural Attaché of our Embassy, I was able to see something of what the Ministry of Education in Colombia was doing to teach the pupils of the schools about their national customs and traditions. The children in the public schools were not asked to collect songs and dances, but they were taught how to perform them. I found that there had been a very considerable collecting activity of songs and dances in the past, and that the Minister of Education was more interested in propagation than in investigation. There is a Division of Popular Culture which undertakes to spread this knowledge in the schools by means of phonograph records and moving pictures, as well as by traveling exhibitions of photographs.

In Bogotá the Museum of Ethnology has now established an archive of folklore. This has been done largely through the influence of Paul Rivet, the great French ethnologist who spent the war years in Bogotá. They seemed to have a very good beginning of an archive of folklore, with good filing systems and a clear-cut plan of action. I found a most interesting plan being elaborated whereby a team of investigators was going out to one of the remote Indian tribes to make a joint study of their ethnology, their tales, legends, songs, dances, and other aspects of their traditional life. This, I understood from Señor Luis Alberto Acuña, who visited us later in Bloomington, turned out to be a most successful expedition. Some of the results have been published in a journal of folklore issued at Bogotá.[1]

Our next real stop was at Lima, where we remained for a good month. This month gave me the opportunity to meet practically all those in Peru interested in folklore. I had had some correspondence with Federico Schwab, of the library of San Marcos University, and he was very helpful in making me acquainted with the folklorists and their activities. Much of the work of the Museum of Culture in Lima concerns all aspects of the life of the Quechua and Aymará Indians, and much that we know about the ancient Inca civilization comes from that museum. The work among the Indians was done mainly by linguists, who incidentally collected much material that interests the folklorist, and, since it happens that several of them studying these indigenous groups had at least a considerable admixture of Indian blood, they were valuable interpreters of the Indian cultures. There was also a folklorist from Arequipa, Miguel Ugarte, who knew a great deal about children's rhymes, and games, songs and folktales of old Spanish tradition.

The Ministry of Education was also interested in folklore; some of their efforts went toward propagation, as in Colombia, but there was also an attempt to have school children collect local traditions, which I felt was not well-handled. The directions and questionnaires were issued by a man who had little knowledge of folklore, and I am afraid that the stories sent in were polished by the schoolteachers. These schoolmasters and mistresses were brought to Lima once a year to attend lectures, some of which were on folklore.

Peru is interesting as still having a great deal of the old Indian population at various locations. We attended the Indian market at Huancayo and found several local enthusiasts who were collecting Indian traditions. Similarly, in Cuzco, the ancient Inca capital, Victor Navarro del Aguila was training a group of young students to take advantage of their strategic location and study the Quechua peoples. Since Navarro's lamented early death this work has been very well carried on by one of his younger disciples, Efraim Morote Best, who has established a good journal of folklore and who is maintaining a first-rate standard of research.[2]

To me one unfortunate aspect of the folklorists in Lima is that they seem hopelessly divided into two groups. One school feels that everything of interest in Peruvian tradition is essentially Indian, and that the Spanish influence has never penetrated far. The other, somewhat smaller, takes exactly the opposite position and contends that very little of the original Indian tradition persists after four centuries of Spanish occupation, either as colonizers or as republican rulers. The latter group has done very little collecting in Peru, but contents itself very largely with repeating the traditions gathered in the many volumes of Ricardo Palma's *Tradiciones Peruanas Completas* (2nd ed., Madrid, 1953).[3]

After leaving Lima we stopped briefly in La Paz, Bolivia, where it seemed to me the efforts to obtain the folklore of this predominantly Indian population were very feeble, and then we traveled on to Argentina. At Tucumán, our first stop, we noticed a placard in the hotel enjoining us to visit the Provincial Folklore Museum. Here was a new museum with a good display of such traditional articles as illustrate the life, past and present, of this section of Argentina. The collection was especially rich in equipment for horses—spurs, stirrups, and saddles, as well as in household utensils of all kinds. In Tucumán there was also a folklorist interested in the traditions of the province, Tobias Rosemberg. He was especially kind to us, taking us not only to see the folklorists of Tucumán, but also on a hundred-mile trip to Santiago del Estero to Oreste di Lullo, a physician and philanthropist who had studied the folk customs of that province. Rosemberg was at that time planning the establishment of a journal of folklore, and in two or three years after our visit he did establish such a journal, which has flourished.[4]

In Buenos Aires we were taken to the Instituto de Tradiciones Nacionales, at that time directed by Juan Alfonso Carrizo, and assisted by Bruno Jacovella. Carrizo had been one of the assiduous collectors of all kinds of folklore from the north and northwest provinces of Argentina.[5] He had specialized in coplas, four-line stanzas by which the Latin-Americans express their aphorisms. Indeed, he was so much immersed in the study of coplas that one was tempted to speak of his organization as El Instituto de Coplas. He had large plans for publication and also for expansion of his activities on a national scale, and had the sponsorship of the Perón government. Looked at after the events of a decade, much of the work of this Institute seems rather futile. The grandiose plans never developed, but with a new regime the first-rate earlier collection of manuscripts which had been made inaccessible by the Peronese group now forms the basis for what seems to be a much more satisfactory national institute. The leading figure from the old days, Ricardo Rojas, was then in complete eclipse, but his scholarship has now been revived.[6]

In spite of the political difficulties, there survived much real folklore interest. One individual folklorist in Buenos Aires has made an international reputation for himself and for the field which he cultivates. Carlos Vega seems to me to carry on his research in the study of folksongs and their musical analysis[7] with more seriousness and ability than almost any other folk musician I have met. He has trained a number of young disciples, and they are helping to bring technical knowledge to several other Latin American countries, notably to Uruguay and Venezuela. One of the delightful parts of our visit to Buenos Aires was the almost continuous association with Vega and his pupils.

As we headed for Chile we stopped at the beautiful city of Mendoza to visit Juan Draghi Lucero, who was living on Paso de Los Andes. He had spent a year in the States, mostly at Chapel Hill, and had learned about our methods and those of European folklorists. He had published a good deal of material from the province of Cuyo, some of it about songs and legends, and some about material folklore.[8] We heard him give a good lecture to his students illustrating the difference between authentic folk artifacts and imitation.

In Chile we found that the folklore activities were rather evenly divided among three groups. There was first of all an excellent folk museum much like that at Tucumán. Then there was the Institute of Folk Music, whose leading spirit was Eugenio Pereira Salas. He was well acquainted with America and with American methods of study, as well as those of Europe. He has assembled a very large collection of recordings of Chilean folksongs, primarily of Spanish tradition. His institute is really a part of the larger National Institute of Music, which maintains a symphony orchestra which plays in all of the provincial towns as well as in Santiago.

The third group in Chile is headed by Yolando Pino Saavedra. This is an institute of general folklore connected with the school of pedagogy of the University of Chile. It actually consists of only a few other persons beside Pino himself, but it is larger now, since I was made an honorary member of this Institute. Pino does have some tales and traditions collected by his pupils, and he has assembled a library. He studied in Germany and knows something of the German methods, but most of his knowledge in this area dates before 1900. Some excellent work in the collecting of Chilean traditions was done a generation or two ago, and I think there is a tendency to feel that that is enough.

From Santiago we flew to Buenos Aires, and then went by boat across the mouth of the La Plata to Montevideo. Of organized effort for the study of folk traditions there seemed to be little sign in Uruguay. In spite of the announcement we received several years ago of the organization of a folklore society there, the efforts of the organizers have apparently failed, and the Society is at least in abeyance. But one of Carlos Vega's disciples, Lauro Ayesterán, had made a large collection of folksongs and had done some analysis of these, and one of the professors in the University, Ildefonso Pereda Valdés, had collected many songs and traditions, both Negro and white.[9] In general he was a specialist in Negro folklore. His wife collected many of what we would call "tall tales."

We had all too short a time to spend in Brazil. In Porto Alegre one of the leaders in the Institute of History, Walter Spaulding (who, by the way, speaks no English), was working on large schemes for the collecting of Brazilian folklore. Much more active in folklore was Dante di Laytano, whose special field is the Brazilian Negro. In Saõ Paulo we found one of the largest collections of recordings of folksongs to be seen anywhere, the Discoteca Municipal. There was also a group from the state of Saõ Paulo who were collecting Indian dances, using both phonographic recordings and moving picture techniques. I saw some of the results of this seven years later on my return trip to Saõ Paulo.

In Rio de Janeiro the Institute for Folklore Investigations was concerned almost entirely with the collecting and analysis of folksongs. In many ways the director, Luís Heitor Correa de Azevedo, was the same type as Carlos Vega of Buenos Aires. He had assembled a group which, as a part of its university work, made a serious study of Brazilian musical traditions. There was also at the University a professor of Ethnology, Artur Ramos, whose interest was primarily the Negro. He had frequently been in the United States and knew the American Negro well. He invited me to lecture before his anthropological groups, and since I speak no Portuguese, I lectured to them in Spanish on "Why We Study Folklore." A third group in Rio before whom I spoke, the Folklore Society of Rio de Janeiro, is much more amateurish and is made up of the general public interested in folklore, under the leadership of Joaquim Ribeiro. Although three folklore groups exist in the city, there was fortunately no feeling of rivalry between them, and their fields of activity are clearly delimited.

The one Brazilian folklorist about whom I had known before going to South America was Luís da Camara Cascudo.[10] We had enjoyed a very cordial correspondence and had exchanged not only publications but also photographs. We made a long detour to Natal to visit with him and his disciples. Cascudo has written books on almost every phase of Brazilian folklore, and is perhaps the principal force uniting the interests of folklorists throughout Brazil. Very shortly after our visit he and his friend Luís Heitor left for Portugal, where they helped work out a plan for a Congress of Portuguese-Brazilian Folklore for the summer of 1948, at the invitation of the Portuguese government.

In the middle of July 1947, I entered my duties as technical advisor for the service of folklore investigations at the Museum of Natural Sciences at Caracas. The Acción Democratica, now at last in control again in Venezuela, had decided that one of the best ways to make their government of real service to the people in the outlying districts was to study their traditions, both those of Spanish origin and those of Negro and Indian origin. When I arrived, the music division of the service was already operating. They were actively collecting in various parts of Venezuela and were bringing the material into the Museum and analyzing it according to the methods of Carlos Vega. Until my arrival, most of the efforts of the service were in this direction. My attempt in the four or five months I was in Venezuela was to broaden the scope of their investigations so as to include not only all kinds of oral traditions, but also dances and material folklore. Fortunately, there were others around who knew about the dances, and that aspect of the work has gone on very well. I lectured to groups in the Museum about the problems of oral folklore, particularly legends, traditions, and folktales. As a result of these lectures, several of the men brought in worth-while collections from their own districts, and I worked with them in editing the material. I also gave public lectures to a group of interested students about twice a week. Though this was a considerable workout for my in-adequate Spanish, I think some of them learned a good deal about folklore tech-niques. At the suggestion of the director, I wrote out a rather elaborate plan for the conduct of the service, based on my experience with European archives. On my re-visit to Caracas in 1954, I was pleased to see that in their new headquarters the Museum had carried out my suggestions with great faithfulness. They had not only developed a well-recognized institute of folklore, but were sponsoring regular publications and a good periodical.

My short return in 1954 took me only to Brazil and Venezuela. The occasion was an international folklore congress at Saõ Paulo being held on the 400th anniver-sary of the founding of the city. Delegates came from many countries of Europe, as well as from the United States, which sent several of us. The International Folk Music Council also had its annual meeting in connection with this Congress. This was, I think, the first time that many of the South American folklorists ever had a chance to meet any of their European colleagues. On the whole, the meeting was decidely worth-while. There was some friction between the various Brazilian folk-lorists, and I was disappointed that my friend, Camara Cascudo, and his disciples were uncooperative. The group which sponsored the Congress is still publishing frequent bulletins, and I think the Congress served as a stimulus for a number of younger men scattered around through Brazil. It was also a pleasure at this meeting to renew acquaintances with folklorists of various parts of South America whom I had seen seven years earlier.

For four months, from November 1960 to March 1961, I was in Latin America on a "specialists" program for the United States State Department, attending a con-gress and lecturing. The month of December was spent in Argentina, where from December 5 to 10 there was held in Buenos Aires an International Folklore Congress. This congress brought together a large number of folklorists from South America, as well as a few from Europe and the United States. It was divided into five commissions which met separately and at which the papers were read. An extraordinary feature of these commissions, to me, was the vote-taking after each paper to decide whether the paper was to be accepted and recommended by the commission. The reports of the various commissions were considered in plenary sessions. As in most congresses of this kind, the important thing was for the various folklorists to get together and to have talks about their mutual problems. Such meetings were made somewhat difficult at this congress because of the Pan American Folk Dance Competition which took place late every evening. It seemed to me that the folk dances were performed with great competence, and if we have anything like them in the United States, I have failed to see them. At the end of the congress a permanent commission was formed to arrange for future international congresses. It is impossible to say at the moment whether these congresses will be truly international or almost exclusively South American.

I also had an opportunity to lecture to a class of sixty women who are studying folklore in a teachers' college. This means that folklore in the public schools is a real part of the Argentine curriculum.

In Uruguay I found no great change since my last visit. In Chile my old friends are still active. Yolando Pino Saavedra has considerably extended the scope of his work in these last years. Shortly after my visit there he began to interest himself in the Chilean folktale, and in several field trips he has made a large collection of newly recorded tales. The first volume of these has now appeared and two more will follow.[11] These are edited with excellent technique, and the relation of all these tales to the folkstories of the world is made clear.

One of the ablest folklorists in South America, Paulo Carvalho Neto of Brazil, is now in the Brazilian Embassy in Quito. I had a good visit with him and found that he is very active in collecting folklore wherever his duties take him, and in writing books on theoretical aspects of the subject.[12] I did not meet any folklorists in Ecuador in my earlier trip, but this time, both at Buenos Aires and later in Guayaquil I saw something of the excellent work in folk music and folk dance that is being done by Justino Cornejo. In Colombia, I lectured in eight different cities, but I did not discover that any particular advance in folklore studies had been made.

In the two weeks we visited Caracas I found practically all my old friends carrying on as they had been seven years before. The Institute of Folklore has now grown considerably, and is located in a new home. They are doing a good deal of fieldwork, and the archiving is on a professional basis.

The rest of the trip consisted of something more than a month in British Guiana, Trinidad, Jamaica, and Guatemala. I found very little folklore work being carried on in British Guiana, though one woman from a remote country district came into Georgetown and showed me a large collection of songs she had collected. I was unable this time to go to Brazil, but I had the feeling from the representation at Buenos Aires that folklore studies were being advanced very vigorously in that country. A group of the leading members of the Congress were invited to the Brazilian Embassy and were presented with the Sylvio Romero medal for their activities in folklore. Publication of books has gone on at a good pace in Brazil in these last years.

Looking at South America as a whole, the folklorist finds it a continent of very diverse interests, everywhere showing enormous potentialities for future work. It may be well to warn folklorists of our country who plan to visit our South American neighbors that they should be able to carry on at least simple conversations in Spanish, for it is a mistaken notion that everyone in South America worth talking to speaks English. They usually read it, but neither speak nor understand it. Without using Spanish it is impossible to come to know any one of the five best-informed folklorists of South America.

NOTES

(This article is expanded from the author's paper on "Folklore in South America" in the *Journal of American Folklore*, LXI [July-September 1948], 256-260.)

1. *Revista de Folklore* (Bogotá, 1947 ff.). A useful listing of South American folklore publications can be found in the annual "Folklore Bibliography" by Ralph S. Boggs in the March issue of *Southern Folklore Quarterly* (1937-60). Beginning in 1961, this department is being conducted by Américo Paredes.

2. *Tradición: Revista Peruana de Folklore* (Cuzco, 1950 ff.). Morote Best is now at the new university at Ayacucho.

3. An extensive bibliography of Peruvian folklore has recently been compiled by Mildred Merino de Zela. This is the *Bibliografía del Folklore Peruano*, Publicación Núm. 230, Instituto Panamericano de Geografía e Historía de la Comisión de Historía de la Publicaciones del Cómite de Folklore (México and Lima, 1960), prologo por Jose Maria Arguedas. Pp. xv + 186.

4. *Boletín de la Asociación Tucumana de Folklore* (Tucumán, 1950 ff.).

5. Carrizo published various *Cancioneros* (Jujuy, La Rioja, Salta, Tucumán), and an important *Antecedentes Hispano-medioevales de la Poesía Tradicional Argentina* (Buenos Aires, 1945).

6. The work of the Instituto has now been taken over by the Instituto Nacional de Investigaciones Folklóricas.

7. Carlos Vega's principal works are: *La Música Popular Argentina*, 2 vols. (1941); *Bailes*

Tradicionales Argentinas, 18 vols. (1946 ff.); *El Origen de las Danzas Folklóricas* (1956); *La Ciencia de Folklore* (1959). All published in Buenos Aires.

8. *Cancionero Popular Cuyano* (Mendoza, Argentina, 1938); *Las Mil y Una Noches Argentinas* (Mendoza, 1940).

9. Important is his *Cancionero Popular Uruguayo* (Montevideo, 1947).

10. Among Luís da Camara Cascudo's many works may be mentioned: *Antologia do Folclore Brasileiro* (Saõ Paulo, 1943); *Lendas-Brasileiras* (Rio de Janeiro, 1945); *Contos Tradicionais do Brasil* (Rio de Janeiro, 1946).

11. Pino Saavedra, *Cuentos Folklóricos de Chile* (Santiago de Chile, 1960).

12. Paulo de Carvalho Neto, *Folklore y Psicoanálisis* (Buenos Aires, 1956); *Folklore y Educacion* (Quito, 1961).

Indiana University
Bloomington, Indiana

ASIA

RICHARD M. DORSON

FOLKLORE RESEARCH IN JAPAN

JAPAN and England present obvious geographical similarities, with implications for the folklorist. Each is a proud island nation facing a vast conglomerate mainland. In both countries insularity has bred a long-lived, homogeneous folk culture, and intellectual energy has produced inquiring folklorists to examine this submerged culture. Japanese folklore theory has indeed been influenced by English rather than continental methods of investigation. But there the analogies end.

In England I knew the language but had come half a century too late to meet the vigorous Victorian folklorists. In Japan I arrived in the midst of the efflorescence of folklore studies, but could neither talk to the folklore scholars nor read their writings veiled in an impenetrable tongue—impenetrable during a ten months stay. As a lesson in establishing relations with foreign folklorists, the experience was invaluable, and not without its ludicrous aspects.

The chain of events that led me to Japan began at a regional meeting of the American Folklore Society in Lexington, Kentucky, in May 1953. During the meeting I received a note from George K. Brady, professor of English at the University of Kentucky, who wished to introduce Masanori Takatsuka, visiting him that year to collaborate on a translation of the Japanese Folklore Dictionary (*Minzokugaku Jiten,* Tokyo, 1951). Professor Brady had spent some months in Japan after the war on government service, and had fallen in love with the land, its people, and its culture. Although approaching retirement, he had expanded his intellectual commitments and course offerings from English bibliography to Japanese culture. Neither Brady nor Takatsuka were folklorists, but their common field of English literature had brought them together, and Brady's colleague Jansen had suggested the cooperative folklore publications of Kunio Yanagita and his Japanese Folklore Institute as worthy subjects for translation.

Among his books and periodicals on Japanese subjects Professor Brady pointed out an article on "Post-War Folklore Research Work in Japan" by Hiroji Naoe.[1] Naoe's survey revealed a ferment of activity and productivity quite unsuspected on this side of the Pacific. When I applied for a Fulbright lectureship in 1956-57, as visiting professor in the department of American Studies at the University of Tokyo, one avowed purpose was making contact with the Japanese folklorists. Teaching duties at the university involved only two lectures a week, with a ten weeks interim between the school years, so my time was relatively free to seek out the folklore scholars.

In order for the reader unfamiliar with the Orient to appreciate the complexities behind this seemingly simple task, a few facts about Tokyo and Japan should be offered. Tokyo is the largest city in the world, with upwards of eight million people, and an antiquated transportation system designed for half that number. One frequently spends two hours traveling from one part of the city to another in the crowded *denshas* (the interurban electric trains, which run on the same tracks as the national railways). The difficulties of communication cannot be exaggerated, and to find one's way about, or even to ask the time of day, may become an interminable chore. Japanese is like no other language, although it has incorporated the Chinese Kanji characters to make its three alphabets more confusing. A Japanese youth spends two more years in school than a Western schoolboy needs to learn his own tongue. Americans who make a stab at the language usually peter out at the sixth lesson, the numeral systems, whose number is legion: there is one method of counting for people, another for animals, one for long thin objects, another for short flat objects—a system more complicated than the Motif-Index. The addition of honorific prefixes to people and objects further baffles the Westerner, and renders the Japanese themselves continually uneasy, for the marks of respect and deference in verbal address and obeisance reflect constant tensions within the culture. For an American, accustomed to the cult of informality and the shibboleth of equality, the protocol in daily Japanese life is a mystery. Yet to gain entree into a given circle the forms must be scrupulously observed: a letter of introduction from a mutual friend precedes the first visit; the great man in the circle—and intellectual activities are knit with interlocking family relationships much like a village kinship group—needs always receive the initial homage. In a highly concentrated society, alert and ambitious, packed in small, mountainous islands (with half the American population, the Japanese occupy an area the size of Montana), the people of Japan compete fiercely for the available jobs, and still cherish their traditions of civility and courtesy which keep life at close quarters tolerable. One slip in protocol can cost the young man his chance for a career.

Communication between Japanese and Westerners is rendered all the more difficult because many Japanese pretend to much more English than they know. English has become the second language in the schools since the war, but the older generation of scholars was trained in German and Chinese, and the teachers of English are themselves in need of instruction. The desire to master English is almost a national obsession, and the American walking down the street may be stopped by a stranger requesting English lessons. Every Fulbright professor, regardless of his subject, ends up teaching English in class, and so do his wife and children at home. But because of the Japanese politeness, the individuals who converse with the Westerner never admit lack of comprehension; and since the structure of Japanese grammar calls for "Yes" where English calls for "No" ("You don't receive the JOURNAL OF AMERICAN FOLKLORE, do you?" "Yes"), a visitor seldom knows where he stands.

A case in point is the occasion on which I had invited two of my most helpful new friends to have dinner at our small dwelling. Both spoke English, but that day at the Japanese Folklore Institute they introduced me to a leading folktale scholar of Japan, who did not. The four of us left the Institute together, but when we came to the *densha* station, my new acquaintance never mounted the steps, but continued to trudge along with the rest of us, while my consternation grew. When we arrived at our abode, I ducked in ahead and barely had time to apprise my wife of the extra guest. Our quarters were simply too small to have more than two dinner guests at a time, so she had to eat at a separate little table with our small son.

These seemingly slight incidents loom large when one is endeavoring to establish lines of communication among alien scholars. This was Asia not Europe, and the culture offered few handholds and many pitfalls for the intruder. Several strokes of good fortune aided me. In the first place, the quarters selected for us by the Fulbright office proved to be a ten minute walk from the Minzokugaku Kenkyusho (the Folklore Research Institute), in the grassy suburb of Seijo-machi. Secondly, a letter sent in advance of my coming by Professor Brady to the director of the Institute, Tokihiko Oto, properly prepared the way. Thirdly, I came in the nick of time, as the Institute closed down the following April 1957, for lack of funds, and for internal political reasons never clearly divulged to an outsider.

The Japanese Folklore Institute was the lengthened shadow of one man, Kunio Yanagita, almost literally, for he not only had founded the whole field of folklore science in Japan and established the Institute in the large library of the house he had given his daughter, but himself lived next door in a smaller, newer, shrubbery-lined home. In October 1956, when I met him, Yanagita *sensei* (professor) was eighty-one, and famous. Every Japanese intellectual I encountered, no matter what his subject, knew the name of Yanagita, and his work in folklore. A member of the Japan Academy, he had published a hundred books and a thousand articles—or more properly, he had permitted his name to be listed as author on those works. The disciples of the great scholar, pursuing their researches under his sponsorship, were delighted to see his name on their work. The director of the Institute, Mr. Oto, showed me the valuable history of the Japanese folklore movement which he had written, and which had been translated into German, and proudly pointed out the acknowledgment to Mr. Oto given by Mr. Yanagita, whose august name appeared as author on the title page.[2] Mr. Oto had even written the acknowledgment to himself!

A letter to Mr. Oto brought a reply inviting me to the Institute at a certain day. Later I learned that a peripheral associate of the group, Naofusa Hirai, had been requested to come from Kokugakuin University for the occasion to act as interpreter. Half a dozen scholars greeted me ceremoniously, presented me with several handsome illustrated volumes of Japanese folklife, and after an exchange of cordialities through Mr. Hirai, conducted me next door to meet Yanagita *sensei*. A sturdy, venerable old man, benign in manner and obviously accustomed to deference, he brought to mind the images of Buddha one saw everywhere, and most impressively as the majestic Daibutsu (Great Buddha) of Kamakura. During my ten months stay, I called at periodic intervals, when an interpreter was available, and the good will of Professor Yanagita made possible the furtherance of any projects I might conceive. In fact it was indispensable.

Physically the Minzokugaku Kenkyusho was a spacious, high-ceilinged, Western-type chamber, lined with books and journals, and cluttered with desks and tables haphazardly arranged. Its heating arrangements were, alas, typically Japanese, consisting of the small charcoal braziers over which a Westerner desperately waved his hands hoping to warm at least his finger tips. Although the Institute had a hardwood floor, all visitors still left their shoes at the door and shuffled into slippers, so one's feet froze sooner than the rest of his torso. During the winter months I sat here almost daily, lacking both animal heat and mental light, surrounded by a treasure house of folklore that was all Japanese to me.

There was one section of books in English, and I was interested to note the strong representation of the English folklorists, in particular George Laurence Gomme. His *Folklore as an Historical Science* (1908) clearly had exerted great influence on Yanagita, who had guided Japanese folklore studies toward problems of historical reconstruction rather than comparative distribution.

In its official brochure the Minzokugaku Kenkyusho announced its aims in language familiar to folklorists everywhere: to collect, preserve, and publish the folk traditions of the land, and to encourage scholarly investigation and research. The main difference between the Japanese Folklore Institute and the American and English Folklore Societies lay in the conception of an institute as a small body of cooperating scholars, usually working with a special library, museum, collection, or archive. Such institutes abounded in Japan, modeled on those in Europe and like them customarily attached to and spawned by universities. In this respect the Minzokugaku Kenkyusho differed from the pattern, for it was independent of any university, a fact which, I heard members say, contributed to its downfall. Small research grants from the Ministry of Education supplemented the budget. The Institute was founded in 1948 and in 1951 began publishing a quarterly journal, *Nippon-Minzokugaku (Journal of Japanese Folklore)*, which was distributed to members of the Japanese Folklore Society, a much larger group than the Institute and open to any interested layman.

A seven page mimeographed statement available in English translation described the scholarly objectives of the Institute, and gave its constitution. The first three pages are copied below.

MINZOKUGAKU KENKYUSHO
(THE FOLKLORE RESEARCH INSTITUTE)
Origin and History

Minzokugaku Kenkyusho (The Folklore Research Institute) was founded in 1948, but the history of the Institute can be traced 22 years back. For a long time Mr. Kunio Yanagita, deeply mindful of the promotion and improvement of folklore science, had been planning various ways and means for the purpose, and at last he originated "Mokuyokai" (the Thursday Association) in September 1933. From that time on, regular meetings of this Association have been held weekly or fortnightly until the present time. As a result of these meetings "Kyodo Seikatsu Kenkyukai" (the Society for the Study of Local Living) and "Minkan Densho no Kai" (the Society for the Folklore) were established. The former society carried on an investigation, extending over four years from 1934, of the life of people in mountain and seaside villages, and submitted a fruitful report to the learned circles. The latter society has a magazine named "Minkan Densho" (the Folklore), and tiding over many difficulties, even during the World War II when almost all the societies were obliged to discontinue their journals, continued to bring it out with unusual devotion and effort. Under these circumstances, the publication of 14 volumes of classified folklore glossaries, the arrangement and compilation of folk tales collected from all over Japan, and the establishment of chairs of Japanese folklore science were successively achieved, enabling the science to tread the path of expansion gradually but steadily.

After the World War II, Mr. Yanagita confirmed his determination to promote the development of folklore science by offering for the use of younger students all his books and materials on folklore studies, which he had been collecting for a long time. A unique institute of folklore science in Japan was thus founded. The institute was then incorporated, and obtaining the authorization of the Ministry of Education, "Zaidan Hojin Minzokugaku Kenkyusho" (the Folklore Research Institute, Inc.) was newly established on 8 April 1948.

The Institute is managed by the common agreement of the representatives elected by members scattering all over the country. As Mr. Yanagita did not accept the position as head of the Institute, it has been arranged that the directors should be responsible for administrative works by the request of the Board of Representatives. The Institute collects members widely from all over Japan, and on application, new members are nominated by the Board of Representatives.

The Institute is maintained by the income from royalties of publications, various kinds of subsidies and subscriptions, etc. However, the Institute is still being liberally supported by Mr. Yanagita himself.

The chief publications of the Institute are:—

Minzokugaku Shinko (New lectures on folklore science). 1947.

Shakaika Sosho (Social study series). 1948—

Kaison Seikatsu no Kenkyu (A study of the life in seaside villages). 1949.

Zenkoku Minzokushi Sosho (Folk customs of all Japan series). 1949—

Minzokugaku no Hanashi (Introduction to folklore science). 1949.

Minzokugaku Kenkyu (Studies in folklore science). Series 1-3. 1950-52.

Minzokugaku Jiten (Dictionary of folklore). 1951.

Nenji Gyoji Zusetsu (Illustrated book of annual observance). 1953.

Minzoku Sensho (Selected books on folklore).

Vol. 1. "Minzokugaku no Hanashi" (Introduction to folklore science). 1954. (Other volumes to follow)

Nihon Minzoku Zuroku (Pictorial record of Japanese folk customs). 1955.

At present, the Institute is engaged with all its might in the compilation and publication of "Sogo Nihon Minzoku Goi" (A comprehensive folklore glossary of Japan). The research activities undertaken by the Institute include the collection and arrangement of folkloristic materials, instruction and training of research members, and holding of meetings for the study, etc. More especially, every effort has been made to pursue the investigation of the life of people in isolated islands (3 years from 1950) and of the culture in southern islands (mainly Okinawa).

As subjects of folklore studies, the Institute is currently dealing with the following questions with great interest.

1. The question of rites concerning the paddy-rice cultivation. Above all, the worship of the Field-deity is the nucleus of beliefs in agricultural deities in Japan, closely connected with various other beliefs.

2. The question of the worship of ancestor-gods: or the burial system and the idea of the future existence. As this field of study has largely remained uncultivated until now, new facts are being revealed one after another with the progress of investigation.

3. The question of marriage customs connected with the kinship system.

4. The question of the line of families possessed by evil spirits. Since the problem of families regarded to be possessed by such spirits is related to serious social problems, close investigations have been carried on, especially in districts where such families are found in large numbers.

Half a dozen older and younger scholars qualifying as research members of the Institute worked regularly at the various desks. None spoke English, save for Professor Toichi Mabuchi of Tokyo Metropolitan University, and Miss Yasuyo Ishiwara, a graduate of Tokyo Women's Christian University, who had worked under Professor Yanagita on several of his projects. Professor Mabuchi was a noted anthropologist, specializing in the ethnology of Formosa; one of his responsibilities at the Institute was translating into English titles of articles for the cover of *Nippon-Minzokugaku*. Miss Ishiwara served as a research assistant for Professor Yanagita and other scholars. Being available when I came to Tokyo, to my great good luck, she assisted me in becoming acquainted with the Japanese field collections.

Only two Westerners came to the Institute during that year. Cornelius Ouwehand was a Dutch ethnologist, curator of the Japanese collections in the National Museum of Ethnology at Leiden. His earlier work in Indonesia had terminated with the independence of those islands, and he had retooled for Japan, adding Japanese to his other languages as a matter of course.[3] Fanny Hagin Mayer was an American, born in Iowa, the daughter of a missionary, who brought her to Japan at the age of one, and took her home again at fifteen (1900-14). During the occupation she returned to Japan to serve as interpreter and Assistant Education Officer for the Civil Affairs Team in Niigata Prefecture. Subsequently she stayed on to work for a doctor's degree in Japanese folk literature at the University of Tokyo. A grandmother living by herself on the Japanese economy, teaching English at a Japanese college (Tokyo Gakugei University), tall, weatherbeaten, and indomitable, her head usually swathed in a thick kerchief, Mrs. Mayer represented the one visible American penetration into Japanese folklore. She knew Professor Yanagita, and had translated one of his books, *Japanese Folk Tales,* an edition simplified for children, but still a selection of traditional texts.[4] Also she had translated, but not published, Professor Yanagita's *Nihon Mukashibanashi Meii* (Classification of Japanese Fairy Tales), depositing a copy with the Institute.

The Institute possessed other valuable scholarly manuscripts in English. These included copies of the unpublished translations completed by Takatsuka and Brady of three major projects directed by Professor Yanagita: the *Japanese Folklore Dictionary,* the *Studies in Mountain Village Life,* and the *Studies in Fishing Village Life.* The Dictionary listed and described items on the popular traditions and concepts of folklore science in Japan, and though on the sketchy side, was of enormous value in furnishing basic data. The other two volumes grew from cooperative surveys based on questionnaires and field investigations of the traditional culture in the isolated village communities in the interior mountains and along the coast and outlying islands. The latter study was interrupted by the war and never yielded as full results as the first.[5] Yet another manuscript on hand was a copy of the dissertation submitted by Hiroko Ikeda for her doctoral degree in folklore at Indiana University in 1955, *A Type and Motif Index of Japanese Folk-Literature.* This thesis classified Japanese traditional narratives from the comparative perspective of Stith Thompson, the thesis director. Dr. Ikeda, beginning as student under Kunio Yanagita (and a classmate of Miss Ishiwara), and ending under Stith Thompson, had moved the gamut from the national to the international classificatory systems.

These five manuscripts provided windows into the content, techniques, and activities of Japanese folklore. The extent of the activity startled a Europe-oriented Westerner. Mr. Oto showed me a volume of one hundred and thirty-eight pages devoted entirely to the bibliography of Japanese folklorists in the ten years (1945-54) since the end of the war.[6] This body of work was practically unknown outside their country, and in fact at my very first visit to the Institute Mr. Oto drew me over to the Funk and Wagnalls *Standard Dictionary of Folklore, Mythology, and Legend,* turned to the article on Japan, and shaking his head with some vehemence sputtered "Awful!" Nothing in English of scholarly substance had appeared since Anesaki's volume on Japan in *The Mythology of All Races* back in 1928.

As a beginning I asked Miss Ishiwara to translate for me the tables of contents of major works. Soon it became evident that the core of Japanese folk tradition was embodied in the *densetsu,* the local legend found everywhere in Japan, from the center of Tokyo to the remotest hamlet. The *densetsu* reflected supernatural belief, historical event, religious observance, household custom, economic practice. Animism, Shintoism, and Buddhism, filtering through the folk mind, contributed elements to legends of mountains, shrines, and temples. The *densetsu* was in effect the narrative expression of *minkan shinko* (folk belief), the tissue of supernatural sanctions enveloping Japanese folklife, and the special object of study by the Japanese scholars. *Minkan shinko* colored peasant songs and village festivals, household images and exvoto offerings, as well as the ubiquitous *densetsu*.

Collectors had assiduously gathered *densetsu*. They published them in journals like *Tabi to Densetsu* (Travels and Legends), the periodical first launched by Yanagita in 1928 to obtain legends from travelers and local residents; in mixed tale collections containing *mukashi-banashi* (fairy tales); and in over fifty volumes entirely devoted to local traditions. Since the leading scholars were attached to universities in Tokyo, the same cleavage prevailed as in Victorian England, though in lesser degree, between the professional folklorists in the capital city and the amateur collectors in the countryside. Schoolteachers, postmasters, political officials, fiction writers all assembled *densetsu*, which were usually published locally, even by banks, as a gesture of cultural good will to the community. Seldom did these books present full scholarly data, such as the names of informants and notes on variants, but they clearly dipped into authentic and pervasive village traditions.

In the end my sessions with Miss Ishiwara produced a manuscript in English translation, *Folk Legends of Japan*, offering representative texts with comparative notes from the rich store of field collections. These translations from print were supplemented with some fresh oral examples, including half a dozen secured by my student at Tokyo University, Kayoko Saito, from her grandmother, who had been born in Shikoku.[7] The literary classics like *Kojiki* and *Nihongi*, modern short stories, and novels like Akutagawa's *Kappa* (1927), the Noh and Kabuki plays, woodblock prints and scroll paintings, all drew freely from the national stocks of local legends.

A second idea for a book useful to American folklorists came to me at the Institute, namely a volume of essays especially written for a Western audience by leading Japanese folklorists on their research fields. Mr. Mabuchi and Mr. Oto responded eagerly to this plan, with Professor Yanagita's blessing. They drew up a list of potential contributors; I called upon Mr. Robert Hall, director of the Asia Foundation in Japan, and obtained a grant of seven hundred dollars to cover translation costs; and all seemed smooth sailing. But the *Studies in Japanese Folklore* ran into the rough waters that apparently lie in wait for all cooperative scholarly translations from the Japanese. When the articles came in, the problem of clarifying the murky literal translation became apparent. Four years later the manuscript wrinkles have finally been ironed out, and for the first time the theoretical work of the Japanese folklorists will be available in English.[8]

All these articles, written by the disciples of Kunio Yanagita, share a concern with *minkan shinko*, and all employ the method of historical reconstruction. A typical essay, for instance, on the double-grave system by Takayoshi Mogami, seeks to reconstruct the earliest form and the sequence of change in the custom of mourning at two graves, one for the body and the other for the spirit of the deceased. The reconstruction is based on examples obtained both in fieldwork and from documentary records, and Mogami compares these instances to determine their archaic traits. Unlike the historical-geographical method of the Finns, this kind of analysis relies on relatively few examples, deals with custom rather than with tale or ballad, and traces temporal relationships, not migratory routes.

These two translation enterprises seemed highly desirable from the viewpoint of Western folklorists. The Japanese scholars in turn welcomed the opportunity to introduce their collections and studies to the English-speaking world. Although I had brought a tape recorder with me, I made no use of it, feeling that the circumstances called not for additional collecting, through interpreters in an alien land, but for partial translation of the extensive collections already published.

In April 1957, while these two projects were well under way, the Institute closed its doors. Subsequent plans called for the transfer of its library to nearby Seijo University, where Mr. Oto lectured on folklore. The *Journal of Japanese Folklore* continued publication from a different address.

In the remaining three months of my stay, I approached Japanese folklore through two new avenues: library resources in Western languages, and trips to distant points where local folklorists resided. Starting first with the monumental *Bibliography of the Japanese Empire,* compiled by Fr. von Wenckstern (vol. 1, Leiden, 1895, et seq.), which contains a section on "Fairy Tales, Folklore, Proverbs and Superstitions" (82 items, pp. 223-227), one can amass a considerable body of scattered publications bearing on Japanese folk tradition. German travelers, French ethnologists, the editors of popular and scholarly periodicals on the Far East, have helped place on record materials pertinent for the folklorist. From the older compendium of *Things Japanese* by Basil Hall Chamberlain, to the moving autobiography of Etsu Sugimoto, *Daughter of the Samurai,* one writer after another on Japanese life and culture touches, almost inescapably, on folk ritual and legend.[9] Here is an early and knowledgeable article in *Lippincott's* of 1874 on "Japanese Fox Myths" by William E. Griffis; the suspicious sounding *Quaint Customs and Manners of Japan* (4 vols., 1951-55) by Mock Joya, beckoning to tourists in every bookshop, nevertheless offers useful capsules of traditional belief and behavior; the journal of Far Eastern ethnology, *Folklore Studies,* contains translated articles and digests of Japanese publications of prime importance to the folklorist, for example the extensive comparative study of the *kappa* by Eiichiro Ishida.[10] The editor of *Folklore Studies,* Dr. Matthias Eder, was an Austrian priest who had taken his doctorate at the University of Berlin in Japanology, anthropology, and Sinology. He founded the journal in 1942 in Peking, and left in 1949 just ahead of the Red army; thoroughly fluent in German, Chinese, Japanese, French, and English, he could translate from one to the other without pausing for breath. It was he who had translated Naoe's "Post-War Folklore Research Work in Japan" in his journal.

The best collection of books and periodicals in English, French, and German on Japanese life was the KBS Library, then housed in the National Diet Library in Tokyo.[11]

The United States Educational Commission in Japan sponsors lecture tours by the visiting Fulbright appointees, as do sister commissions in other countries, and these trips seemed to offer an opportunity to meet collectors in the outlying districts. The first trip I took, one week in May, through the southernmost main island of Kyushu, proved a comedy of mishaps. After speaking on American Folklore at the anchor city of Fukuoka, I was placed on a train for Miyazaki, and whisked down the inland coast of Kyushu past the beckoning spa of Beppu to a country where Western tourists rarely ventured. Nine hours later, sitting all the while without food in a cramped (for an American) third class compartment, I reached Miyazaki to discover that the local Japanese in the American Cultural Center had only just been notified of my coming, and could not arrange any lectures. On the next leg, to lovely Kagoshima at the southern tip of Kyushu, the situation reversed itself, for my hosts first informed me that I would simply address casual remarks to a small, informal group, and then next morning took me to Kagoshima University and thrust me into an auditorium where the entire student body of over a thousand youths was assembled, to hear me discourse, a sentence at a time, while the interpreter conveyed the message, about the genuineness of Davy Crockett and the artificiality of Paul Bunyan. Spirited back to the train before I could hunt out the local folklorists, I was next borne up the ocean coast to the populous city of Kumamoto. Five minutes before my talk at the junior college of Kumamoto, the faculty member who was to introduce me approached and inquired my name and topic. On learning my identity he expressed a surprise immediately matched by my own, for he was Manabu Maruyama, the only Japanese folklorist to attend the 1950 Midcentury Folklore Institute at Indiana University.

In spite of the confusion and comic misunderstandings marking this trip, it revealed the possibilities for a monolingual visitor to gain entree into the hinterland. From the beachheads of the American Cultural Centers in the various cities, and through the channel of the public lecture, one could advertise his mission. Even this initial trip yielded some valuable contacts. At Miyazaki my hosts introduced me to Chihei Nakamura, a well-known author who levied upon local traditions, and who presented me with a copy of his volume, *Hyuga Minwa Shu (Collection of Folktales from Hyuga,* Miyazaki, 1954), from which I had several selections translated for the *Folk Legends of Japan.* Nakamura was partial to legends of the *kappa,* the boyish Japanese goblin carrying water in his saucer-shaped head, whose sinister reputation developed in Kyushu, and the writer displayed on his mantelpiece an extensive collection of *kappa* figurines and carvings. At Kumamoto I met Professor Toshiaki Harada of Kumamoto University, whose name had been given me by Mr. Oto, and saw his many photographs of the *o-hake,* a tall bamboo rod planted outside Japanese dwellings in Kyushu; Harada was studying the role of the *o-hake* in the worship of *uji-gami,* the Japanese household religion. In Fukuoka, on my return there after completing the circle around Kyushu, I looked up Teigo Yoshida, lecturer in sociology at the University of Kyushu, who had come to my lecture the first day of the trip. Yoshida had spent a year at the University of Oregon, belonged to the American Anthropological Association, and was investigating the factors of social change corroding the old agricultural folk beliefs. In his fieldwork he had located a village where *kappa* was still revered as a river god.

On the basis of this trip and its experiences, I planned a second lecture tour with maximum advance notice to the American Culture Centers to alert the local folklorists. This second excursion, in July, to the northwestern coast of Honshu fronting the Japan Sea, did indeed prove that each province possessed its folklore collectors and enthusiasts, and that they could be located with the help of the Centers. On the first leg of this foray I benefited from the company of Fanny Hagin Mayer, who knew intimately our first stop, Niigata, having served there as interpreter for the occupation forces. At Niigata, in the heart of the "snow country," the announcements from the American Culture Center had instigated a group meeting of folklorists in the prefecture to confer with the visitor, and I was able to see the character of a local society. In the group were the grand old man, venerable and arthritic, Zon Kobayashi, who openly dared challenge some of the theories of Yanagita; a schoolteacher, Kenichi Mizusawa, who through his students had uncovered some excellent tellers of *mukashi-banashi* in the back country, publishing their tales in *Mukashi Attantengana (Once Upon-a-Time Stories,* Nagaoka, 1956); a political party official, Shogo Nakano, whose substantial collection *Densetsu no Echigo to Sado (Echigo and Sado in Legends,* 2 vols., Niigata-shi, 1923-24) Miss Ishiwara had earlier brought to my attention. Among the others were a railroad employee with a hobby of mountain-climbing, who had become interested in the religious folk taboos of mountain-village farmers; a professor of agriculture whose training for the Buddhist priesthood led him into a study of Buddhist signs and hand gestures in folktales; an amateur ethnologist who presented me with a sheaf of mounted photographs he had taken on the small offshore and inbred island of Awashima, population 881, connected with Honshu only by an irregular and infrequent boat service. These were representative members of the Niigata folklore group.

Three hours by ferry from Niigata lay Sado Island, where Mrs. Mayer also had friends, one being the president and prime mover of a Sado folklore society. We called at his home, and Shunosuke Yamamoto related to us from his book *Sado no Shima* (*The Island of Sado,* Sado-gun, 1953), the celebrated island legend of Okesa the geisha. When a poor old couple befriended a homeless cat, the cat turned into a geisha and danced to make money for them. The Okesa dance and costume are known throughout Japan, and the shops on Sado were filled with figurines in wood and stone, designs on fabrics, and paintings on pottery of the dancing Okesa for the tourist trade—the Japanese tourists, as Westerners go only to Kyoto, Nara, Nikko, and Karuizawa.

After leaving Mrs. Mayer, who was to accompany Mr. Mizusowa on a collecting trip (which she subsequently described in *Midwest Folklore*),[12] I traveled next to Nagano, where the bright Japanese youth in charge of the American Culture Center assured me that no folklore activity existed in his prefecture. He showed me a film of William Faulkner, who had visited Nagano for a week's lecture in 1955, a visit already legendary in itself; a book has been published giving a day-by-day account of the visit, and the lovely inn where he stayed (and in which I occupied the room he had slept in) displayed a framed testimonial from the famous author.

In Nagano the imposing Zenko-ji Temple attracted worshippers and tourists, and portrayed on one of its friezes the scene of a celebrated tradition. A greedy peasant woman ran after an ox (or cow) which had impaled a cloth she was washing on its horn. The ox led her all the way to Zenko-ji, where the spirit of Buddha entered her heart. Hence the saying "Driven to Zenko-ji by a cow," told of a person who undergoes a spiritual repentance.

Reasonably certain that Nagano possessed its legend collectors, I renewed my plea in the lecture at the Center for contact with local folklorists. After the talk an elderly member of the audience requested an interview, but it turned out that he merely wished me to pronounce English words in his lesson book; he was a retired farmer who came faithfully to all the Center lectures to hear the sound of English, which he could reproduce accurately, although he knew no meanings of words. Another lead proved more fruitful, and brought me in touch the next day with Masaharu Murai, a high-school teacher of English who had translated fifty-one legends from *Shinshu no Densetsu* (*Legends of Nagano,* Nagano, 1929), twenty-one of which were published in a small book of ninety-eight pages printed at the local newspaper press under the title *Legends and Folktales of Shinshu* (Shinano Mainichi Press, 1949). The remainder were in typescript. Mr. Murai gave me a copy of the book and the typescript, and these were the only English translations of field-collected *densetsu* I unearthed in Japan.

The final stop on this trip was the windy city of Kanazawa guarding the Noto Peninsula, which Percival Lowell in 1891 had described in his *Noto.* Here the director of the Center had arranged meetings for me with two local folklore study groups. A Japanese youth on the staff of the Center, Masaaki Miyasaki, grandson of a samurai, dictated two family traditions to me of fox and *tengu* magic (now printed in *Folk Legends of Japan*). Knowing from the Japanese Folklore Institute that a former Tokyo member, Manabu Ogura, now lived in Kanazawa, I was able to arrange a breakfast session with him, during which he explained, through a Center interpreter, his collecting activities of the past ten years in the Noto area. Ogura was especially interested in the legends of "drifted deities" that abounded on that rocky coast; boulders washed ashore had in an earlier time been considered gods of the sea, and annual festivals honored these deities. By attending the village festivals, Ogura was able to hear and write down the legendary traditions recalled on those festal days. He had visited every Shinto shrine in Noto in his search for accounts of drifted deities.

On August 3, 1957, we left Japan. The associations formed during those ten months have prospered in the intervening years. Professor and Mrs. Hori, Professor Mabuchi, and Kayoko Saito have visited in our home during their trips to the United States, and discussed our manuscript on *Studies in Japanese Folklore*. A student from Washington, Robert J. Adams, who worked with Professor Keigo Seki in Japan, and has translated the texts of his comprehensive classification of Japanese folktales, entered the graduate school of Indiana University in September 1961, to pursue comparative folklore studies.

The situation in Japan appears without counterpart in national folklore studies. In the centers of folklore research, particularly the European capitals, scholars are in close touch with each other. In the areas of the world where oral literature and traditional culture still flourish—represented in our volume by Polynesia, Africa, and to a lesser extent, South America—scholarship is proportionally underdeveloped, and the main emphasis falls on fieldwork. Among the new nations and old civilizations of Asia, like India and Pakistan, only a handful of lonely folklorists can presently be found. But in Japan, where the ancient folk culture and modern ways commingle, a vigorous folklore scholarship has developed in virtual isolation from the rest of the world.

NOTES

1. *Folklore Studies*, VIII (Peking, 1949), 277-284. Translated from the Japanese by Matthias Eder. Subsequently I arranged for its reprinting in *Midwest Folklore*, III (Winter, 1953), 213-222.

2. "Die Japanische Volkskunde: ihre Vorgeschichte, Entwicklung und Gegenwärtige Lage," *Folklore Studies*, III (Peking, 1944), 1-76. German translation by Matthias Eder. See also Matsumoto Nobuhiro, "L'état actuel des études de folklore au Japon," *Japon et Extrême-Orient*, no. 10 (Paris: October, 1924), 228-239.

3. Ouwehand has since published "Some Notes on the God Susa-no-o," *Monumenta Nipponica*, XIV (Tokyo, 1958-59), 384-407, based on his researches into Japanese mythological beliefs.

4. (Tokyo, 1954, translated from *Nippon no Mukashi-banashi*, rev. ed., 1942; first published, 1030.)

5. All three translations are now available in the University of Kentucky Press Microcard Series A, *Modern Language Series, 1, 2,* and *18* (1954, 1958). The Japanese Folklore Dictionary was modeled on the *Wörterbuch der deutschen Volkskunde*, by Oswald A. Erich and Richard Beitl (Leipzig, 1936).

6. *Nihon Minzokugaku Bunken Mokuroku (Japanese Folklore Bibliographical Index*, Tokyo: Japan Science Council, 1955). Compiled by the staff of the Minzokugaku Kenkyusho: Taro Wakamori, editor-in-chief.

7. This book is being published this year (1962) by the Charles E. Tuttle Company of Tokyo, Japan, and Rutland, Vermont. Charles Tuttle has become an outstanding American publisher in Japan, and his motto, "Books to Span the East and West," succinctly expresses his major contribution to closer cultural relations between Americans and Japanese. His two-story office building at

15 Edogawa-cho, Bunkyo-ku, Tokyo, his staff of seventy employees, and his half dozen bookshops handle all aspects of the book business: original publishing, translations, reprints of books published abroad, distribution of books and periodicals in Asia, printing for other presses, retail sales of books of all publishers and out-of-print books. These operations had grown from a vision of Tuttle's when he was stationed in Japan after the war and saw opportunities to develop an export-import side to the long established rare-book business he had inherited in Vermont. The publishing aspect, which by now dominates this trans-Pacific business, began with slender volumes of cartoons and jokes aimed at the GI market (*Baby-san* was his first best-seller), and climbed toward its present list of beautifully printed and illustrated works on Japanese art, literature, and culture. For the folklorist several titles are pertinent: for instance, the eye-catching *The Folk Arts of Japan* by Hugo Munsterberg (1958), with the cover fabric and end papers made by folk craftsmen, and *Japanese Folk-Plays: The Ink-Smeared Lady and Other Kyogen,* translated by Shio Sakanishi (1960).

Tuttle was my classmate and close friend at both Exeter and Harvard, and his career was another factor stimulating my interest in Japan.

8. *Studies in Japanese Folklore* will be issued as Publication 17 in the Indiana University Folklore Series.

9. A discussion of the Western-language bibliography on Japanese folklore will be given in my introduction, "Bridges between Japanese and American Folklorists," in the volume mentioned above.

10. "The *Kappa* Legend: A Comparative Ethnological Study on the Japanese Water-Spirit *Kappa,* and Its Habit of Trying to Lure Horses into the Water," *Folklore Studies,* IX (Peking, 1950), 1-152.

11. KBS stands for Kokusai Bunka Shinkokai (The Society for International Cultural Relations). It is now housed in new headquarters at Shirogane Daimachi, near Meguro station.

12. "Collecting Folk Tales in Niigata, Japan," *Midwest Folklore,* IX (Summer, 1959), 103-109.

Indiana University
Bloomington, Indiana

EDWIN C. KIRKLAND

A PROJECTED BIBLIOGRAPHY OF THE FOLKLORE OF INDIA

A BIBLIOGRAPHY of the folklore of India is needed to bring together the vast amount of material beginning with the Jatakas, traditional stories current some two thousand years before the Grimm brothers made their collection. These traditional tales have not entirely disappeared from oral circulation today as "Br' Rabbit and the Tarbaby" testifies. During the second half of the nineteenth century and the first three decades of the twentieth century many books and articles on Indian folklore appeared. Since Indian independence a number of books, many in the languages of India, and a number of journals, notably *The Eastern Anthropologist* and *Indian Folklore,* have given evidence of increased interest and activity in collections and scholarly publications.

No one expects to get a full and complete picture of Indian folklore from any one source, or from several; however, I feel that a fairly adequate over-all picture of Indian folklore can be found in three sources. One of these is a sixty-nine page booklet, *An Outline of Indian Folklore* by Durga Bhagwat, published by The Popular Book Depot, Bombay, India, in 1958. This is a brief outline and condensation of her Marathi book, *Loksāhityact Rūprekhā,* published in 1956 by the Mumbai Marathi Grantha-Sangrahalaya. Miss Bhagwat puts the emphasis on the Great Tradition, the literary tradition. "Indian culture," she says, "as represented in folklore, has been of one and the same quality, texture, and strength, since Vedic times. . . . Whether you study a proverb, or a myth, or a riddle, or a song, you almost certainly find its prototype either in Vedic, Buddhist-Jain literature, or in the epics and the Purānas" (pp. 1-2). Anyone acquainted with Indian folklore will recognize the truth of her statement. However, Miss Bhagwat clearly appreciates that Indian folklore is not as simple as the foregoing statement would seem to those unfamiliar with the culture of India. The folk culture of India is very complex due to the juxtaposition of various races, starting with Dravidian and Aryan, and of various religions, Hindu, Islam, Buddhism, Jain, and others. Yet all races and all religions in addition to their individual cultures have absorbed some of the old Vedic and Sanskrit tradition, and this tradition does give a unity to Indian folklore. Miss Bhagwat points out the early societies and journals. Perhaps she will include late developments in the comprehensive monograph which she announces in her preface. She outlines ten divisions of the Indian folk tradition, and summarizes briefly various types, such as myth, tale, legend, fable, and riddle. In a very brief space she has given a compact survey of much of Indian folklore.

The second reference which contributes to the over-all picture of Indian folklore is K. D. Upadhyaya, "A General Survey of Folklore Activities in India," *Midwest Folklore,* IV (1954), 201-212. He emphasizes the diversity and contrast of cultures: Aryan versus Dravidian, patriarchal versus matriarchal, monogamous versus polyandrous. The many tribes and religions intensify the diversity and contrast. The very title of his article limits the material to the modern and to what is folklore in a restricted sense rather than in the sense which blends with anthropology. Lines between folklore and anthropology can never be precisely drawn, and certainly the best interests of both require cooperative efforts rather than separation. Without bringing up this issue at all, Mr. Upadhyaya is nevertheless largely concerned with activities in the area of popular literature, such as tales, songs, and riddles. He names a number of British civil servants and missionaries who started the activity, and then lists some dozen societies, practically all with their periodicals or plans for publication, and all very recently established.

In this activity of founding new societies, organizations and periodicals, I see something that is typical of the new India, of independent India, of India since 1947. The desire to found new societies rather than build on the old is typical, I believe, of many areas of Indian life. Also, the founders of these new societies, the editors of the new periodicals, and the authors of modern books of folklore are no longer practically all missionaries or British civil servants but they are Indians: Acharya N. Deva, Hajari Prasad Dwivedi, D. N. Majumdar, and Banarasi D. Chaturvedi. I also see in the titles of the periodicals and books the new independent India. Instead of titles such as *Journal of the Royal Asiatic Society, Indian Antiquary,* and *Man in India,* the newly established periodicals have not English titles but Indian: *Braj Bharati, Janapada, Lok-Varta,* and *Rajasthan Bharati.* Many of the articles and books on folklore are now being published in the languages of India. Thus in folklore scholarship we see the spirit of nationalism, the new India. How far the shift in language will go and what effect it will have on the folklore scholarship of India is a problem too vast and at present too speculative to discuss here.

Both Miss Bhagwat and Mr. Upadhyaya have given very brief, but usefully compact and accurate, pictures of Indian folklore. The one emphasizes the old, the anthropological, the Vedic, and the literary tradition. The other emphasizes the modern, the folklore, and the oral aspects. The two pictures are not contradictory, and I believe their authors would not want them contradictory but complementary. To overlook either would give a distorted picture of Indian folklore.

The third reference which I would give for a general over-all picture of Indian folklore, or Indian tradition, is the JOURNAL OF AMERICAN FOLKLORE, LXXI, No. 281 (July-September 1958), titled "Traditional India: Structure and Change." The entire issue presents the research of some twenty scholars. In no other one place will one find such breadth and depth in presenting the caste, class, tribal, and occupational traditions. Since most of the twenty contributing scholars are in the fields of anthropology, sociology, or Sanskrit literature, naturally the traditional material which falls within these disciplines has been extensively covered by persons well prepared to present the results of their research. The wealth of material in this number (also issued as vol. 10 in the Bibliographical and Special Series of the American Folklore Society) of the JOURNAL OF AMERICAN FOLKLORE is basic to a study of Indian folklore. Milton Singer as guest editor for this issue has brought together the work of outstanding Indian and American scholars.

I first began to prepare a bibliography of the folklore of India for my own use. It has grown into a major project, and I intend to present it for publication. At the present I have about fifteen hundred items, and when all available sources have been examined the total will be well over two thousand. In addition to giving full bibliographical references for each item, I plan to give the geographical area covered (Assam, Kashmir, Punjab, etc.), the linguistic or cultural area (Bengali, Gujerati, Telegu, etc.), and the types of folklore presented (customs, songs, tales, proverbs, etc.). Occasionally an additional notation will be given to note significant content. Furthermore, I hope to list a library in India and one in the United States where each item is located. Naturally, this is an ideal goal, and I can only strive to approach it as closely as possible.

A number of limited bibliographies found as parts of scholarly studies are most useful, and from these I made my beginning. The folktale has received as much attention as any form, and a number of articles and books on this genre have bibliographies. One of these is W. Norman Brown, "The Pañcatantra in Modern Indian Folklore, Part I," *Journal of the American Oriental Society,* XXXIX (1919), 1-54. Many items not found in other bibliographies are listed here, and I am also indebted to Dr. Brown for his personal assistance. Verrier Elwin in *Myths of Middle India* (Madras, 1949) and *Tribal Myths of Orissa* (Bombay, 1954) has important lists. Stith Thompson and Jonas Balys have an extensive list in *The Oral Tales of India,* Indiana University Press, 1958. Stith Thompson and Warren E. Roberts in *Types of Indic Oral Tales,* FF Communications, No. 180 (1960), have a similar list. James G. Frazer in the twelfth volume of *The Golden Bough* has a most extensive bibliography with many items dealing with the folklore of India. The fullest listing, however, is found in Elizabeth von Fürer-Haimendorf's *An Anthropological Bibliography of South Asia* (Paris: Mouton and Co., 1958). All of these are invaluable. Catalogues of the Library of Congress, the British Museum, and the National Library of Calcutta have added many items. Such periodicals as *Indian Antiquary, Man in India, Eastern Anthropologist,* and *Folk-Lore* are filled with pertinent material; the JOURNAL OF AMERICAN FOLKLORE has a little; and even such unlikely sources as the *Southern Folklore Quarterly* and *Midwest Folklore* contribute something. The library of the University of Pennsylvania is very rich in Asian material. I am indebted to Dr. Rudolph Hirsch, Assistant Director, for his assistance to me. The list of references which I have given is not to be taken as inclusive or final; many are yet to be examined, and all indications point to a considerable increase in the size and extent of my bibliography.

I shall give a few items to illustrate the scope and form. Some of these have not been verified.

1. Abbott, John. *The Keys of Power, a Study of Indian Ritual and Belief.* New York, E. P. Dutton, 1932.
   Belief, ritual.
   New York Public Library.

2. Accappa, H. S., ed. *Kannada Gādegalu.* Mysore, the editor, 1958.
   Kannada, proverbs.
   National Library Calcutta.

3. Asboe, Walter, "Social Festivals in Ladakh, Kashmir," *Folk-Lore,* XLIX (1938), 376-389.
   Kashmir, Ladakh, festivals, rhymes.
   Library of Congress.

4. Bābar, Sarojinī. *Marathi Lokakathā.* Poona, A. V. Naik, 1957.
   Marathi, tales.
   National Library Calcutta.

5. Bezbaroa, Sahitya Rathi Lakshminath. *Tales of a Grandfather from Assam.* Translated by Aruna Devi Mukerjea. Bangalore, Indian Institute of Culture, 1955.
Assam, tales.
New York Public Library.

6. Bhagwat, Durga. *Lokṣāhityacī Rūprekhā.* Sangrahalaya, Mumbai Marathi Grantha, 1956. Translated and condensed by Durga Bhagwat as *An Outline of Indian Folklore,* Bombay, Popular Book Depot, 1958.

7. Bolton, H. Carrington, "The Counting-out Rhymes of Children," JAF, I (1888), 31-37.
Marathi, rhymes.

8. Brewster, Paul G., "Four Games of Tag from India," *Midwest Folklore,* I, no. 4 (1951), 239-241.
Games.

9. Brown, W. Norman, "The Pañcatantra in Modern Indian Folklore," *Journal of the American Oriental Society,* XXXIX (1919), 1-54.
Tales.
New York Public Library.

10. Crooke, C. William, "The Dasahra, an Autumn Festival of the Hindus," *Folk-Lore,* XXVI (1915), 28-59.
Festival.
Library of Congress.

11. Dev, Som, "Some Folk Songs of Gorakhpur District," *The Eastern Anthropologist,* II, no. 4 (June 1949), 206-208.
Gorakhpur, songs.

12. Elwin, Verrier. *Folk-songs of Chhattisgarh.* Bombay, Oxford University Press, 1946.
Chhattisgarh, songs.
New York Public Library.

13. Emeneau, M. B. and Archer Taylor, "Annamese, Arabic, and Panjabi Riddles," JAF, LVIII (1945), 12-20.
Punjab, riddles.

14. Frere, Mary Eliza Isabella. *Old Deccan Days, or Hindoo Fairy Legends Current in Southern India.* London, J. Murray, 1868.
Tales.
New York Public Library.

15. Lang, Andrew, "The Indian Origin of Popular Tales," *The Academy,* XLI, no. 1028 (January 16, 1892), 63-64.
Tales.

16. Majumdar, D. N. *Field Songs of Chhattisgarh.* Lucknow, Universal Publishers, 1947. Folk-Culture Series, no. 2.
Bihar, Chhattisgarh, songs, tales.

17. Mookherjee, Ajit, "Indian Crafts," *Indian Folklore,* I, no. 2 (April-June, 1958), 77-78.
Crafts.

18. Naik, T. B., "Khayana Songs of Gujarat," *The Eastern Anthropologist,* II, no. 3 (March 1949), 161-162.
Gujarat, songs.

19. Ramanujan, A. K., "Some Folktales from India," *Southern Folklore Quarterly,* XX (1956), 154-163.
Tales.

20. Sambamoorthy, P., "South Indian Folk-Music," *Indian Art and Letters,* N. S., VI, no. 1 (1932), 32-34.
Music.

21. Sarma, S., "An Interesting Custom in the Holi Festival of Assam," *Journal of the University of Gauhati,* VI (1955), 217-219.
Assam, festival.

22. Satyarthi, Devendra, "Indian Children's Rhymes and Chants," *Orient Review,* IV, no. 8 (August 1958), 7-13.
Rhymes.

23. Satyarthi, Devendra, "New Songs of Andhra Peasant," *The Rural India,* V (1942), 369-372.
Andhra, songs.

24. Schanzlin, G., "Omens in Indian Folk Lore," *Visva-Bharati Quarterly,* IV (1926), 136-143.
Omens.

25. Sethupillai, R. P., "Place Names of Agricultural Regions," *Tamil Culture,* IV (October 1955), 323-336.
Place names.

26. Sen, P., "A Basali Folk-Song," *Man in India,* XII (1932), 175-180.
Basali, song.

27. Taylor, Archer, "Twenty-Three Telugu Riddles from Nellore," JAF, LIV (1941), 72-75.
Telugu, riddles.

28. Thompson, Stith and Warren E. Roberts. *Types of Indic Oral Tales, India, Pakistan, and Ceylon.* FF Communications, No. 180. Helsinki, Suomalainen Tiedeakatemia Academica Scientiarum Fennica, 1960.

29. Wood, Casey A., "Sinhalese and South Indian Ceremonials in the Prevention and Treatment of Disease," *Annals of Medical History,* N. S., VI (1934), 483-490.
Sinhalese, medicine.

An index composed of the notations on geographical, linguistic, and cultural areas, and types of folklore will be included. Each item in the index will carry numbers which refer to the bibliography. For example, if we use the sample given above in the index we would have: Tales: 4, 5, 8, 14, 19, 28.

Many problems arise. One is geographical; at the present I am including Kashmir, Pakistan, Tibet, and Ceylon. A greater difficulty comes when we attempt to determine what is folklore and where to draw the line between folklore and anthropology, sociology, nonfolk literature, and other closely related areas. I have seen no satisfactory solution to this problem, and I have none to offer. Whenever I am in doubt about including an item which is only remotely related to folklore I shall probably include it, preferring to draw down upon my head harsh judgments rather than to deprive someone of a reference which may be most important to him. My doubts may arise from several situations. As far as possible I hope to examine, or have examined, every item in the bibliography. However, this is again an ideal. Some of the items undoubtedly cannot be located and verified. Then, I shall have to depend upon the title alone for judging the contents, and shall often be in doubt. However, even when I have ample opportunity to examine certain works fully, I shall many times be in doubt, and my only reply to why a certain article or book is included will be that made famous by Samuel Johnson. Persons whose primary interest is folklore may well say that too many items that are purely anthropology have been included. And the persons whose primary interest is anthropology may well say that many items have been left out that should have been included.

Again persons who limit folklore to the oral and folk may well feel that much literary material that is not folk is included. In India the content of Vedic literature permeates the oral and folk to such an extent that much of the material that could be nonfolk in cultures outside of India does have a definite relation here. Again, when doubt arises, I have included the items.[1]

The material available only in India needs to be checked before the project is adequately completed, material available in such libraries as the National Library at Calcutta, the Library of the Asiatic Society at Bombay, the library of the Deccan College Post-Graduate and Research Institute at Poona, and the libraries at the Universities of Bombay, Calcutta, Delhi, and Madras.[2]

NOTES

1. I expect to have covered the bulk of the material in the United States by the end of the summer of 1961. This will be possible because of special assistance and a research grant from the University of Florida, specifically from the Department of English, Dr. C. A. Robertson, chairman, and from the Research Council, Dean L. E. Grinter, chairman.

2. I am indebted to a number of individuals who have already given assistance: Dr. W. Norman Brown and Dr. Rudolph Hirsch of the University of Pennsylvania, Dr. S. M. Katre, Director of the Deccan College and Post-Graduate Research Institute, and Miss Durga Bhagwat. Before the project is completed I shall need further assistance, particularly from the scholars of India.

University of Florida
Gainesville, Florida

Oceania
and
Australia

KATHARINE LUOMALA

SURVEY OF RESEARCH ON POLYNESIAN PROSE AND POETRY

INTRODUCTION

THE MATERIAL to be surveyed here covers only the oral narratives and chants of Polynesia. Excluded from consideration, except for occasional passing mention, is research on Polynesian music and dance, closely related though these subjects are to the narratives and chants.

Included in the phrase "oral prose and poetry" is a variety of stylistic forms which in each archipelago are sometimes designated by specific terms that, unfortunately, are not widely, clearly, and consistently enough used throughout Polynesia to serve now to designate native categories of oral narrative art. My brief glance at "Western Polynesian Classification of Prose Forms"[1] showed that Samoans, Tongans, Uveans, Futunans, Rotumans, and Ellice Islanders apply terms to categories that we would call myth, cosmogony, legend, traditional history, folktale, animal tale, explanatory tale, cante-fable, riddle, riddling tale, proverb, hero saga, charm, oration, artistic conversation, and subtypes of these. The eastern region has comparable categories.

The line between rhythmic narrative prose and chanting is often hard to draw, but the Maoris of New Zealand, to single out one group as representative, have hundreds of terms relating to chants and rhythmic verbal formulae. Subject, function, form, or other criteria determine the native name for a type of chant. Many narratives include chants.

Obviously the Polynesians have a noticeable awareness of verbal art; have nebulous standards, more felt than defined, of aesthetic quality and form; and have innumerable named, though vague, categories of artistic verbal communication. A native's ordinary exposition of ethnographic information to an investigator, though it reflects his cultural style of communication, should be distinguished from the studied, self-conscious, stylistic forms that originated in the past.

Polynesia, the geographical and cultural area to be surveyed, means "Many Islands" and extends from the Hawaiian Islands in the north to Easter Island in the east, New Zealand and Chathams in the south, and the Samoan, Tongan, and Ellice Islands in the west. Besides the islands named which are on the boundaries of the area, there are also such major groups as the Society Islands, the Tuamotus, the Marquesas, the Australs including Rapa, the Northern and Southern Cook Islands, and many scattered, isolated islands.

Some of the narrative motifs and the stylistic forms found within Polynesia are present in the adjacent culture areas of Micronesia and Melanesia, especially in those islands with so predominantly a Polynesian culture or physical type, or both, as to be called "Polynesian outliers." Some motifs can be traced back through Indonesia to the Asiatic mainland. With Australia, however, Polynesian folkloristic connections are slight.

Despite Polynesian relationships with adjoining areas, it is useful in a short survey to focus upon the one area, Polynesia, and a particular phase of its culture, the oral chants and narratives, and to bring in peripheral subjects and areas only incidentally. But although the geographical boundaries customarily defined for Polynesia are a working convenience, they should never become a straitjacket to lead us to ignore the diffusion of similar content and style over the south Pacific.

Chronologically the collection and study of Polynesian prose and poetry has covered four major periods. These periods have no rigid dates but are distinguishable by the predominance of a certain type of collector or approach to the collecting and analyzing of Polynesian narratives and poetry. First, there were the European discoverers and explorers and also the earliest settlers who published a few "bits and pieces" of native stories, or short summaries and comments about them, in reminiscences of their impressions and experiences in Polynesia. Second, as the European occupation and development increased, there were the dedicated amateur anthropologists who, in the course of their administrative and professional duties for governments and religious missions, interested themselves in the native languages and cultures, and collected and published entire myths and chants with the native-language versions and European-language translations. The bulk of the source material on myths and chants comes from this period. Third, there were the professional anthropologists who salvaged additional versions from the native peoples and further swelled the total number of versions and variants by rescuing from oblivion, and probably eventual destruction, manuscript collections by both native and foreign residents in the islands. Finally, there is the present.

Each of these four eras will be discussed more fully, but only a few representatives of each period will be named, for it would be impossible in a short article to name all who have recorded Polynesian chants and narratives. But first a glance at helpful bibliographies.

BIBLIOGRAPHIES

Unfortunately, there is no comprehensive or up-to-date bibliography of the publications and manuscripts of collections of Polynesian oral narrative art and the analytical studies of them. Works dating from the last two periods that include long bibliographies which the student may find useful as starting points are Roland B. Dixon's *Oceanic Mythology* (Boston, 1916), which was Volume 9 of *The Mythology of All Races,* edited by Louis H. Gray; Martha Warren Beckwith's *Hawaiian Mythology* (New Haven, 1940); and my *Maui-of-a-thousand-tricks: His Oceanic and European Biographers* (Honolulu, 1949), which was Bulletin 198 published by the Bernice P. Bishop Museum. Some of the published surveys of the content and character of Polynesian oral art will be mentioned later in this article. However, these three works will provide examples of the lore as well as bibliography. The third reference, which also discusses the collectors in particular archipelagoes and the theorists using Polynesian lore, will provide more detail on these phases than is possible here. The demigod Maui was so popular with storytellers, collectors, and theorists that he is a key mythological figure in the area.

Robert W. Williamson's *Religious and Cosmic Beliefs of Central Polynesia* (2 vols., Cambridge, England, 1933) has a long bibliography together with abstracts of myths, Williamson's theories, and an introductory essay on theories of Polynesian origin and history that students unfamiliar with the area or this subject will find informative. Probably in no other area in the world have native oral narratives and chants been so much used as a direct source of history by investigators of the subject as in Polynesia.

A special and important group of collectors of tales and of other cultural data is discussed, and a bibliography given, in my article on "Missionary Contributions to Polynesian Anthropology."[2]

Other long bibliographies have appeared which, like the two just named, have more than the oral narrative art as the purpose of their compilation. *Introduction to Polynesian Anthropology* (Honolulu, 1945), by Peter H. Buck (Te Rangi Hiroa was his Maori name), published as Bulletin 187 by Bishop Museum, is a survey of research in general anthropology of the area and of particular archipelagoes within it. Its general and regional items include many relevant to Polynesian lore. Valuable orientation is provided by the discussion of the various groups and individuals who have contributed to knowledge of Polynesian culture. Buck tells about the explorers, the first settlers, the traders, the government officials, the native informants, and the missionaries. Also of special interest to those working on myths and chants is Buck's consideration of the problems relating to translations and interpretations and to the publishing of native texts. The history of the formation of ethnological societies in Polynesia and of the work of individual ethnographers and of special expeditions from the Bishop Museum in Honolulu will also guide the newcomer in the field to sources of value. The study now needs to be revised and corrected in details.

Purely bibliographical and more extensive in subject and area is the compilation by C. R. H. Taylor, *A Pacific Bibliography: Printed Matter Relating to Native Peoples of Polynesia, Melanesia, and Micronesia* (Wellington, N. Z., 1951), published as Memoir 24 in 1951 by the Polynesian Society. The work is elaborately subdivided by area, archipelago and subject matter. However, more than the items under "Folklore" should be consulted because much on the subject is scattered in works classified under "Religion"; "Music, Arts, Recreation"; "Traditional History"; and other headings. Taylor also includes a list of bibliographies pertinent to Oceanic research. He also prepared an index, published by the Polynesian Society, to the first fifty volumes of its *Journal*. This is an important aid because the Society, founded in 1892, has published in its quarterly journals and memoirs many collections of narrative art as well as much else of ethnographical interest. Polynesia, particularly New Zealand, is best represented, but the Society also publishes occasional articles and monographs on other Pacific areas.

Other serials and periodicals will be mentioned later. However, La Société des Études Océaniennes (Papeete, Tahiti) should be mentioned now because of its "Bibliographie de l'Océanie" which appears in its *Journal* and includes items of Polynesian lore. The compilers are Patrick O'Reilly and Edouard Reitman. The *Journal* (formerly called the *Bulletin*) also publishes articles on narrative art from French Polynesia, for example, from such groups as the Societies, Marquesas, Tuamotus, and Mangareva.

Intensive surveys of research on the oral narratives and chants of particular archipelagoes with bibliographies as complete as possible are rare. Amos P. Leib has inevitably surveyed the history of collection in the Hawaiian Islands in the course of discussing translators and retellers of tales and of presenting an annotated bibliography of their publications in English through 1948. Titled *Hawaiian Legends in English: An Annotated Bibliography,* Leib's work was published by the University of Hawaii Press, Honolulu, in 1949.

For other archipelagoes it is necessary to compile one's own bibliographies of legends from the general bibliographies already mentioned. Should the latter be un-available, one can consult the ethnographies of particular islands or archipelagoes published by Bishop Museum because they usually include extensive lists of pub-lished works and manuscripts relating to the region discussed, and the authors often present myths and chants with occasional considerations of their cultural content and role. A comprehensive survey of collections and analyses of narrative art in New Zealand is much needed because of the amount of material from there and the uneven quality. So far only occasional evaluative articles on individual collectors and trans-lators have appeared.

THE FIRST PERIOD

Although the first Polynesian islands, the Marquesas, were discovered by Mendaña in 1595, the student of narrative art will find little for his field in the journals of dis-covery and exploration until the last quarter of the eighteenth century. Then Captain Cook and his companions (for example, George and J. R. Forster and especially Wil-liam Anderson who provided the captain with much information) published from the three voyages a few brief, repetitive, and often garbled references to names and deeds of gods and heroes.[3] The information was culled from within their own group or from accounts of earlier voyages. Sometimes they noted with regret that they did not know enough of the native languages even to skim the wealth of lore, religious and popular, which they recognized existed, or they thought the stories they heard too absurd to record. Their interpreters did not know enough English to communicate what they knew, and because they were nonliterate they could not write even in their own language. Time also pressed too much on the voyagers to permit them to make intensive inquiries into subjects not immediately significant.

It should also be remembered that no scientific study of culture, let alone folk-lore, existed at this time to stimulate inquiry. The voyagers' descriptions, as a matter of fact, inspired curiosity about strange peoples and cultures and were a factor in the development of anthropology. Their material about gods and heroes provides us now with a minimum date for the presence of certain mythological incidents, names, and details—in other words, of motifs—and sometimes gives us a clue to their function and relative importance in the lives of the people. Further to add interest to their books, the writers sometimes described how the narrators behaved as they functioned as entertainers, magicians, or educators. These fugitive impressions, for all their sub-jectivity, are to me one of the major values and charms of the records of this first period. They have the pristine freshness of the European's first glimpse at this alien world before he began to change it. Few such revealing glimpses come later, even of the changing culture.

Explorers of the early nineteenth century give us references to lore as poor in quality and quantity as those of the preceding century. One must scan page after page, volume after volume, to glean a mythological name or incident. The volumes of the United States Exploring Expedition commanded by Charles Wilkes, 1838 to 1841, come to mind as one example.[4]

This paucity also characterizes the travel books by pioneer settlers, administrators, missionaries, and visitors less transient than the discoverers. New Zealand had a spate of these books, with J. L. Nicholas publishing in 1817, J. S. Polack in 1838 and 1840, W. Yate in 1835, E. Dieffenbach in 1843, and W. Brodie in 1845.[5] Edward Shortland's volumes are more productive of material on prose and poetry than most of these others because Shortland often gives fuller versions and sometimes the Maori texts of chants, translated, however, to eliminate what might be objectionable to those unable to read the Maori beside it. Shortland's *Traditions and Superstitions of the New Zealanders* was published in London in 1854.

Other archipelagoes have books like these Maori travel volumes. Of special interest because of its intimate knowledge of Tongan culture is the account published in 1817 that the young seaman, William Mariner, gave to Dr. John Martin.[6] The book, which includes scraps of lore and examples in Tongan of chants, is about Mariner's experiences and knowledge of Tongan life during his four year enforced stay in the archipelago. In 1855 Sarah S. Farmer gave some fuller Tongan stories in her book on Tongan customs for which she had the benefit of notes by the missionary John Thomas.[7]

Some missionaries and their literate converts were gathering material at this time, but until the mid-century such of it that was published or prepared for publication consisted of general accounts of the vanishing old culture and of the history of the mission. The main purpose was to interest the general public in supporting these outposts of missions and empires. Of the published works, Rev. William Ellis' *Polynesian Researches* (2 vols., London, 1829), which went through several editions, is one of the most valuable for the anthropologist in regard to central Polynesia, particularly the Society Islands. The specialist in narrative art, however, will find, as in other works of this era, only a sprinkling of references to heroes and gods, some abstracts of stories, and now and then a chant to illustrate the language. The same applies to Ellis' *Journal of a Tour Around Hawaii* (Boston and New York, 1825), also often reprinted but with the title of *Narrative of a Tour Through Hawaii* or included as an additional volume with *Polynesian Researches*.

Ellis, who represented the London Missionary Society, probably helped a little on his two visits to the Hawaiian Islands to interest the American Board missionaries in collecting information about native culture. An important development was the movement begun by Rev. S. Dibble of the Lahainaluna School on the island of Maui to get some of his pupils like D. Malo and S. M. Kamakau to write in Hawaiian about the old culture. In 1841 the group organized the Royal Hawaiian Historical Society with Kamehameha III as one of the charter members. The Hawaiian-language newspapers in which much of this material appeared became a mine of information in the twentieth century for both scholars and popular writers, and even before then some of it was translated and published in English. However, there is still very little in the way of full versions of narratives and chants in this early period, beyond the type of material characteristic of the era and the interesting reinterpretations of ancient beliefs by intense converts to Christianity.

THE SECOND PERIOD

A new period with a new approach opened in 1855 with the publication in London of Sir George Grey's *Polynesian Mythology and Ancient Traditional History of the New Zealand Race.* J. A. Davies contributed an appendix "On the Native Songs of New Zealand." It was the first book, so far as I know, devoted entirely to the mythology of a Polynesian group and with the narratives given in their entirety in English and in the native language. Earlier, in 1853, Grey had brought out the Maori texts of some songs and chants, and in 1854 the Maori texts of ancestral traditions.[8] The latter publication went into a third edition in 1928 when the Board of Maori

Ethnological Research reprinted it with revisions and corrections by H. W. Williams.[9] One of Grey's interpreters, C. O. B. Davis, included chants in his *Maori Mementos* that was published in Auckland, New Zealand, in 1855, the same year as Grey's *Polynesian Mythology*. However, it was *Polynesian Mythology* which caught the attention of both the general public and scholars in England and on the continent.

Although one can appreciate the reason for it since, like the books of the preceding era, it was intended mainly for the general public, the first part of the title is too inclusive for a collection from only the Maoris of New Zealand. The collector-translator in his preface tells how as Governor General he began to learn the language and to collect the mythology so that he might govern more wisely the native people through understanding the lore which they cited to support their claims. Unfortunately, the native application of the lore is not illustrated. Grey obtained his narratives by a method increasingly used. High-ranking Maoris were asked to dictate or to write down in notebooks their traditions and chants in the native language. Grey himself took down some of the dictation.

Despite criticisms that have come with later knowledge and standards, Grey's *Polynesian Mythology* remains a minor classic because of its position as a milestone in Polynesian research; its importance for reference until his original notebooks are retranslated; and its good selection of narratives for the casual reader of Maori mythology. The book continues to be reissued.

The late Sir Peter Buck, in order to illustrate the liberties that Grey took with his material in this work and that led later to misinterpretations of Maori cultural history, has presented an example in *The Coming of the Maori* (Wellington, N. Z., 1949, p. 45). In two parallel columns he gives first the Maori text of a passage with its literal translation and then Grey's version of the passage, which includes not only translation but interpolation of his own interpretation which he did not keep separate. Also, Grey omitted or altered incidents that might offend the European unable to read Maori or that showed European influence on the Maori narrators. He pieced together different incomplete versions, and rearranged or substituted incidents. He admits in his preface that he made alterations that seemed justified to him. He did not specify the tribes or narrators from which specific selections came.

Modern scholars of Maori linguistics and mythology have had the opportunity only since 1922 and 1923 to study the original notebooks because Grey, who had also served as an administrator in south Africa, had given this treasure, of which only parts were ever published, to a library in Capetown. Now this original source material has been transferred to the Auckland Public Library. Recently Bruce Biggs has begun to study and retranslate the narratives. He finds that Grey made many alterations as described above and also for no apparent reason frequently revised his Maori informants' Maori sentence constructions. Biggs confirms, as had been conjectured, that most of the narratives in *Polynesian Mythology* came from Wi Maihi te Rangikaheke, or, as he was also called, Wiremu Marsh, a chief of the great Arawa tribe of North Island, New Zealand. Biggs's article on "The Translation and Publishing of Maori Material in the Auckland Public Library"[10] is important in understanding research in Maori traditions.

Grey by no means initiated the collecting of Polynesian myths in their entirety in the native language. Others in Polynesia, Europeans and literate natives alike, had been doing it too. However, Grey's prestige as Governor General probably helped get his selection of myths published and thus set a precedent that opened the way for others to get entire myths published also. Grey broke the ice, but the ice was ready to be broken. One direction taken by the interest aroused during the period of discovery in the Noble Savage—the Polynesian being a favorite example—was toward the development of a science of folklore and ethnology. The year 1812 had marked the first publication of a collection of tales in Germany by the Grimm brothers, who had presented them as the peasant storytellers had told them, except that Wilhelm Grimm occasionally pieced together fragments as Grey was to do later. Previously the romantic interest in myths and songs of savages and peasants had served only to inspire poets with themes for their creative interpretations or to spice the pages of travelers' books. The more objective spirit of the Grimm brothers and the interest in the tales for themselves and as narratives from an alien culture took hold slowly. However, enough headway had been made for Grey to find an audience when his *Polynesian Mythology* appeared and to lead E. B. Tylor, the great pioneer English anthropologist, to correspond with Grey and to mention this correspondence, involving more literal translations of passages of certain stories, in his classic *Primitive Culture*.

Perhaps had the objective spirit been as strong when Ellis' *Polynesian Researches* appeared, he might have gathered up for publication the collections of chants and narratives that he and his colleages of the London Missionary Society had been making since the establishment of the mission in the Society Islands in 1797. Ellis, with J. M. Orsmond, the most indefatigable collector of lore, arrived in 1817. Instead of his book meeting with a scientific spirit it encountered the persisting romantic spirit of the time. Ellis, an unusually capable and intelligent observer, reacted to the admiration of Wordsworth and Southey, by discussing with them his long, romantic narrative poem based on a Polynesian theme. Orsmond's massive collections remained unpublished except for brief excerpts for at least a century. In 1928 Bishop Museum published *Ancient Tahiti* (Bulletin 48) based on what Teuira Henry, Orsmond's granddaughter, could salvage from his remaining notes and her own research. Orsmond's original, completed manuscript, which he had given to the French when Tahiti became French, was lost somewhere in Paris. The major purpose of the missionaries who made early collections was to learn the language, prepare dictionaries and grammars (which helped to lay the foundation for the science of linguistics), translate the Bible into native languages, and incidentally to learn something of the native culture.

In Mangareva in 1856 Father Honoré Laval, a pioneer Catholic missionary, was also preparing a manuscript on the culture of that island with the aid of one convert, Tiripone, in particular. Copies of this manuscript, and copies of copies, circulated widely, some getting into print before Laval's copy, titled *Mangareva,* was published in 1938 at Braine-le-Comte by the mission and with the support also of Bishop Museum. The problem of repetitive publication recurs in research on Polynesian mythology. Examples are discussed in my article, "Documentary Research in Polynesian Mythology."[11]

In later decades of this second period the rich vein of public interest in South Sea heathen customs and tales continued to be exploited. Outstanding among the later L.M.S. missionaries for his interest in chants and narratives and ability to attract readers to collections of myths was William Wyatt Gill, a voluminous writer of ethnographical items, but best known for his charming selection, unfortunately never reprinted, called *Myths and Songs from the South Pacific* (London, 1876). Like most of his information the material came from the Cook Islands, but, as often was the case even in this period, the island origin is not always made clear. Revealing of the spirit and stage of mythology as a science at this time is the fact that the preface was by Max Müller, who gloried in the opportunity given by Gill's stories and songs to step backwards into a time and stage of culture gone from the western world. It was, Müller wrote, as if the zoologist could see the megatheria alive, and the botanist walk among the waving plumes of the coal forests of the past.

Gill through his jottings saved many fugitive items of lore, such as his converts' sermons using native proverbs and tales to point Christian morals, native reminiscences of heathen times, and many, many chants. The latter, which usually were the only items given in the native language, should be retranslated. Gill translated them very freely to make them readily comprehensible and attractive to the general reader. Extracts from Gill's unpublished materials, in texts and translations, some by later translators than Gill, appeared in 1915 in the *Journal of the Polynesian Society* and later in the Reprint Series as *Rarotongan Records*.

The third important published collection of myths and tales in this era to have a wide circulation, besides Grey's and Gill's two major books, came from the northern end of Polynesia and was credited by its editor R. M. Daggett to King Kalakaua of Hawaii. Daggett, who had been U. S. Minister to the Hawaiian Kingdom, retold *The Legends and Myths of Hawaii* (New York, 1888) in the florid English of the time, and selected his stories from a variety of published and unpublished sources incompletely acknowledged in his preface.

Other collectors published in the journals and bulletins of the scientific societies that were springing up. In New Zealand these societies include the New Zealand Institute (later called the Royal Society), the Dominion Museum, and later, the Board of Maori Ethnological Research; in Australia, the Royal Society of New South Wales and the Australasian Association for the Advancement of Science; and in the Hawaiian Islands, the Hawaiian Historical Society. Popular books of reminiscences and descriptions by missionaries, administrators, and travelers continued to appear with examples of native tales. One worth mentioning, because it comes from an out of the way archipelago, is Mrs. Edgeworth David's *Funafuti, or Three Months on a Coral Island* (London, 1899). Like Gill, Mrs. David had a flair for including ephemeral local color, such as the popular songs based on Biblical themes that the Ellice Islanders were singing.

In Samoa, the missionary Thomas Powell first published some of his collected material in free poetic translations through the Victoria Institute. Later his colleague, Rev. George Pratt, with John Frazer, translated Powell's material more literally and added explanatory notes. Most of these translations appeared under one or more of the three names, principally in the journals of the Royal Society of New South Wales during the early 1890's and later in the journals of the Polynesian Society. Some of Pratt's translations appeared in *Folk-Lore* under the name of J. Abercromby.[12] The general books on Samoa by John B. Stair and George Turner, also missionaries, include some myths not only from Samoa but occasionally from archipelagoes to the north where the L.M.S. had stations.[13] Indicative of what the writers drew on for their popular accounts are Stair's "Jottings on the Mythology and Spirit-lore of Old Samoa."[14]

In New Zealand, Grey's former secretary and interpreter, John White, brought out six volumes of texts and translations of *The Ancient History of the Maori* (Wellington, N. Z., 1887-91). The traditions and chants were garnered from many sources, published and unpublished, which White mentioned in the prefaces of the volumes. Among the sources were his own collections, Grey's manuscripts, and published articles or manuscripts by other collectors, such as Rev. J. F. H. Wohlers, who, in 1874 and 1875, published some texts with very free translations (of what he thought was not too silly or obscene) in *Transactions of the New Zealand Institute.*[15] White's volumes are a major reference work despite criticisms of it by his colleagues. An evaluation of the work and of the criticisms appears in an informative appendix to J. Prytz Johansen's *The Maori and His Religion in its Non-Ritualistic Aspects* (Copenhagen, 1954). Others works, like *The Lore of the Whare-Wananga, or Teachings of the Maori College on Religion, Cosmogony, and History* (New Plymouth, N. Z., 1913-15), are also discussed there.

The two volumes of *The Lore* were edited, annotated, and translated by S. Percy Smith, appearing as Memoirs 3 and 4 of the Polynesian Society. In the mid-nineteenth century a gathering of East Coast Maoris decided to record their elders' knowledge, and one sage in particular dictated to two young Maoris the material preserved in *The Lore.* Smith also made, or acquired, collections in Rarotonga, Niue, and many other parts of Polynesia. Usually the Polynesian Society, of which he was long the editor, published his chants, narratives, and ethnographical descriptions. Smith had much confidence in the value of the traditions and genealogies as direct sources of history on the origin, customs, and migrations of the Polynesians into their present island homes. In "Hawaiki: The Whence of the Maori," which first appeared in the *Journal* and later in book form that went through four revised editions, the last in 1921,[16] Smith drew upon the traditional material, particularly from Rarotonga and New Zealand, to trace the Polynesians back to India, which he believed to have been their homeland. His enthusiasm for his theory led, some critics claim, to his asking informants leading questions to which they gave the answers he wanted. Smith, although untrained in anthropology, knew Polynesians and their culture well, and whatever criticisms later standards of research have given rise to, he stands in this second era as one of the two major theorists and collectors, or preservers, of collections of Polynesian traditions. The other is Abraham Fornander of the Hawaiian Islands.

Fornander in his *An Account of the Polynesian Race* (3 vols., London, 1878-85) used his Hawaiian collections to expound his theory that the Polynesians were a "chip of the same block" as the Aryan-speaking peoples of southwest Asia. In general his theory was not too different from Smith's except that he favored Semitic Arabia rather than India as the place of Polynesian exodus. Fornander's and Smith's time schedules for Polynesian migrations, which they based on comparisons of genealogies and traditions, have continued in use for lack of anything better. But in recent years comparative studies of Polynesian languages and radiocarbon dating have begun to alter our time perspective on Polynesian settlement of the eastern Pacific.

The greatest of all assemblages of Hawaiian lore—Fornander's Hawaiian texts of narratives, chants, and ethnography, obtained from informants, from manuscripts of foreign residents and literate natives, and from Hawaiians whom he sent out to gather material—was not published until the next period. In the third period that I have distinguished, Bishop Museum from 1916 to 1920 published as Memoirs 4, 5, and 6, each with Parts, the *Fornander Collection of Hawaiian Antiquities and Folklore,* containing both texts and translations. Thomas G. Thrum, a businessman who had become interested in Hawaiian culture, served as editor and one of the translators. It was Thrum who published the *Hawaiian Almanac and Annual,* usually called

Thrum's Annual, in which from 1875 on he printed in each volume one or more articles or bits of old Hawaiiana obtained from a variety of contributors, including himself. In 1907 and 1923 his two principal books of selections from the *Annual* or from translations made from Hawaiian-language newspapers were published in Chicago to reach a larger group of readers.[17] In the production of popular books of selections of Hawaiian lore he was surpassed in quantity after 1910 by Rev. W. D. Westervelt.[18]

With the start of the twentieth century and Hawaiian annexation as a territory of the United States, interest in this foreign possession led to much writing about it. One of the most valuable and attractive books is *The Unwritten Literature of Hawaii,* which the Bureau of American Ethnology published as Bulletin 38 in 1909. The hula chants in the collection had been translated and abundantly annotated by Rev. N. B. Emerson. In 1915, in Honolulu, Emerson published *Pele and Hiiaka,* his synthesis into a connected story of some narratives and chants about the volcano goddess and her younger sister.

Among other important collectors of the second era was Elsdon Best, who published voluminously in New Zealand, with the Tuhoe tribes of North Island as his principal subject. Packed with fascinating information, some of his books are nonetheless hard to follow for they frequently sound like field notebooks transferred to the printed page, but other volumes are organized around selected activities in Maori life.[19] Myths, chants, and tales are usually combined with all kinds of ethnographical data. Even though one may puzzle as to what to make of them at times, collections of narratives from this era generally consist of more than dead bones which are unrelatable to any existence they once had or still retained in native life. Other collectors in New Zealand, to name but two more from many, Edward Tregear and, later, James Cowan, brought out occasional books of Maori narratives and chants but published most of their material in the scientific journals of New Zealand.[20]

The turn of the century also saw much collecting and publishing of myths and chants with other ethnographical information by Germans holding government positions in Western Samoa, then a German colony. W. von Bülow published myths in 1898 and 1899 in the *Internationales Archiv für Ethnographie* and from 1895 to 1897 in *Globus.* O. Sierich from 1900 through 1905 also published many "Samoanische Märchen" in the *Archiv.* In 1896, O. Stuebel published *Samoanische Texte* as the fourth volume of the *Veröffentlichungen aus dem Königlichen Museum für Völkerkunde.* A. Krämer in 1902 and 1903 published in Stuttgart two large volumes called *Die Samoa-Inseln* which included many texts and translations into German of chants and narratives. An English translation was mimeographed in 1942 by the government, now British, in Apia, the capital of Western Samoa. E. Schultz included Samoan proverbs with commentaries in his general ethnographic research while serving the government, but the proverbs were only recently published, translated from German into English by Brother Herman, through the Polynesian Society, appearing first, as is often customary in this Society, through the journals and then in a memoir. Schultz's *Proverbial Expressions of the Samoans* (1953) is Memoir 27.

Most of the collections from French Polynesia were printed, as was noted above, in the publications of La Société des Etudes Océaniennes. Hervé Audran was a frequent contributor. L. G. Seurat, an administrative official, sent much material in 1905 and 1906, mostly on the Tuamotus, to *Revue des Traditions Populaires.*[21] A.-C. E. Caillot between 1909 and 1932 brought out four books on Polynesian myths and traditional history, but he is never explicit about his sources of information. Some may have been native manuscripts or records published in native-language newspapers. In my *Maui-of-a-thousand-tricks* I cite an example of the repetitive publication of an identical cycle of stories about Maui from Tonga. Caillot published the cycle with a French translation. P. Reiter, a missionary, also published it with a French translation in *Anthropos*. E. E. V. Collocott, another missionary, published a free account in English in *Folk-Lore* and later in the same journal a more literal translation. The first publication was in a native-language magazine of a Tongan mission school.[22]

This second period, noticeably the latter part of it which extends into the first two decades of the twentieth century, was dominated by highly educated or at least unusually intelligent, persistent, sympathetic, and observant amateur anthropologists whose personal interest in Polynesians and their culture sometimes led them to devote most of their time to writing on the subject. Many of these writers held government positions and often served the government in a variety of capacities. Among the most versatile were Krämer, a medical doctor by profession, Smith, a surveyor, and Fornander, who also served for a time as a surveyor and later as an inspector of schools and a circuit judge.

Only occasionally in this period did a professional anthropologist, someone not too common then anyway, visit Polynesia and write about it. Adolf Bastian (who else!) stopped by on his way to Asia and as usual uncovered a treasure and managed to interest a few local people in what lay about them. In addition he brought out in 1881, 1883, and 1884 books about Hawaiian and Samoan mythology.[23] When he heard that King Kalakaua had a manuscript of the Kumulipo, the family genealogical chant, he borrowed it and published part of it with his translation. He probably inspired the king to publish the Hawaiian form in its entirety. Later Queen Liliuokalani translated it into English for publication.[24] Karl von den Steinen, who as early as 1898 had published a few snatches of stories in his writings on Marquesan native art, published more with comparative notes and abstracts in the mid-1930's in *Zeitschrift für Ethnologie*. A. Baessler published Tahitian legends in the same journal in 1905 and in *Globus* in 1897 and 1898.

Professional scholars in Europe and England incorporated references from publications on Polynesia into their syntheses and analyses of culture. Theodor Waitz included a discussion of narrative art in his survey of Polynesian culture in the sixth volume of his *Anthropologie der Naturvölker* (Leipzig, 1872). T. Achelis wrote essays and a book on native myths and gods.[25] The first comparative study of Polynesian mythology, limited to the Maori, was C. Schirren's *Die Wandersagen der Neuseeländer und der Mauimythos* (Riga, 1856), published one year after Grey's *Polynesian Mythology*. Schirren abstracted the scattered references to Maori lore and presented his theory that the Maori traditions were not historically valid but were really symbolic descriptions of the sun in its rising and setting. Solar, evolutionary, and etymological theories, blended together, prevail in the theories of foreign scholars studying Polynesian lore. They are also evident in the writings of Smith, Fornander, and other Polynesian-based scholars who, however, usually preferred to follow in the footsteps of Euhemerus.

During the early twentieth century both Frobenius and Graebner also analyzed some of the Polynesian narratives in terms of their Old World relationships or as evidence of the presence in Polynesia of elements of certain evolutionary blocks of cultural traits or concepts.[26] These varied theories are reviewed in my *Maui-of-a-thousand-tricks*.

THE THIRD PERIOD

The flow of manuscripts relating to myths and chants reached flood tide during the first two decades of the twentieth century when the second era gradually drew to a close. To fix a date when a new era seems to be initiated is naturally an arbitrary procedure. However, 1916 seems to me to signalize through the publication of Dixon's *Oceanic Mythology* the start of a new era, the third in my divisions, when professionally trained anthropologists, usually with experience in more than one culture area of the world, became markedly more frequent among the contributors to collections of Polynesian verbal art.

Dixon's *Oceanic Mythology* was the first book of the twentieth century to attain as wide and influential an acceptance as a classic in the field as Grey's *Polynesian Mythology,* different as the two are. As Dixon pointed out in his Preface, no one before him had tried to bring together all the available materials from the Pacific region or to discuss the relation of the myths of the various areas to one another and to adjacent areas. The book surveyed the narrative art, mainly the prose, of Polynesia, Micronesia, Australia, and Indonesia. Polynesia, which Dixon discussed first, was given more attention than any other of the areas. However, Indonesia received only a half dozen pages less.

Despite the fact that the book was meant for the general reader and the narratives were retold, Dixon provided not only a long bibliography, mainly of original works, but, most valuable of all for the professional student of narrative prose and poetry, thirty-three pages of notes that cite the exact reference for each incident referred to in his book and add its occurrences elsewhere in the Pacific. Fairly new in Polynesian research on narratives was his use of individual incidents rather than entire stories as units of comparison.

For each of the five areas Dixon had a chapter on its myths of origins and the deluge; then one or more chapters on its major types of myths; and a chapter of its miscellaneous tales that he hoped were a fair sample of types with the widest distribution and interest. At the end of each section devoted to an area he discussed the probable origin of some of the myths and the evidences for their diffusion. The statistics that he mentioned using to shape his conclusions are given only in the most general way. Dixon theorized that a series of waves of migration from the Asiatic mainland had spread through the Pacific, each wave covering its predecessor more or less, and modifying it and being modified. What one misses in this fine and useful book is anything at all about the cultural context of the narratives. The illustrations, photographs of museum specimens, contribute to the lifeless quality that the lively characters in the narratives can scarcely counteract.

In 1919 another professional anthropologist, Martha Warren Beckwith, published her literal translation of the *Hawaiian Romance of Laieikawai with Introduction and Translation,* in the thirty-third annual report for 1911-12 of the Bureau of American Ethnology. S. N. Haleole, a Lahainaluna School graduate of the preceding era, had vastly elaborated a native legend in the hope of creating a new Hawaiian literature and had published the romance serially in a Hawaiian-language newspaper. Miss Beckwith's introductory essay on Polynesian literary style is one of the first, and still one of the principal, discussions of this subject, and her summaries of the long Fornander myths are useful. This work, rather than Dixon's book, might perhaps be singled out to mark the beginning of a new era. The study of Laieikawai is meant for the scholar as is evident from the uncompromisingly literal translations, the abundant explanatory notes, the abstracts of myths, the impressive and lively introductory essay, and the publication in a scientific series. Yet for these very reasons it is less well known than Dixon's work and less influential except among a small handful of students of narrative art.

Subsequently, working with others, Beckwith translated the work of another Lahainaluna graduate, S. M. Kamakau, *Ruling Chiefs of Hawaii* (Honolulu, 1961). Her translation of *Kepelino's Traditions of Hawaii,* an account of old Hawaiian customs as seen by a Christian convert like Kamakau, was published by Bishop Museum as Bulletin 95 in 1932.

Through the Folklore Foundation of Vassar College with which she was associated until her retirement, Beckwith also saw through the press volumes of Hawaiian tales, often with original and translated texts, collected either by herself on her frequent returns to her childhood home, or by Laura Green and Mary K. Pukui.[27] During her years as a professor of comparative literature at Vassar, Beckwith carried on ethnographical fieldwork and tale-collecting among Caribbean islanders and American Indians. This suggests the broad perspective she brought to her Polynesian studies.

The same broad perspective was also being brought to south Pacific research by other professional ethnographers engaged in making reconnaissance studies of Polynesian culture as part of a great program of the 1920's and 1930's carried on by Bishop Museum. This increased activity at the Museum is also one of the highlights of this new period. While Americans predominated in the program other countries were represented. During these years Dr. Peter H. Buck left behind him his medical and political career in New Zealand to spend full time on Polynesian anthropology on which he had been publishing a mounting number of articles and monographs. Later he became Director of Bishop Museum, a position he held until his death in 1951. Oddly enough, although he found much personal enjoyment in narrative art, he never devoted a book entirely to the subject. However, in most of his ethnological monographs, even those on material culture, he frequently retold stories and beliefs connected with the manufacture and use of an artifact. His *Anthropology and Religion* (New Haven, 1939) provides helpful orientation in the mazes of the Polynesian pantheons and cosmogonies. Of his many ethnographies published by the Museum which include Samoa, Tongareva, Manihiki and Rakahanga, Mangaia, and Cook Islands, one of the most fascinating from the standpoint of narrative art is his *Ethnology of Mangareva* (Honolulu, 1938, Bulletin 157). Here he gives the texts of chants but not of the prose narratives; he has much about the role of the narrators.

In the same year two other New Zealanders, Ernest and Pearl Beaglehole, published their *Ethnology of Pukapuka* (Honolulu, 1938, Bulletin 150), which has some myths and chants too. Ernest Beaglehole's popular book, *Islands of Danger* (Wellington, N. Z., 1944), has a provocative chapter on translating native chants. Also to Bishop Museum came A. Métraux from fieldwork on South American Indian tribes to do *Ethnology of Easter Island* (Honolulu, 1940, Bulletin 160), with many myths and chants that leave no doubt of this remote island's affiliation with Polynesian culture. Métraux's popular book, *Easter Island* (New York, 1957), should also be consulted for examples and description of the cultural role of chants and tales. Both books have long bibliographies in which are listed several important collections in the Spanish language.

Among the Americans whose general ethnologies, published by the Museum, also included examples of narrative art and relevant bibliographies are Robert T. Aitken who worked on Tubuai Island; Edwin G. Burrows whose field reports were on Futuna and on Uvea, and whose monographs on native music were also published by the Museum; Edwin M. Loeb with a monograph on Niue; Gordon Macgregor with a Tokelau report; and Margaret Mead on Samoa.[28] E. W. Gifford in addition to other monographs on Tonga published *Tongan Myths and Tales* (Honolulu, 1924, Bulletin 8) in which he included a numerical comparison of Tongan mythological similarities with Melanesia and Micronesia, for which he used especially Dixon's book and L. Fison's *Tales from Old Fiji* (London, 1907). E. S. C. Handy, besides his other works on Marquesas, prepared *Marquesan Legends* and wrote other monographs on this theory of Polynesian origins in Asia.[29] Even the monographs on archaeology have occasional tales or information that relates to traditions and chants.

Customarily the shorter papers by these ethnographers, if not published by the Museum in its Occasional Papers, appeared in the journals of the Polynesian Society. Other journals, of course, were also used as outlets. Beckwith, for example, has several articles of value to the student of narrative art in the *American Anthropologist.*[30]

The interest of the Museum in rescuing manuscripts of the previous eras has been mentioned. What was too long for the ethnographers to incorporate in their monographs appeared separately. Henry's *Ancient Tahiti* and the *Fornander Collection* are two examples. Nonprofessional anthropologists also contributed their collections, such as W. H. Rice's *Hawaiian Legends* (Bulletin 3, 1923) and Rev. H. P. Judd's *Hawaiian Proverbs and Riddles* (Bulletin 77, 1930). From the Tuamotus came J. F. Stimson's *Legends of Maui and Tahaki* (Bulletin 127, 1934) and *Tuamotuan Legends, Island of Anaa* (Bulletin 148, 1937). Rev. E. E. V. Collocott's *Tales and Poems of Tonga* (Bulletin 46, 1928) followed his joint publication with John Havea, a Tongan, of *Proverbial Sayings of the Tongans* (Occasional Paper 8, 1922).

Besides the unpublished myths and chants from this period that have been mentioned, Kenneth P. Emory has some from the Tuamotus. His articles for the Polynesian Society have incorporated some of the Tuamotuan and Tahitian lore he has collected, and some also appears in his archaeological reports.[31] M. K. Pukui's translations from Hawaiian newspapers have been published only in part. Collecting proverbial sayings has been one of her sidelines of interest. She has been of much help to others working in this archipelago through her knowledge of Hawaiian language and custom derived from experience and reading.

Donald G. Kennedy, a government administrator, included examples of the native prose and poetry he had collected in his *Field Notes on the Culture of Vaitupu, Ellice Islands* (New Plymouth, N. Z., 1931, Polynesian Society Memoir 9). In 1928 and 1929 Sir Apirana Nagata published untranslated Maori chants with notes, which, since 1957, have appeared with English translations in the journals of the Polynesian Society.[32] From Rotuma, a Polynesian outlier north of Fiji, came C. Maxwell Churchward's *Tales of a Lonely Island,* first published serially in *Oceania.*[33] As Fijian lore has much in common with Polynesian, particularly the Tongan, it is unfortunate that so little has been collected. Buell Quain's *The Flight-of-the-Chiefs* (New York, 1942) shows what richness is there. Besides Fison's collection there is T. R. St. Johnston's *The Lau Islands (Fiji) and their Fairy Tales and Folk-lore* (London, 1918). Among A. M. Hocart's unpublished papers in the Turnbull Library, Wellington, New Zealand, are some collections of Fijian tales and legends.[34]

Among general surveys of Polynesian chants and myths of this era are H. M. and

N. K. Chadwick's discussion in the third volume of *The Growth of Literature* (Cambridge, Eng., 1940); Johannes Carl Andersen's popular selection *Myths and Legends of the Polynesians* (London, 1928); and Paul Hambruch's selection in German which includes other Pacific areas besides Polynesia.[35] While I have tried in this paper to limit references to those works, whether meant for the general public or the scientific world, that include original material, the name of Padraic Colum, who retold Hawaiian tales in Irish style, should still be mentioned. For the noteworthy fact is that the Hawaiian Legislature appointed a Hawaiian Legend and Folklore Commission to sponsor, in cooperation with the Yale University Press, a reteller of Hawaiian tales for children. Colum was the person appointed.[36]

THE FOURTH PERIOD

The fourth era in research on Polynesian narrative art extends from the period of World War II into the present. Probably Beckwith's comprehensive *Hawaiian Mythology* with its over-all view of the content and sources of Hawaiian lore and its relationship with tradition elsewhere in the Pacific serves to mark 1940 as the time when analyses and syntheses of collections of narrative art begin to appear, not for the first time, of course, but more frequently than in the previous periods. In the same year my analysis of *Oceanic, American Indian, and African Myths of Snaring the Sun* was published by Bishop Museum as Bulletin 168. My work on Polynesian narrative art had begun in 1936 when as a graduate student at the University of California I went from Berkeley to Bishop Museum to work with Miss Beckwith on her *Hawaiian Mythology*. At that time I became interested in the Maui hero cycle in which the snaring of the sun is one of the adventures. In 1949 the Museum published my general study of the hero. In the same year the University of Hawaii published Leib's annotated Hawaiian bibliography.

In 1951 Beckwith, who died early in 1959, published her last work, a major undertaking on which she had worked a long time. This was *The Kumulipo, a Hawaiian Creation Chant,* published by the University of Chicago Press. The author presented not only her translation with extensive commentary but also several chapters on its social and historical background and on Polynesian chants of creation in general. The book sets a model for the retranslation and re-examination so much needed of many of the works recorded in earlier periods.

Some retranslating has been taking place in New Zealand. The work of Bruce Biggs, a trained linguist, has been mentioned in connection with Grey's manuscripts. Biggs has also made recordings of many Maori chants, copies of which are in the folklore archives of Indiana University. These archives also contain more untranslated and unpublished recordings of chants from other parts of Polynesia.

Samuel H. Elbert, also a trained linguist, joined the University of Hawaii faculty after the war and prepared with Mary Kawena Pukui a new *Hawaiian-English Dictionary* published by the University of Hawaii Press in 1957. He has interested several students and faculty members, by no means only those of native Hawaiian stock, in studying the language and attempting retranslations. Often his students practice on Fornander's texts. Helen Topham of the English Department published some chants from the story of the hero Kawelo in the *Journal of Oriental Literature* in 1955.[37] This student-maintained publication which publishes both Pacific and Asian material appears intermittently. Ruby Kinney, who has contributed an article on narration to it, also recorded Hawaiiana for Bishop Museum in 1956. A mimeographed statement was prepared on the tapes she obtained in a district on Hawaii. Now Mrs. Pukui and Eleanor Williamson have continued with this work in the archipelago and show that there is still much to be obtained by the collector. The Museum has also been recopying many of its older recordings made in the previous period by various expeditions.

Elbert's study, "The Chief in Hawaiian Mythology," appeared serially in 1956 and 1957 in the JOURNAL OF AMERICAN FOLKLORE. His valuable article on "Hawaiian Literary Style and Culture" appeared in the *American Anthropologist* in 1951. His collection of Marquesan chants and narratives remains unpublished except for some chants and love songs that the *Journal of the Polynesian Society* published in 1941. His collection from Kapingamarangi and Nukuoro, Polynesian outliers in western Micronesia, were mimeographed by CIMA (Coordinated Investigation of Micronesian Anthropology) but some appeared as "Uta-Matua and Other Tales of Kapingamarangi," in the "Pacific Issue" of the JOURNAL OF AMERICAN FOLKLORE in 1949 under my editorship.[38] Despite the inclusive title of this issue most of the material came mainly from Micronesia and Polynesia north of the equator as my efforts to get the southern islands represented proved unavailing. Elbert, who returned in 1957 from Rennell Island, an outlier in Melanesia, reports that he obtained narratives there, including some about the demigod Maui. A motif-index of the area was prepared by Bacil F. Kirtley in 1955 at Indiana University.[39]

Since 1946 when I joined the Anthropology Department of the University of Hawaii, I have given almost every year a general course on Folklore for which one of the student assignments is to collect narratives and chants from any of the numerous national and native groups represented in the Hawaiian Islands. Some of this material has appeared in the JOURNAL OF AMERICAN FOLKLORE, of which I was an editor for two years, but much still must be sorted, analyzed, and evaluated. I have written some survey articles on the narrative art of Pacific areas for the *Encyclopedia of Literature* in 1946 and for the Funk & Wagnalls *Standard Dictionary of Folklore, Mythology, and Legend* in 1949 and 1950. My book, *Voices on the Wind,* retelling and discussing some of the principal characters within the context of Polynesian culture and literary style, was published in 1955 by Bishop Museum.

The continued collecting in the Hawaiian Islands is paralleled in some other archipelagoes. In Tonga, for example, Queen Salote has sponsored within the last few years the collection of traditions which members of families have been asked to write down for her. What is included in this material is not known to me nor what plans, if any, have been made for its publication or permanent preservation. In other archipelagoes, like Samoa, I hear of families holding notebooks filled with family traditions. This is also true in the Hawaiian Islands. Often there is reluctance toward allowing this material to be examined, partly from an exaggerated idea of its commercial value, fear of supernatural retaliation from family spirits, unwillingness to reveal cherished family secrets to strangers, and other reasons.

The need felt to collect and to preserve these records of the past was typically expressed in an editorial in the *Fiji Times* of March 4, 1958. Headed "Losing a Priceless Fiji Heritage," the editorial declared that the present director of the local museum should be assisted by one or two full-time fieldworkers to gather legends and examine them. The article mentioned that the first governor of Fiji, Sir Arthur Gordon, offered a cash prize for the best collection of legends and traditions. Although the response was poor, one collection, obtained from a Mr. Hedemann, was later preserved in the

Stanmore Papers, the whereabouts of which are now unknown. The editorial noted further that the old Native Lands Commission performed a valuable service in preserving legends and historical material. A few collections were also made by individuals, including an unnamed early Methodist missionary. Whether this editorial produced any results has not been reported.

SUMMARY

In this survey of what has been done on Polynesian narrative art, I have distinguished four main periods, none of which has any sharply definable dates. Each, however, is characterized by the predominance of a certain approach to the subject. The first period, the stage of pioneer discovery and settlement, produced only fragments of native prose and poetry. Then, as Polynesia became more settled, both the Europeans and the literate natives began to write down more completely the narratives and chants of the native cultures and to publish them, frequently with texts and translations, in scientific journals and occasionally in works directed toward the general public. This second period dominated by the amateur anthropologist produced most of the material we now have. The third period is that of the professional anthropologist, although the dedicated amateur is still represented. The anthropologists, besides collecting more material, including that preserved in local archives, also began some extensive comparative work on the myths, but with few exceptions, they did not undertake to make large-scale reconstructions of Polynesian history on the basis of the narratives and chants. They usually preferred to limit their reconstructions to inter-archipelago connections in contrast to the writers of the previous era. The fourth period has continued along the lines of the former, but it is probably producing more re-evaluations and comparative studies of single characters or motifs than the previous era. Collections continue to be made. The field is wide open for many different approaches to the collected material, but the trained workers are lacking.

NOTES

1. *Journal of Oriental Literature*, VI (April 1955), 16-23.

2. In *Specialized Studies in Polynesian Anthropology*, Bernice P. Bishop Museum, Bulletin 193 (Honolulu, 1947).

3. References of this kind appear within Anon., *A Journal of a Voyage Round the World, in His Majesty's Ship Endeavour, 1768-1771* (1771); James Cook, *A Voyage to the Pacific Ocean . . . in his Majesty's Ships the Resolution and Discovery, 1776-1780* (3 vols., 1784); George Forster, *A Voyage Round the World in his Britannic Majesty's Sloop, Resolution, Commanded by Capt. James Cook . . . 1772-1775* (2 vols., 1777); and John Reinhold Forster, *Observations Made During A Voyage Round the World, on Physical Geography, Natural History, and Ethnic Philosophy* (1778). All published in London. William Anderson published no account of his own.

4. Charles Wilkes, *Narrative of the United States Exploring Expedition* (5 vols., Philadelphia, 1844).

5. J. L. Nicholas, *Narrative of a Voyage to New Zealand* (2 vols., 1817); J. S. Polack, *New Zealand: Being a Narrative of Travels and Adventures* (1838), and his *Manners and Customs of the New Zealanders* (2 vols., 1840); William Yate, *An Account of New Zealand* (1835); Ernest Dieffenbach, *Travels in New Zealand* (2 vols., 1843); and Walter Brodie, *Remarks on the Past and Present State of New Zealand* (1845). All published in London.

6. John Martin, *An Account of the Natives of the Tongan Islands . . .* compiled and arranged from the extensive communications of Mr. William Mariner (2 vols., London, 1817).

7. Sarah S. Farmer, *Tonga and the Friendly Islands* (London, 1855).

8. Sir George Grey, *Ko nga Moteatea, me nga Hakirara o nga Maori (Poems, Traditions, and Chants of the Maoris)* (Wellington, N. Z., 1853); and *Ko nga Mahinga a Nga Tupuna Maori (Mythology and Traditions of the New Zealanders)* (London, 1854).

9. New Plymouth, N. Z., 1928. A photo-offset reprint has appeared since then, entitled *Nga Mahi a Nga Tupuna* (Wellington, N. Z., 1953).

10. *Journal of the Polynesian Society,* LXI (1952), 171-191.

11. Ibid., XLIX (1940), 175-195.

12. See, e.g., Thomas Powell, "A Samoan Tradition of Creation and the Deluge," *Journal of the Transactions of the Victoria Institute of Great Britain,* XX (1887), 145-147; Powell and George Pratt, "Some Folk-Songs and Myths from Samoa," *Journal of the Royal Society of New South Wales,* XXIV (1890), 195-217; Pratt, "The Genealogy of the Sun, A Samoan Legend," *Reports of the Australasian Association for the Advancement of Science,* I (1889), 447-463; Pratt and John Fraser, "Some Folk-Songs and Myths from Samoa," *Journal of the Royal Society of New South Wales,* XXV (1891), 70-86, 96-121, 121-146, 241-286; XXVI (1892), 264-301; J. Abercromby, "Samoan Stories," and "Samoan Tales," *Folk-Lore,* II (1891), 455-467; and III (1892), 158-165.

13. See Stair's *Old Samoa* (Oxford, 1897); Turner's *Nineteen Years in Polynesia* (London, 1861); and the latter author's *Samoa a Hundred Years Ago and Long Before* (London, 1884).

14. *Journal of the Polynesian Society,* V (1896), 33-57.

15. Titled "The Mythology and Traditions of the Maori in New Zealand," Wohler's collections appear in vols. VII, 3-53, and VIII, 108-123, of the *Transactions.*

16. *Journal of the Polynesian Society,* VII (1898), 137-177; *Hawaiki: The Original Home of the Maori* (London, 1921).

17. Thrum's books are entitled *Hawaiian Folk Tales* and *More Hawaiian Folk Tales.*

18. See, e.g., Westervelt's *Legends of Maui—A Demi-god of Polynesia and of his Mother Hina* (Melbourne, Australia, n.d., and Honolulu, 1910), and his *Legends of Old Honolulu* (Boston, 1915).

19. Best's publications include "The Diversions of the Whare Tapere," *Transactions of the New Zealand Institute,* XXXIV (1901), 34-69; *Games and Pastimes of the Maori,* and *Maori Agriculture* (Dominion Museum, Bulletins 8 and 9, Wellington, N. Z., 1924, 1925); "The Polynesian Method of Generating Fire," *Journal of the Polynesian Society,* XXXIII (1924), 87-102, 151-161; "Te Rehu-o-Tainui: The Evolution of a Maori Atua," ibid., VI (1897), 41-66; and *Tuhoe; the Children of the Mist,* Polynesian Society, Memoir 6 (Wellington, N. Z., 1925).

20. Tregear's works include *A Dictionary of Mangareva (or Gambier Islands)* (Wellington, N. Z., 1899); *The Maori-Polynesian Comparative Dictionary* (Wellington, N. Z., 1891); *The Maori Race* (Wanganui, N. Z., 1904); and "Polynesian Folklore—Part II: The Origin of Fire," *Transactions of the New Zealand Institute,* XX (1887), 369-399. Among Cowan's publications are *Legends of the Maori* (2 vols., Wellington, N. Z., 1930); *The Maoris of New Zealand* (Christchurch, N. Z., 1910); "The Patu-paiarahe. Notes on Maori Folk-Tales of the Fairy People," *Journal of the Polynesian Society,* XXX (1921), 142-151; and "The Story of Niue," ibid., XXXII (1923), 238-243.

21. In this journal Seurat's "Légendes des Paumotos" appear in XX (1905), 433-440, 481-488; XXI (1906), 125-131.

22. Caillot's publications are *Les Polynésiens orientaux au contact de la civilisation* (Paris, 1909); *Mythes, Légendes et Traditions des Polynésiens* (Paris, 1914); *Histoire de l'Ik Uparo ou Rapa* (Paris, 1932). For Reiter's French translations of the Maui cycle, titled "Traditions tonguiennes," see *Anthropos,* II (1907), 230-240, 438-448, 743-754; XII-XIII (1917-1918), 1026-2046; and XIV-XV (1919-1920), 125-142. Collocott's versions in *Folk-Lore* are "A Tongan Theogony," XXX (1919), 234-238; "Legends from Tonga," XXXII (1921), 45-58; and "Tongan Myths and Legends," XXXV (1924), 275-283, 372-378.

23. The work of Bastian is discussed by Robert H. Lowie in *A History of Ethnological Theory* (New York, 1937), ch. IV, pp. 30-38.

24. Liliuokalani, *An Account of the Creation of the World* (Boston, 1897).

25. See, e.g., by Achelis, "Der Maui-Mythus," in *Festschrift für Adolf Bastian* (Berlin, 1896), pp. 541-555; "Die Stellung Tangaloas in der polynesiaschen Mythologie," *Globus,* LXVII (1894), 229-231, 249-251, 270-272; and *Über Mythologie und Cultus von Hawaii* (Braunschweig, 1895).

26. See, e.g., Leo Frobenius, *Das Zeitalter des Sonnengottes* (Berlin, 1904), and F. Graebner, "Thor und Maui," *Anthropos,* XIV-XV (1919-1920), 1099-1119.

27. Martha Warren Beckwith, *Hawaiian Mythology* (New Haven, 1940); and *The Kumulipo. A Hawaiian Creation Chant,* tr. and ed. with commentary by M. W. Beckwith (Chicago, 1951).

28. See, e.g., Aitken's *Ethnology of Tubuai,* Bulletin 70 (1930); Burrows' *Ethnology of Futuna,* Bulletin 138 (1936), *Ethnology of Urea (Wallis Island),* Bulletin 145 (1937), and *Native Music of the Tuamotus,* Bulletin 109 (1933); Loeb's *History and Traditions of Niue,* Bulletin 32 (1926); Macgregor's *Ethnology of Tokelau Islands,* Bulletin 146 (1937); and Mead's *Social Organization of Manua,* Bulletin 76 (1930). All published in Honolulu.

29. Handy's *Marquesan Legends* (1930) is Bulletin 69. Other works by him include *The Native Culture in the Marquesas,* Bulletin 9 (1923); *History and Culture in the Society Islands,* Bulletin 79 (1930); and *Polynesian Religion,* Bulletin 34 (1927). All published in Honolulu.

30. See Beckwith's "Hawaiian Riddling," *American Anthropologist,* XXIV (1922), 311-331, and her "Hawaiian Shark Aumakua," ibid., XIX (1917), 503-517. See also the following articles

in the same journal by Laura S. Green and Beckwith: "Hawaiian Customs and Beliefs Relating to Sickness and Death," XXVIII (1926), 176-208; and "Hawaiian Household Customs," XXX (1928), 1-17. All of these articles contain examples of narrative art.

31. See, e.g., Emory's "The Tahitian Account of Creation by Mare," *Journal of the Polynesian Society,* XLVII (1938), 45-63; "Tuamotuan Concepts of Creation," ibid., XIL (1940), 69-136; and "The Tuamotuan Creation Charts by Paiore," ibid., XLVIII (1939), 1-29. Emory's unpublished "Translations of Vahitahi Island Legends" is still on deposit in the Bishop Museum, as is his also unpublished "Bishop Museum Tuamotu Expedition Field Notebooks, 1929-1930, 1934."

32. See, e.g., Nagata's *Nga Moteatea,* Parts I and II, Maori Purposes Fund Board (2 vols., Wellington, N. Z., 1928-29).

33. Titled "Rotuman Legends," the serial version appears in *Oceania,* VIII (1937-38), 104-116, 247-260, 351-368, 482-497. The book was issued as Oceania Monographs No. 4 (Sydney, Australia, 1940).

34. Anon., "The Hocart Papers in Turnbull Library," *Journal of the Polynesian Society,* LIX (1950), 69-272.

35. *Südseemärchen aus Australien, Neu-Guinea, Fidji, Karolinen, Samoa, Tonga, Hawaii, Neu-Seeland* (Jena, 1921).

36. See Colum's *At the Gateway of the Day* (New Haven, 1924); *The Bright Islands* (New Haven, 1925); and *Legends of Hawaii* (New Haven, 1937).

37. "The Function of the Chant in the Legend of Kawelo," *Journal of Oriental Literature,* VI (April 1955), 24-31.

38. For the articles cited for Elbert, see *Journal of American Folklore,* LXIX (1956), 99-113, 341-355; LXX (1957), 264-276, 306-322; LXII (1949), 240-246; *American Anthropologist,* LIII (1951), 345-354; and "Chants and Love Songs of the Marquesas Islands, French Oceania," *Journal of the Polynesian Society,* L (1941), 53-91.

39. Kirtley's *A Motif-Index of Polynesian, Melanesian, and Micronesian Narratives* (diss., 2 vols., Indiana University, Bloomington, Ind., 1955) appears as Publication No. 14,660, University Microfilms, Ann Arbor, Michigan.

University of Hawaii
Honolulu, Hawaii

JOHN GREENWAY

FOLKLORE SCHOLARSHIP IN AUSTRALIA

I. The Aborigines

IN 1688, during a recession in piracy in the southern oceans, William Dampier nosed his corsair into a bay on the bleak northwest coast of the unknown continent of Australia and fell upon the poor, hapless, naked, fly-blown, rat-eating Bard tribe for an ethnographical survey. "The inhabitants of this Country are the miserablest People in the world," he wrote later; "they all of them have the most unpleasant Looks and the worst Features of any People that I ever saw, though I have seen great Variety of Savages."[1] Jonathan Swift got hold of the report and used the Bard people as a basis for his Yahoos in the fourth book of *Gulliver's Travels;* thus folklore began about aboriginal Australia.

From Dampier's time to this, Australia has been a producer of primary folklore rather than secondary, scientific, solid analysis of folklore, just as one might expect in a country where fish climb trees, mice are marsupials, Midsummer Day falls in the middle of winter, and dentists have been known to fill Americans' teeth free. Some of the most fantastic stories outside Tibet have emanated from this continent—no Yeti, of course (unless the bunyip could be placed in that taxonomy), but web-footed sea dwellers, marsupial people, and several of those hopelessly lost tribes of Israel. The layman cannot be expected to disbelieve the fallacy of the returning boomerang, but even anthropologists have perpetuated such fakelore: only a half-century ago Sergi was willing to put the Tasmanians into a separate genus of primates, *Hesperanthropus tasmanianus,*[2] and today aboriginal telepathy is still believed in by many in the profession.[3] Only occasionally is it possible to find the fact beneath the fancy; in one of his egalitarian statements about race a famous American physical anthropologist and popular lecturer on the creamed chicken circuit argued the mental superiority of Australian aborigines by the case of the "abo" who supposedly was chess champion of Australia. What this scholar did not realize was that even before the story reached him it was well grounded in fantasy—the truth of the matter was that the aboriginal in question had not competed in a chess tournament, but a checker tournament; it was not the national championship, but a local competition sponsored by the Melbourne Draughts Club; and far from emerging as Champion, he failed to win a single game.[4]

The study of Australian aboriginal mythology and religious concepts, explanatory tales, and other lore has lacked only a systematic and scientific examination; there has been no want of reporters. Next to the outlandish nature of the people themselves, nothing has caught the attention of the invading observers more than the traditional customs which we will here arbitrarily call folklore. The mariners of the eighteenth century rarely stayed long enough ashore to do more than confirm Dampier's jaundiced opinion of the natives' looks and perhaps to contribute a few original imaginings—like Tasman hearing trumpets and Bligh seeing wigwams—but the overland explorers who spread out over the arid wilderness of the interior after the Blue Mountains were pierced in 1813 made more copious notes on the folk-lore of the natives. The major explorer-commentators were John Molesworth Oxley, Charles Sturt, Thomas Livingstone Mitchell, Edward John Eyre, Ludwig Leich-hardt, Augustus Charles Gregory, Edmund Besley Court Kennedy, Peter Egerton Warburton, John McDougall Stuart, Robert O'Hara Burke, William John Wills, John Forrest, and Edward Giles. However, it was the missionaries who first went to live with these most primitive people on earth, and who assembled the first extensive reports on native groups that were only a few years short of extinction. The most important missionary writer in the first half of the nineteenth century was Lancelot Edward Threlkeld, who, after settling among the Awabakal people on the beautiful shores of Lake Macquarie, was fired by the London Missionary Society for spending too much time on ethnographic and linguistic observations and too little on the sal-vation of the autochthones.[5] Missionaries like Threlkeld, James Robert Beattie Love,[6] William Ridley, George Taplin, J. H. Sexton, and Pater Wilhelm Schmidt (whose work on the beginning of religion is internationally renowned[7]) are unusual among the thousands of workers in the spiritual vineyards of sterile Australia. Most members of Threlkeld's profession stuck grimly to their lasts, despite an almost unspotted record of no conversions, and instead of preserving aboriginal mythology, inculcated their own in such books as *Tjujurpa Jesunja Pakantjala Malangka (Post-Resurrection Stories in the Pitjandjara Language)*[8] and *Testamenta Marra Jesuni Christuni Ngant-jani Jaura Ninaia Rarithmalkana Wonti Dieri Jaurani (The New Testament in the Dieri Language).*[9] Even in Threlkeld's first book Bishop W. G. Broughton intruded with an Awabakal translation of the Book of Common Prayer. This seeding brought fruit; the Creator gods like Baiame are thought to have a European origin. At the present time the missionaries are saving the most innocuous of the aboriginal stories and publishing them in religious or ameliorative periodicals like *Our Aim,* the *Austra-lian Board of Missions Review,* and *Dawn,* but these tales are on the level of "How the Fish Got Their Tails."

The missionaries more than the anthropologists recognized the truth, for Australia at least, of Émile Durkheim's brilliant insight that religion is society sanctified, and that mythology is the means of preserving religious beliefs.[10] The aborigines made little distinction between the secular and the spiritual dimensions, and since mythology was the charter of the latter, it twined inextricably with the former. The missionaries suffered neither to grow until the harvest, but eradicated both. Fortunately the mis-sionaries by no means had the field to themselves. In the 272 years that have passed since Dampier slandered the Bards, thousands of writers have recorded snippets of aboriginal folklore and published them everywhere. Even the South Australian Min-istry of Works included a significant collection in their published survey of a local coalfield;[11] and the Archdeacon C. C. Greenway printed a number of aboriginal folktales in *Science of Man* at the beginning of this century.

But by men who in a later day would have been professional anthropologists, col-lection was desultory until the appearance of the polymathic Scot, Andrew Lang. That he managed to write forty-six books and articles on the religion and mythology of the Australian aborigines while occupying himself full time with a half-dozen other intellectual pursuits (such as writing novels and fairy tales) is astounding; more astounding still was his effrontery in attempting to confute scholars who had spent years studying the aborigines—men like Samuel Gason, Alfred Howitt, Arnold van Gennep, F. B. Jevons, and R. H. Mathews.[12] The only writer on Australian mythology who came within his range and was not demolished was harmless Mrs. Langloh Parker—possibly because her books on the stories of the Euahlayi of New South Wales appealed to him as fairy tales. The books of Mrs. Parker (actually Catherine Somerville Stow) will probably outlast those of her more competent and disputatious colleagues since they are simple and honest collections of the tales of a people who are now extinct. Her books have even been pirated in Russia.[13]

Though peaceful and unobtrusive until Lang, a great amount of ethnographic writing eliciting conclusions from mythology appeared before anthropology became a recognized academic discipline at Australian universities. One might cite even theoretical work like William Bleek's "On Resemblances in Bushmen and Australian Mythology,"[14] but order, basic training in the principles of anthropology, techniques in reliable collecting, and ability to recognize the genuine from the spurious were only sporadic until the first chair of Australian anthropology was established at the University of Sydney in 1926. The works of Spencer and Gillen, however, are outstanding examples of classical anthropology in the early years of this century.[15]

Ruefully it must be admitted that the founding of the first university department of anthropology in Australia was not prompted by a desire to save the culture of the fast-vanishing tribes. Though more altruistic motives suggested formation of such a department a quarter of a century earlier, it was not until the mandating of southeastern New Guinea to Australia after World War I and the consequent acknowledgment of the expediency of training qualified administrators and police officers to keep the cannibalistic Papuans in good behavior before the eyes of the world, that the Commonwealth and State governments provided the funds to create the department. As a matter of embarrassing fact, Sir John Hubert Murray, one of the founding fathers, warned the new department against "preoccupation with scientific investigation."[16]

Fortunately the teaching profession's impracticality prevailed, and much work was done on the folklore of the aborigines. By the third number of *Oceania* (the chief journal of Australian aboriginal studies, published by the Department of Anthropology at the University of Sydney), A. R. Radcliffe-Brown, the first Professor of Anthropology, was writing on the Rainbow Serpent myth, and was joined by several of his students who had collected in various parts of the continent.[17] His successor in the Chair, Adolphus Peter Elkin, included many studies of aboriginal mythology, legend, and music (Elkin is the chief collector and publisher of aboriginal song and music) among his 240 published titles; significantly, his dissertation at Sydney was on "The Religion of the Australian Aborigines." Later Sydney anthropologists who have collected mythology extensively are Arthur Essex Capell, Mervyn Meggitt, C. W. M. Hart, Phyllis Kaberry (the authority on women's folklore in Arnhem Land and elsewhere), Frederick McCarthy (now Curator of Anthropology of the Australian Museum, Sydney, and principal authority on aboriginal rock carvings and paintings, on which he has published more than one hundred books and articles), and Ursula McConnel, whose work has been chiefly in the interpretation of legends, mythology, and ritual among the Cape York tribes.[18]

Though Sydney is the official anthropological center, the most valuable and stimulating work in all fields is going on along the Park Lands side of North Terrace, Adelaide, where the South Australian Museum, the Royal Society of South Australia, the South Australian Archives, the Public Library of South Australia, and the University of Adelaide are clustered together. The leading scholar among the excellent men in this enclave is Norman Bartlett Tindale, probably the world's outstanding authority on the Australian natives, who has written more than a hundred substantial articles, many of them on aboriginal folklore.[19] Equally prolific is Charles Pearcy Mountford, nearly all of whose writing has been on art, myth, and symbolism; he contends with McCarthy of Sydney as the international authority in this area.[20] At Adelaide also is Theodor George Henry Strehlow, bilingual in Aranda and English, son of Carl Strehlow, the founding pastor-ethnologist of the famous Hermannsburg Mission in central Australia.[21]

At this writing the only other department of anthropology outside Sydney is at the National University, Canberra (Australian Capital Territory). The National University is of chief interest to folklorists because it is officially the nation's archive center—though most of the materials are in the world's largest repository of Australiana, the Mitchell Library at Sydney. Though the country's libraries are comparatively poor in holdings (the National Library, equivalent in intent to the American Library of Congress, had in 1957 only 400,000 volumes), the museums which hold the tangible products of folklore are good. Six of the seven capital cities—Sydney, Melbourne, Brisbane, Canberra, Adelaide, and Perth—have a State Museum; there are two local museums worthy of mention, at Narrandera and Medlow Bath, and several university museums.

At Melbourne D. S. Thomson rests between field trips to central and north Australia. Thomson has collected considerable lore of a popular sort, though he is a biologist at the University of Melbourne, but of his seventy articles, not one appears in an Australian scholarly journal.

Next to Adelaide, the University of Western Australia is the place where the most exciting work is being done; here Ronald M. Berndt and Catherine H. Berndt conduct a subdepartment of anthropology in the department of psychology. Many of their seventy books and articles concern aboriginal folklore and its interpretation; perhaps to a larger extent than any other Australian researchers, the Berndts are concerned with theoretical analysis and synthesis of their materials.[22]

Because most Australian academicians have been only casually interested in aboriginal folklore, the great bulk of the published collections has been made by amateurs—literary ladies, antiquarians, retired and retiring clergymen, local historians, poets, and humanitarians—and by foreign writers. Of the ladies, none exceeded the venerable Daisy Bates in any respect; she published more articles than any other writer (274) and among these were several that established her authority in aboriginal folklore (for example, her series on native stellar myths, which appeared in *The Australasian* and several other similar weekly periodicals in 1924). Dame Mary Gilmore is chief among the poets, who include also A. Gross, John Hicks, William Linklater, and Roland Robinson. Robinson's books, *Legend and Dreaming* and *The Feathered Serpent* (Sydney, 1955, 1956) are perhaps the most beautiful translations and illustrations of aboriginal oral and graphic literature.

As in other areas of Australian anthropology, the most vital research and synthesis in aboriginal folklore have been accomplished by foreign scholars. Ernest Worms in a half-dozen very important articles in scattered anthropological journals sought diffusionary significance in aboriginal mythology[23]; major workers in this area are the Americans D. S. Davidson and W. L. Warner; the latter's *A Black Civilization* (New York and London, 1937) is classic. Following his countryman Émile Durkheim as an anthropological gadfly, Lucien Levy-Brühl suggested a promising theoretical approach in his *La Mythologie Primitive* (Paris, 1935); another French writer who probed symbolism in the natives stories is J. Guiart.[24] But certainly no foreign writer on Australian mythology and its symbolism has had the impact of Sigmund Freud (principally his *Totem and Taboo*) and his followers, of whom the most extreme and irrepressible was Geza Róheim.[25]

And at the end of all this roll-call of writers on Australian aboriginal folklore, there is one Australian aboriginal: the tragicomic figure of David Unaipon, who wrote two slim books, *Aboriginal Legends* and *Native Legends* (Adelaide, 1926, 1930).[26]

II. THE SETTLERS

Before a people can accept their folklore (the vestiges of their time of unsophistication and innocence), they must achieve acceptance of self; that is, they must feel unassailable self-confidence and pride in their ethnic uniqueness and unity. It took a long time for Americans to look upon their folklore without shame and even guilt; it will take a long time for Negroes to tell one another Rastus jokes. Australians are at least half a century behind Americans in national maturity. They speak with bitterness of the arrogance of their British cousins, yet they are eagerly solicitous of British approbation. Much of their pro-American sentiment grows out of the supercilious attitude with which the English regard them.

Long before folklore is accepted as a legitimate occupation of a country's scholars, the sophisticated arts must be established. In America Charles Brockden Brown had to precede Washington Irving (and it should be remembered that Irving was importing an alien folklore); a succession of Richard Wrights will arise before a Negro folklorist attains eminence. In Australia the important university posts still are occupied by Englishmen or native anglophiliacs, who regard indigenous Australian culture as second-rate and unworthy of their attention. At this writing there is thus in no Australian university a department of either Australian history or Australian literature; and therefore, aside from anthropologists dealing with aboriginal traditions, there are no university folklorists. Though the Ph.D. is so highly regarded by the Australians that it enabled me to have lunch with Arnold Toynbee, and though I came with that and other testimonials of my position in American academic life, my field of folklore disqualified me for any participation in Australian university activity. I was officially attached to the faculty of Sydney University, but the only time I spoke there my invitation came from a group of young moral and political anarchists who sandwiched my talk in between lectures on "The Case against God" and "Sex: How Far Should One Go?"

To understand this curious situation, one should know how Australia became a nation. Australia's colonizers came from the poorest element of late eighteenth-century British society, an element that could hardly be said to represent English culture. Though Lord Bacon advised that "it is a shameful and unblessed thing to take the scrum of people and wicked condemned men to be the people with whom you plant," the continent of Australia was opened as a dumping ground for tens of thousands of convicts who had vainly awaited transportation to the New World after the anticipated British victory in the American Revolution. They were, as one of the first lot of transportees to Botany Bay wrote:

> True patriots all; for, be it understood,
> We left our country for our country's good.[27]

The free settlers who accompanied the transported felons on the First Fleet of

1788 and later were probably as bad as the imprisoned criminals, but as time went on these became the upper level of Australia's two-strata society, and the convicts, their descendants, and their free followers from poorest England became the proletariat. Though the early free settlers were rapacious, they were sophisticated; they brought educated ideas, not tropismatic folklore, to the new country; and for the superstitious, ignorant, and generally unwashed canaille, they had only contempt. The two strata and the contempt are apparent today; academicians, drawn from the upper class by a really admirable system of self-perpetuation through education, see nothing commendable in either an artistic or moral way in the lore of the people.

This is not to say that no collecting of white folklore was made in Australia in years past but rather that it was made for the most part without sympathy and regard for the material. A. B. "Banjo" Paterson was the first to collect Australian folksongs,[28] but he was only a journalist with a near-monomania for horse racing, and even he thought little of his material. His putative composition—Australia's most famous song "Waltzing Matilda"—he sold to his publishers together with what he called a "lot of old junk" of the same sort. His superiors in the use of native material, Adam Lindsay Gordon and Henry Lawson, have the literary reputation of Edgar A. Guest.

Australian folksongs are remarkably like American folksongs, paralleling the same situations, developing the same themes—those of a hard, uneducated, virile lower class battling a hostile frontier. The historical situation was in neither case one to assure the better people of domestic tranquility. The important difference between the two countries, and therefore between their attitudes, is that in Australia the frontier still exists—and Jesse James alive in America today would seem about as heroic to us as Al Capone; in Australia no one is sure that another Ned Kelly will not come bursting, armor-plated, into some outback pub.

Therefore, in surveying publications on Australian folklore and folksong it is not necessary to select painstakingly a cross section of scholarship; one can give nearly the lot of it. Following Paterson's *Old Bush Songs* at some distance in time and quality are Will Lawson's *Australian Bush Songs and Ballads* (Sydney, 1944) and Douglas Stewart and Nancy Keesing's *Australian Bush Ballads* (Sydney, 1955), the latter consisting mainly of infraliterary pieces. Less comprehensive collections are John Manifold's *Bandicoot Ballads* (Brisbane and Melbourne, 1954-56), a sheaf of sixteen broadsides; Hugh Anderson's *Colonial Ballads* (Ferntree Gully, 1955) and *Goldrush Songster* (Ferntree Gully, 1958); nine "Black Bull Chapbooks" produced by R. G. Edwards of The Rams Skull Press,[29] who, under his own name, published *The Overlander Song Book* (Ferntree Gully, 1956); *Old Australian Bush Ballads* (Melbourne, 1951), a small collection of prettified songs edited by Vance Palmer and Margaret Sutherland; and by far the best collection of Australian folksongs yet printed, Stewart and Keesing's enlargement of Paterson's pioneer collection, *Old Bush Songs and Rhymes of Colonial Times Enlarged and Revised from the Collection of A. B. Paterson* (Sydney, 1957). These are just about the whole of published books on Australian settlers' folksong.

The new medium of records is usurping books as a means of issuing and preserving collections of folksong, though again the amount of material is surprisingly small. A recent issue of an American folklore journal took only five pages to review all the recorded folksong of both white and aboriginal Australia.[30] Not surprisingly, the first recorded collection of Australian folksongs was made by an Englishman (A. L. Lloyd) on an American record (Riverside RLP 12-606, "Australian Bush Songs").

Lloyd has since made several other records, and these in sum are the best representation of Australian bush songs, as folksongs are called in Australia. Important for its stimulation of the Australians to hear and enjoy their own folk music is Burl Ives's "Australian Folk Songs" (Decca DL 8749). Possibly worth mentioning among the remaining foreigners who have sung Australian songs on microgroove records is John Greenway, whose "Australian Folksongs and Ballads" (Folkways FW 8718) has the virtue of being a carefully chosen cross section of material, fully described and annotated for the listener whose interest is mainly scholarly.

An Australian company, Wattle Records of 131 Cathedral Street, Sydney, has over the last five years issued about a half-dozen records of native Australians singing native songs, many of which were collected by the one internationally trained folklorist in Australia, Edgar Waters (who is one of the company's founding partners), and by John Meredith, the most important Australian collector (who sings on some of these records).[31] Only one record of "traditional singers"—comparable to the performers on our Library of Congress discs—has been issued: "Australian Traditional Singers and Musicians" (Wattle C7); and only about a dozen or so Australian "hillbilly" records (on Regal-Zonophone) stand against the tens of thousands of commercially published records that have followed Fiddlin' John Carson's first record in this country.[32]

Of books on folklore, there are even fewer. There is of course a fair amount of ephemeral material in the popular press, notably the series of outback stories in the *Australasian Post* by Bill Wannan, but the bound books could be carried under one arm—and of these, the only worth-while ones are the works of Bill Beatty.[33]

The few people in Australia who support the publication of these books and records have two nominally national societies: The Bush Music Club (headquarters in Sydney, branches elsewhere) and The Australian Folklore Society. The Bush Music Club publishes a small monthly journal, *Singabout,* patterned closely upon its overseas matrices (the British *Sing* and the American *Sing Out!*) in political philosophy, format, selection of material, and personality of contributors. The Australian Folklore Society sporadically issues a mimeographed journal, *Speewa.*

Though the situation is poor at the moment, there are hopeful signs. Two academic grants actually have been made in folk studies, both by the forward-looking National University: one a graduate research scholarship to Edgar Waters, and the other a fund for collecting to Russel Ward, historian at the New England University in Armidale, New South Wales.[34]

Most promising of all is the recent publication of the best book in Australian folklore scholarship, Russel Ward's *The Australian Legend* (Melbourne and New York, 1958). Ward, frustrated in his effort to write a history of the outback pastoral worker in the nineteenth century by the lack of documents (a lack attributable to the attitude of the upper-stratum historical writers of the time), was inspired to go to the only preserved expression of the proletariat's ethos, its folksong. The result, which earned him a Ph.D. at the National University, is not only the classic Australian folk study, but a model for the next generation of folklorists in every country.

NOTES

1. William Dampier, *Dampier's Voyages* (New York, 1906), I, 463; II, 440.
2. Giuseppi Sergi, *Europa: L'Origine del Popoli d'Africa, d'Asia, e d'Oceania* (Milan, 1908).
3. See, e.g., Lyndon and Ronald Rose, "Aborigines and Extra-Sensory Perception," *Mankind,*

XVI (Sept. 1950), 18-20; and Ronald Rose, *Living Magic: The Realities Underlying the Psychical Practices and Beliefs of Australian Aborigines* (London, 1957).

4. John Greenway, "An Anthropologist at Large," *The Bulletin* (Sydney), August 28, 1957, pp. 35, 56-57.

5. See, e.g., Threlkeld's *Specimens of a Dialect of the Aborigines of New South Wales* (1827); *An Australian Grammar* (1834); *A Key to the Structure of the Aboriginal Language* (1850); and *An Australian Language as Spoken by the Awabakal* (1892). All published in Sydney.

6. Love's writings total 29 important titles. Among them is *Stone-Age Bushmen of To-day* (London and Glasgow, 1936).

7. Wilhelm Schmidt, *Der Ursprung der Gottesidee* (1926), *Die Religionen der Urvölker Asiens und Australiens* (1931), and *Das Eigentum in den Urkulturen* (1937). All published in Munich.

8. Published by the Presbyterian Church of Australia Board of Missions (Melbourne, n. d.).

9. Carl Strehlow and J. G. Reuther (Tanunda, South Australia, 1897).

10. Emile Durkheim, *Les formes élementaires de la Vie réligieuse* (1912), translated by Joseph Ward Swain as *The Elementary Forms of the Religious Life* (London, 1915).

11. G. G. Poole, *Leigh Creek Coalfield* (Adelaide, 1946).

12. See Gason, *The Dieyerie Tribe of Australian Aborigines: Their Manners and Customs* (Adelaide, 1874), and *The Native Tribes of South Australia* (Adelaide, 1879); Howitt, *The Native Tribes of South-East Australia* (London, 1904), and (with Lorimer Fison) *Kamilaroi and Kurnai* (Melbourne, 1880); van Gennep, *Mythes et Legends d'Australie* (Paris, 1906); Jevons, *Religion in Evolution* (London, 1906); Mathews, 185 titles, including *Folk-Lore of the Australian Aborigines* (Sydney, 1899). Lang's relevant work includes *Custom and Myth* (London, 1884), *Myth, Ritual and Religion* (2 vols., 1887), *Magic and Religion* (1901), *The Secret of the Totem* (1905), and *Social Origins* (1903). All published in London.

13. See, e.g., *Avstraliiskie Legendy* (Moscow, 1903). The latest publication of Mrs. Parker, a selection of the best of her four books, is *Australian Legendary Tales Collected by K. Langloh Parker,* ed. H. Drake Brockman (Sydney, 1955).

14. *Cape Monthly Magazine,* VIII (1874), 98-102.

15. Baldwin Spencer and F. J. Gillen, *The Native Tribes of Central Australia* (1899); *The Northern Tribes of Central Australia* (1904); *Across Australia* (1912); and *The Arunta* (1927). All published in London.

16. Sir John Hubert Murray, *Papua of Today* (London, 1924), pp. 250-251.

17. A. R. Radcliffe-Brown, "The Rainbow-Serpent Myth in South-East Australia," *Oceania,* I (1930), 342-347; Ursula McConnel, "The Rainbow Serpent in North Queensland," ibid., 347-349; A. P. Elkin, "The Rainbow-Serpent in North-West Australia," ibid., 349-352; and Ralph Piddington, "The Water-Serpent in Karadjeri Mythology," ibid., 352-354.

18. Ursula H. McConnel, *Myths of the Mungkan* (Carlton, Victoria, 1957); "The Significance of the Snake in Dreams," *Psyche,* VI (1926), 12-21; "The Symbol in Legend," *Psyche,* XIII (1933), 94-137; and "Totemic Hero Cults in Cape York Peninsula, North Queensland," *Oceania,* VI (1936), 452-477, and VII (1937), 69-105.

19. See, e.g., Tindale's "Initiation Among the Pitjandjara Natives of the Mann and Tomkinson Ranges in South Australia," *Oceania,* VI (1935), 199-224, and his "Legend of the Wati Kutjara, Warburton Range, Western Australia," ibid., VII (1936), 169-185.

20. Mountford's latest and most important book is *Art, Myth and Symbolism in Arnhem Land, Records of the American-Australian Expedition to Arnhem Land,* Vol. I (Melbourne, 1956).

21. See, e.g., T. G. H. Strehlow's *Aranda Traditions* (Melbourne, 1947).

22. Ronald Berndt's most important books in this area are *Kunapipi, a Study of an Australian Aboriginal Cult* (Melbourne, 1951), and *Djanggawul: an Aboriginal Religious Cult of North-Eastern Arnhem Land* (Melbourne and London, 1952). See also, R. M. and C. H. Berndt's "Sacred Figures of Ancestral Beings of Arnhem Land," *Oceania,* XVIII (1948), 308-326, and C. Berndt's "A Drama of North-Eastern Arnhem Land," ibid., XXII (1952), 216-239, 275-289.

23. See, e.g., Worms's "Aboriginal Place Names in Kimberley, Western Australia," *Oceania,* XIV (1944), 284-310.

24. J. Guiart, "Rhombes et Tjurungas Australiens: Etude des Motifs decoratifs et de leur Symbolique," *Études Melanesiens,* n.s. III (Jan. 1951), 47-56.

25. Geza Róheim, *Australian Totemism: a Psycho-Analytic Study in Anthropology* (London, 1925); *The Riddle of the Sphinx* (London, 1934); *The Eternal Ones of the Dream: a Psycho-Analytic Interpretation of Australian Myth and Ritual* (New York, 1945); *War, Crime, and the Covenant* (Monticello, N. Y., 1945); and *Psychoanalysis and Anthropology, Culture Personality, and the Unconscious* (New York, 1950). Róheim's *The Eternal Ones of the Dream* is discussed analytically by the Berndts (see n. 22 above) in their "The Eternal Ones of the Dream," *Oceania,* XVII (1946), 67-78.

26. Tag-ending this survey are some unclassifiable general collections: Frank C. Bray, *The World of Myths* (New York, 1935), pp. 227-237; F. H. Lee, *Folk Tales of All Nations* (New York, 1930), pp. 134-161; Charles W. Peck, *Australian Legends: Tales Handed Down from the Remote Times by the Autochthonous Inhabitants of Our Land* (Sydney, 1925); W. J. Thomas, *Some Myths and Legends of the Australian Aborigines* (Melbourne, 1923); William Ramsay Smith, *Myths and Legends of the Australian Aboriginals* (New York, 1930); Charles Barrett, *The Bunyip and other Mythical Monsters and Legends of the Australian Aborigines* (Melbourne, 1946); and R. B. Dixon, "Oceanic" in *Mythology of all Races,* IX (Boston, 1916).

27. Attributed to George Barrington, pickpocket and playwright.

28. A. B. Paterson, *The Old Bush Songs, Composed and Sung in the Bushranging, Digging, and Overlanding Days* (Sydney, 1898).

29. Hugh Anderson has edited five of the Chapbooks: *The Dying Stockman* (1954); *Two Songs of '57* (1954); *Botany Bay Broadsides* (1956); *Songs of Billy Barlow* (1956); and the very important *Australian Song Index, 1828-1956* (1957). The remaining works in the series to date are Russel Ward's *Three Street Ballads* (1957), and J. S. Manifold's *The Violin, The Banjo, and The Bones* (1957). All bear the imprint of Ferntree Gully.

30. John Greenway, *"Sammelreferat:* Australian Folk Songs," *Western Folklore,* XIX (1960), 294-298.

31. A real pioneer collector, who assembled on his own long before the current, politically inspired interest manifested itself, is Percy Jones, of Melbourne. Jones' collections were used by Burl Ives and others.

32. Among the Regal-Zonophone performers are Chad Morgan, "The Sheik of Scrubby Creek" (G25487); Slim Dusty, "The Dusty Trail Yodeler" (G25405); and Smoky Dawson, "The Cowboy Folk Singer" (G25320).

33. Wannan has reprinted much of his material in his *The Australian: Yarns, Ballads, Legends, Traditions of the Australian People* (3rd ed., Melbourne, 1958). Beatty's volumes are *Come a Waltzing-Matilda* (Sydney, 1955), and *A Treasury of Australian Folk Tales and Traditions* (London, 1960).

34. Received during proofreading of this article was the news that the University of Sydney has created a section of the University Archives for Primitive and Folk Music.

University of Colorado
Boulder, Colorado

AFRICA

MELVILLE J. HERSKOVITS

THE STUDY OF AFRICAN ORAL ART

ANY DISCUSSION under the terms of reference of this Seminar of what is currently being done in the field of folklore in world areas must take on a particular form when Africa is considered. If the outline that has guided the treatment of the other topics were to be followed, our subject could be simply disposed of by stating that very little research is being done there at the present time. However, the resources for such study are greater than one would at first glance imagine, while the potentialities are very great indeed. If one is willing to utilize abstracts of tales, it is possible to accumulate an impressive bibliography of African materials, and while there are relatively few complete texts in hand, nonetheless we can, for example, quite satisfactorily assess the distribution of motifs and analyze underlying unities, even though studies in depth must await the future.

When we treat of the African data, it is essential that the meaning of the word "folklore" be clarified, since its applicability here is limited by certain special considerations. It is, first of all, a word that literate Africans feel has a pejorative connotation. Historically, the field of folklore developed as the result of antiquarian interest in the quaint customs of peasants, or in the oral narratives of peoples regarded as not having the same degree of "civilization" as the European city dweller. In this it is like the term "primitive," another word which must be used with great caution in reference to modern Africa, not only because of its scientific disutility, but also because of the susceptibilities of Africans which this usage violates. For these and various other reasons, in the context of African studies the term "narrative" is preferable to "folktale," just as "nonliterate" is to be used in preference to "primitive." It can be taken as a basic principle of scholarship that only words which hold no invidious connotations are to be used, since this is essential if we are to examine data without the emotional responses that come from using more "loaded" terms. The same postulate is also valid when practical considerations of field research are kept in mind, since the avoidance of these terms can make those who can be of help in gathering data more amenable to providing the data the student seeks.

Another point must be made when delimiting our terms of reference—the difference between what in the study of African cultures would be called "folklore" and "ethnography." This is the differentiation that Stith Thompson has drawn in the case of the American Indians. Perhaps when folklore was defined as the study of customs that represented survivals of another day in certain segments of European societies, the term could have been equated with ethnography. But we are confronted with cultures that, coming out of their own historic past, have developed full-blown ways of life that are peculiar to themselves; here the term "folklore" can no longer be held synonymous with "custom." This is why the history of folklore studies in the United States took quite a different turn than it did in Europe, and why the word in Africa cannot be applied to all aspects of the living cultures we find there. For if one defines folklore as custom, then this practically allocates to folklore the whole field of tradition, something that goes far beyond the claims of even the most enthusiastic folklorist. We must emphasize the fact that African ways of life do not in any sense represent "survivals" of earlier custom, but comprise complete and functioning cultures with the full autonomy of their range of sanctioned behavior.

Because of our approach to the use of the term "folklore," we may ask how, in this context, we should delimit its meaning. Granting that a full body of custom becomes the total culture of a people, we can see that an important part of each culture is that aspect of their creative expression that is verbal. It is these verbal aspects of the creative life of the people, their artistic traditions found in the tale, the proverb and the riddle, that students of culture call "folklore"; and this is what we shall discuss here. An example of this delimitation is to be found in a work by Mrs. Herskovits and myself called *Dahomean Narrative* (Evanston, Ill., 1958). The book treats of the myths, tales and other forms of verbal art of this West African people. It analyzes these narratives in the same way as a short story or a novel might be analyzed, taking into account such aspects of these narratives as plot construction, character development and other points that a literary critic or student of comparative literature would consider. In other words, these narratives represent an oral literature, and it is these literary forms that most students of nonliterate societies think of when the word "folklore" is used.

Over the continent as a whole, African literary expression takes on certain characteristic forms. These forms can be classified as tales (a category in which myth is to be included as a subclass), proverbs, riddles and poetry. This last category, it should be noted, has been almost completely neglected, perhaps because African poetry is most often encountered as words to songs. Yet one of the most intriguing problems lies in this field, that of analyzing the way in which effects are gained through the use of the tonal values of words, so that patterns of rhyme and meter may be cast in tonal configurations rather than in the conventions of phonetic agreement. Obviously, such research has the broadest implications for the study of comparative literature, since it involves the introduction of quite a new conception of poetic structure, on a level that neither literary critics nor students of poetry seem to have apprehended.

Reorientation is also essential in the study of African tales. This involves recognition of the fact that these terms do not necessarily deal with the doings of animals, particularly with the activities of the small creature who plays the role of trickster. The reason for the conventional idea of what "pure" African tales must be is historically interesting for, as I have pointed out elsewhere, it derives from the popularity of the Uncle Remus tales.[1] Even European and British students who have recorded tales in Africa have tended to refer them back to the Uncle Remus stories, holding them to be the "typical" form of African narrative expression. Yet nothing could be more incorrect. Animal tales are found everywhere, but this is quite a different matter from holding that the typical African story has to do with animals. If one will read almost any collection of African tales, it will soon become apparent that the narratives in which the characters are human beings are quite as numerous, if not more so, than those in which they are animals.

What is important here is the fact that in so many cases the conception of the animal story as the "true" African tale tended to skew the work of collectors. Indeed, one comparative study of African tales has gone so far as to categorize all nonanimal stories in African collections as "intrusive." It is one of the minor ironies of our literary history that the assumption implicit in this approach derives directly from a misreading of the facts because one particular kind of African tale popularized by the American writer, Joel Chandler Harris, had been carried over in relatively pure form.

Like all human groups, Africans are interested in their past. Their accounts take us into the mythical realm of ancestors and gods, to explain the relations of these beings with men. In African myths we find many explanations of a cosmogonic order, which tell how the world was constituted and the sequence of events that made it what it is. The theological concepts which validate the demands human beings make on the supernatural are also given explicit statement. "Historical" tales likewise abound, but these recount more recent events, dealing with the adventures and achievements of culture heroes and kings, detailing happenings that are held to have actually happened. Many stories point to a moral, and are used as educational devices for inculcating in the children the value-system of the people. And, as everywhere, we find the explanatory tales, these being the stories in which animal characters abound. One of the most fascinating aspects of the study of these tales is the analysis of how motifs are worked and reworked. Identical elements are found in simple stories used to teach the young, and in the most sacred myths where, though they serve different purposes, they yet remain quite recognizable.

African tales are not necessarily historical or cosmogonic, nor need they point a moral, nor be explanatory in character. Some tales are told just for fun. Africans savor the *double entendre* no less than other peoples; for whatever psychological reason, the off-color tale brings an immediate response. The skilled use of the hidden obscenities is particularly striking in riddles, which on their face are so innocent that the children who tell them have no idea of their obscene implications. Narrative forms of this kind are frequently encountered at funeral rites, the rationalization behind this being that one does not moralize or preach to the dead, but rather tries to amuse them so that their souls will depart in the best possible frame of mind. What all this implies is that for a valid understanding of these African literary forms, social intent and function must be taken into full account. Here we come once more to the need of realizing that we are dealing with a fully participating part of the total way of life of the people, and that the meaning and role of the data we study can be ascertained as can no body of antiquarian survivals of earlier living customs.

The proverb gives us an excellent example of how revealing the analysis of social context can be. In African societies it is a mark of elegance to be able to interlard one's speech with these aphorisms. Proverbs are cited in the native courts in much the same way as our lawyers cite precedent. It is held boorish for a younger man to employ proverbs in discussions with an elder. The morals they point give insights into the basic values of society; they teach us what is held to be right and wrong. They are, indeed, an index to accepted canons of thought and action.

This brings us to another important aspect of the study of African verbal forms: the analysis of the manner of telling them. There is no question that there are considerable methodological difficulties in the way of studying this phase of the problem, but this in no way negates its significance. In Africa tales are essentially modes of dramatic expression, even to the extent that in some instances stories are enacted by tellers for an audience, though this is rather the exception than the rule. More often, one finds the kind of participation by an audience that is to be heard in American Negro shouting churches, where responses of the congregation to the preacher take the form of interjections such as "Yes, Lord!" "That's right!" "You're sayin' it!" almost as a litany. This pattern is deeply rooted in behavior, for not only do African listeners react to a storyteller in this way, but, in general, African conventions of politeness do not approve of permitting anyone to talk into a void of silence. Hence the affirmations by the audience as a story unfolds are essential to the telling of a tale.

Tales are also interspersed with songs, which all know and in the singing of which everyone joins. The presentation of a tale is a bit of acting in itself; when the trickster is in a difficult situation, his whining plea for help is heard. So cleverly can the storyteller act out the parts of the characters that the only way fully to convey how these stories are told would be to have a talking motion picture, which would capture the total setting of teller and audience, the gestures, the play of facial expression, and in total effect would not be very dissimilar from drama as we know it on the stage.

An outstanding aspect of African tales is how widespread some of the stories are found to be. This has long been realized in the case of the animal tales. The resemblances they show to cognates even in Europe and Asia are so great that, for example, many years ago Wilhelm H. I. Bleek entitled his collection of stories from the Bushmen of South Africa, *Reynard the Fox in South Africa*. This unity, not only of tales, but of the patterns which govern their telling, is striking. Thus in Livingstone, Northern Rhodesia, some four thousand miles from West Africa, among people with quite a different culture, there could be found the same manner of beginning a tale with a riddle, the same responses by the auditors, the same interpolation of song with which one is familiar in the Guinea Coast, so far to the west. Nor is this all. As the tales succeeded one another, it was surprising how many of them were those familiar from the West Coast—not only the animal stories, but such a one as "The Flight up the Tree," which was told almost in its identical West Coast form.

We perceive another example of the unity of these tales in the morals they teach. The story of how a small or slow animal, who has his brothers stationed along the way, tricks a swift large one into believing he has lost a contest between them, is a familiar one. Here is an example of such an ending from Dahomey in West Africa: "Frog now went to see the King and said, 'I ran a race with Horse, and here I am, the first to arrive. If you do not believe me, you can send your men and they will find Horse lying dead on the road.' The King called together all of his people and he said, 'No man can quarrel with another who has a large family.'" And the tale goes on to say: "To this day, when a man who has no family argues with one who has, he is told, 'Are you forgetting the story of horse and frog?'"

Compare this with the following story from the Kwango area in southwestern Congo: "There was a man, and he had a daughter. A suitor came to ask for the hand of this daughter, bringing the usual bride-wealth as marriage gifts. He brought the customary three bundles of raffia cloth, and said, 'I want to marry your daughter.' The father replied, 'The man who marries my daughter must eat three calabashes of meat and three calabashes of meal, and drink three calabashes of wine, all at one time.'" This point is elaborated in great detail for each succeeding episode since, again characteristically, the African storyteller favors gaining emphasis through repetition. In this case, the failure of each suitor to meet the tests is recounted in full. Then the story continues: "So Lion comes, and then another animal. Finally Monkey came with the three bundles of raffia and says, 'I wish to marry your daughter.' King says, 'No, I will not give my daughter for three bundles of raffia. The man who marries my daughter must eat three calabashes of meat, and three calabashes of grain, and drink three calabashes of wine.' So Monkey said, 'Let me think' "—again, a typical African reaction, since it is characteristic of African psychology that important decisions are only made after being given full consideration. "Monkey went to his village, summoned all his brothers, and stationed them in the bush around the man's village. When he had finished one calabash of meat, he said, 'Excuse me. I must go and relieve myself.' He went into the bush, and soon afterward one of his brothers, who looks just like him, emerges and eats the second calabash. He repeats the performance, and so does the next, and the next, until the last monkey has gone to the bush after drinking the last calabash of wine. Then Monkey returns, and marries the King's daughter. And that is why you must have a large family if you are going to be successful in life."[2]

These suggestions but indicate possibilities. If we are ever to be able to grasp the unities in African oral art, and take advantage of the insights they yield into such questions as the nature of artistic creativity, the influence of cultural borrowing, to say nothing of other problems in the analyses of human culture that go beyond literary forms, we are going to need far better data than we have at present. For, in truth, little work is being done there. We take it for granted that our own students in anthropology will collect myths, tales, riddles, proverbs; and a number of them have made significant collections. But this, one regrets to say, is by no means the general rule, and the study of narrative, like that of other humanistic aspects of African culture, as we shall see, has been eclipsed by emphasis laid on the study of social institutions. Yet for any student interested in understanding almost any aspect of social behavior, it would seem to be highly advantageous to make collections of the oral literature of the people he studies. Both in the tales and in the manner of their telling, situation after situation occurs which leads easily and naturally into discussions of what people actually do and what their belief systems are, all of which throw much light on the total culture. Even where collecting may be tangential to a primary objective of research, it is an extremely important tool, in that it produces data equally valuable for students of literary forms and for students of human behavior.

Much of the work now being carried on in this field derives, interestingly enough, from the interest of historians in African history. Traditionally, the literary forms of African peoples have been collected in connection with anthropological studies, since this was considered to be a phase of culture for which anthropologists should have active concern. In Great Britain, in recent years, however, and to a certain extent elsewhere, a field known as "social anthropology" has developed, which has been concerned primarily with the study of kinship and related structures, and interested more in institutions than in people. It utilizes a highly restricted approach, focusing on society rather than culture. Because it is so restricted, fine work has been done by social anthropologists in analyzing social structures, especially in Africa. By the same token they have done little to give us a rounded view of the life of any people.

There is another way in which social anthropologists differ from their colleagues who have been interested in the holistic study of culture, which is particularly relevant in this context. This has to do with the fact that anthropologists who study all aspects of culture are in general historically oriented, while social anthropologists are not. In consequence, this latter ahistorically oriented group, which has done much of the recent anthropological work in Africa, has left a vacuum in the study of nonliterate, which is to say nonhistorical societies, into which the historians have been drawn.

Historians of Africa are therefore now engaged in developing what is coming to be known as ethnohistory, welding documentation to archaeological finds and oral tradition, and, it is to be hoped, to comparative ethnographic studies. Whatever the case, this new concern with oral tradition means that our resources in this aspect of the study of narrative should be augmented by fresh data.

We are beginning to witness some very important archaeological discoveries in Africa; concomitant with this has been the development of nationalistic movements, whose leaders are greatly interested in finding out their historic past. This has done much to encourage the study of oral tradition. The problem of the degree to which oral tradition is historically valid or not cannot be taken up here, since this involves difficult technical considerations, though these materials constitute a factor to be taken into account when backed up by archaeological materials and by written historical records of some antiquity, records that in certain instances go back almost twelve hundred years if one considers the early Arab, Persian and Chinese travelers. The point is that most African peoples possess such historical tales. There are, for example, relatively few of them who have no account of the path of migration which brought them to their present location, who their early rulers were, what these rulers did, the battles they fought against other peoples, and so on. This kind of information is sometimes presented in great detail, and it affords to the student of unwritten narrative data that go beyond whatever value they may hold for the reconstruction of the history of African peoples.

These, then, are some of the aspects of the study of African oral art that present themselves to the student who would work in this field. As has been indicated, one can assemble a very considerable bibliography of such materials, even though much of the data consists of abstracts rather than complete titles. In the work written by Mrs. Herskovits and myself, *Suriname Folk-Lore,* can be found titles of most of the works that contain significant collections of tales, proverbs and riddles from Western and Central Africa up to about 1935,[3] while the bibliography in Dr. Klipple's study of motifs in African tales extends the list.[4] Not much has been collected since these became available. In the works named in these bibliographies can be found some four to five thousand tales, given in either fairly full form or in abstract. But it is clear that this is a very limited selection of the materials that are to be found. Certainly from Central Africa, from East Africa, from Southern Africa, from Angola and Mozambique, and from the Congo, we have minimal data.

The field, it is apparent, is a rich one; it is not too much to say that it is there to be made. As was indicated at the outset of this discussion, it is a challenge and an opportunity to students who would understand the power of the creative drive and the nature of artistic expression in verbal form, not only in African, but in all human societies.

NOTES

1. "Some Next Steps in the Study of Negro Folklore," *Journal of American Folklore,* LVI (1943), 1.

2. This tale was recorded among the Basuku by Dr. I. Kopytoff in 1959.

3. Melville J. and Frances S. Herskovits, *Suriname Folk-Lore,* Columbia University Contributions to Anthropology, Vol. XXVII (New York, 1936), "References," pp. 761-766.

4. See the unpubl. diss. (Indiana University, 1938) by May Augusta Klipple, "African Folktales with Foreign Analogues," 2 vols.

Northwestern University
Evanston, Illinois

DANIEL J. CROWLEY

FOLKLORE RESEARCH IN THE CONGO

ALTHOUGH current news reports scarcely encourage research planning, the former Belgian Congo is virtually *terra incognita* for the scientific folklorist. This is not for lack of collecting, since an average of twenty articles or books containing Congolese folk materials has been listed each year in the *Bibliographie Ethnographique du Congo Belge*[1] since its inception in 1925. But with few exceptions, these collections are short and fragmentary, and gathered incidental to other activities by administrators, missionaries, and travelers. More often than not, basic ethnographic information is lacking, to say nothing of descriptions of the functions of the folklore in the local culture. For example, John H. Weeks, a missionary among the Bangala and Bakongo, has published the record number of 57 Congo tales, but their value is vitiated by minimal background data, imprecise methods of collection, and the use of deviant or second-hand informants. His texts were "culled from the pages of a native [mission] magazine," or "written for me by the teachers and boys of the Wathen Mission School," or "told me by a friend who lived for many years among the Balolo tribe."[2] Such details as the name of the narrator, his age, position in the community, stylistic techniques, rapport with his audience, or any attempt at a literal translation or stylistic facsimile of his tale are omitted. A few scholars such as van Caeneghem[3] have published texts in a local language with translation in a European language, and have made some attempts to analyze the data. Many of these more valuable papers have been published in *Grands Lacs, Kongo-Overzee, Artes Africanae,* and other journals available only in very large or specialized libraries. For the most part, past collections will serve only for crude analyses of type and motif variation in space and time.

Coverage of the estimated two hundred distinct tribal groups in the Congo is equally incomplete. Following the adage that missionaries first save the souls in the most accessible regions, folklore collectors have worked most extensively in the Europeanized Bas-Congo from the Atlantic to Leopoldville, in the Kasai Basin, and in the Katanga and Ruanda-Urundi highlands. The huge provinces of Equateur, Orientale, and Kivu remain almost unknown except for incomplete collections among the Mangbetu, the Pygmies, and other scattered groups. Klipple in her survey of African folktales with foreign analogues[4] found only 22 publications containing 28 examples of 16 tale types from the former Belgian territory. Five of the publications do not specify the tribal sources of the folklore, but the provinces of the eighteen tribes listed in the remaining publications are shown in the table on page 458.

As elsewhere in Africa, the political frontiers of the Congo bear no relationship to tribal affiliation. As a result, the most complete collections of folklore of Congo peoples have been made outside her borders. Thus Dennett's collection of Fjort tales[5] and Pechuël-Loesche's Loango collection,[6] both from the former French Congo, can be assumed to be similar to the folklore of adjacent regions of the former Belgian Congo and Angola, since all of these areas are inhabited by Bakongo. Similarly, the Lamba studied by Doke[7] in Northern Rhodesia also inhabit southeastern Katanga.

LEO	KASAI	KATANGA	ELSEWHERE	UNKNOWN
Kongo	Kanioka	Bena Matembo (Mitumba-Luba?)	Mangbetu (in north Orientale)	Bena Buimukullu
Yombe	Lulua			Bena Mukini
		Kioke (Chokwe)		
Pende	Bena Mai (Bakete)			Bena Mwula (all probably Luba)
	Kuba	Luba	Mbunda (from Angola, now migrants in Katanga)	
	Luba	Lunda		
	Songe			
	Tetela			

Chatelain's Umbundu tales,[8] although collected far from the Congo in central Angola, show cultural affinities with tribes in southern Leopoldville Province and in western Katanga.

The dearth of analytical studies of Congolese folklore probably reflects the relatively low status of folklore as a discipline among French-speaking scholars, though this is less true in the Flemish-speaking parts of Belgium where linguistic nationalism has encouraged folklore research. In any case, the Musée Royal du Congo Belge at Tervuren, although definitive in ethnography, natural sciences, and art, has neither a folklore archive nor a folklore series among its publications. The only archive known to me which contains Congo materials is that at the private museum of the Companhia de Diamantes de Angola situated at Dundo, Angola, just south of the Congo border near Tshikapa. It contains music and folklore recordings made in Angola among Chokwe, Lunda, Luena, and other border tribes, and some material from Luba, Lulua, and Kongo from the Kasai who have migrated into Angola to work in the diamond mines. Belgian linguists such as Jacobs, van den Eynde, and others have made collections of texts for purposes of linguistic analysis. The future status of advanced research and graduate study at the Université de Lovanium at Leopoldville remains uncertain, but the Centre Interfacultaire d'Anthropologie et de Linguistique Africaine established by Jacques J. Maquet at the Université Officielle du Congo Belge et du Ruanda-Urundi (now Université de l'Etat à Elisabethville) is already a casualty of Tshombe's crash program in education, wherein there is little place for disinterested long-term research.

If the present political chaos can be resolved through a federation of provinces and/or factions, or through United Nations administration, it will again be possible to consider research. While the much maligned Belgians did not build many secondary schools, primary education was available to most children. As a result, an estimated forty per cent of the Congolese are literate. These are mostly boys and young men, and they are usually literate in one or more local languages, of which there are roughly one hundred and fifty in the Congo. Most of these vernaculars belong to the Niger-Congo or Bantu family, so that a speaker of one language may learn another without too much difficulty. For practical purposes most people have learned to speak at least one of the four relatively simple trade languages, Kikongo ("Fiote") in and around Leopoldville, Chiluba ("Kituba") in the Kasai Province, Lingala on the upper

Congo River, and Kiswahili throughout the east and south. A number of books have been published in these languages, including some folktales used in reading primers. Most of the vernaculars have also been reduced to writing in the last fifty years in a fairly rational manner, but with occasional French spelling such as *Kaloulou* or *Tshombe*. The prestige of French is great because its speakers have access to such desired positions as postal clerk, bank teller, and customs officer, and it is more and more common to hear French used as a trade language among educated Congolese of different tribes. Indeed, members of the same tribe sometimes use French by preference in conversation, and Tshombe has recently ruled that all schooling in Katanga must be conducted in French. Since most schools are run by Flemish Catholic priests and nuns, or by British or American Protestant missionaries, Congolese French often has a curiously archaic and stilted quality.

Doubtless this complex linguistic situation has been a factor limiting folklore research, but at the same time the relatively high level of linguistic skills among the Congolese makes possible some useful experiments in folklore creation and transmission. French-speaking informants would nearly always be men, since few women know French except in urban areas. English-speaking informant-interpreters might be found among immigrants from Uganda or miners who had worked on the Rhodesian Copperbelt, but such people are rare in the bush villages where folklore can still be studied in its traditional milieu.

The availability of literate multilingual informants makes possible badly needed experiments on such matters as tale transmission, range of individual variation permitted within traditional limits, methods of creativity, efforts of narration versus written composition, and verbalizations on esthetic values in storytelling. The Congolese have most kinds of folklore including tales, myths, legends, traditional histories, proverbs, songs, riddles, and many other forms carefully distinguished by local terms. In view of the relative similarity of languages and cultures, the charting of distribution of each folklore form could in itself be productive of important new ideas about folklore dissemination in relationship to language, urbanization, and cultural receptivity to innovation. The traditional histories combined with anthropology and historical documentation could give a clearer picture of pre-Belgian times, and might help coalesce scattered tribes into larger politically viable groups based on a shared past. Careful studies of Congolese verbal expression could replace the current torture-rape-and-cannibalism theme in the press with stimulating subjects which more fairly represent these peoples. Such studies might also help explain the resilience of tribal and family structures in hostile urban environments, and the ability of these cultures to absorb and "domesticate" some Western institutions which have been seriously disruptive elsewhere.

Assuming that a stable government is soon established, the situation for research in the Congo could again be encouraging. The Belgians bequeathed a fairly efficient system of internal transport combining river steamers, trains, and a network of gravel roads that range from very good to impassable. With a car or jeep one can reach most areas except during the rainy season. Whether or not it will be safe for non-Congolese to travel in small parties in the bush will probably depend more on area and tribe than on the nationality of the travelers. In spite of the protestations of some African members of the United Nations, most Congolese consider all aliens as equally foreign. Moroccan and Ethiopian troops are described by the Chokwe as *Chindele*, the term usually translated as "white" or "European." East Indians, Chinese, and even mulattoes are considered no closer to local people because of their darker skins. And for that matter, a Congolese from an enemy tribe may be far less welcome in a village than any complete outsider. In the Katanga, Congolese seem to evaluate each alien individual for what he offers the local community. On this scale the doctors, teachers, nurses, and some administrators rate very highly, while policemen, soldiers, and merchants are considerably less popular.

There is no reason why a folklorist who carefully establishes rapport and disassociates himself from local politics could not collect as much material as he could ever analyze. Of all research subjects, folklore is the most innocuous, the problem usually being to explain why any sane individual would concern himself with such "trivia" when he might be studying social structure, economics, or politics. Since this attitude is not unknown in our own culture, the folklorist will have ample opportunity to develop a repertory of suitable devastating rejoinders before leaving for the Congo. For the scholar who can arrange for the necessary finances and fortitude, the future of folklore research in the Congo offers unlimited possibilities.

NOTES

1. Musée du Congo Belge, *Bibliographie Ethnographique du Congo Belge et des Regions Avoisinantes,* Publications du Bureau de Documentation, Serie I, Vols. I-VI (1925-50) and yearly to present; from 1945-46, compiled by Olga Boone.

2. John H. Weeks, *Congo Life and Jungle Stories* (London, 1923), p. 362; *Among Congo Cannibals* (London, 1913), p. 218; also see "The Leopard and the Maize Farm: A Lower Congo Folk-Tale," *Folk-Lore,* XX (1909), 209-211; *Congo Life and Folklore* (London, 1911); *Among the Primitive Bakongo* (London, 1914), pp. 134-140.

3. R. van Caeneghem, "De bruidschat en de verloving in de spreekwoorden der Lulua- en Baluba-menschen," *Congo,* I, nos. 3-4 (1937), 287-326, 384-424.

4. May Augusta Klipple, "African Folktales with Foreign Analogues" (unpubl. diss., Indiana University, 1938, 20 ff.).

5. R. E. Dennett, *Notes on the Folk-Lore of the Fjort (French Congo),* Publications of the Folk-Lore Society, XLI (London, 1897).

6. E. Pechuël-Loesche, *Volkskunde von Loango* (Stuttgart, 1907).

7. Clement M. Doke, *Lamba Folk Lore,* Memoirs of the American Folklore Society, XX (1927).

8. Heli Chatelain, *Folk Tales of Angola,* Memoirs of the American Folklore Society, I (1894).

University of California
Davis, California

INDEX

(The editor is grateful to Pamela Casagrande for assistance in preparing the index for this Monograph edition.)